HERMENEUTICS

PRINCIPLES AND PROCESSES
OF BIBLICAL INTERPRETATION

Second Edition

HENRY A. VIRKLER
AND KARELYNNE GERBER AYAYO

Baker Academic
Grand Rapids, Michigan

© 1981 by Baker Book House Company;
2007 by Henry A. Virkler and Karelynne Gerber Ayayo

Published by Baker Academic
a division of Baker Publishing Group
P.O. Box 6287, Grand Rapids, MI 49516-6287
www.bakeracademic.com

Printed in the United States of America

Library of Congress Cataloging-in-Publication Data
Virkler, Henry A.
    Hermeneutics: principles and processes of Biblical interpretation / Henry A. Virkler and Karelynne Gerber Ayayo.—2nd ed.
        p.   cm.
    Includes bibliographical references and index.
    ISBN 10: 0-8010-3138-9 (pbk.)
    ISBN: 978-0-8010-3138-0 (pbk.)
    1. Bible—Hermeneutics. I. Ayayo, Karelynne Gerber, 1975– II. Title.
BS476.V54 2007
220.601—dc22
                                                                2007021639

14 15 16   10 9 8

To Mary,
whose interpretation of God's Word
through her life is a constant source
of encouragement to me

To Michael,
who models devotion
to the authoritative proclamation
of Scripture in word and deed

CONTENTS

ACKNOWLEDGMENTS

We would like to thank the many people whose contributions have made this book better. We would especially like to thank Betty DeVries, Diane Zimmerman, Jim Kinney, Arika Theule-Van Dam, and Jeremy Cunningham of Baker Academic for their fine editorial assistance.

We would also like to thank the following publishers for permission to quote from their books:

Baker: *Protestant Biblical Interpretation*, 3rd rev. ed., by Bernard Ramm, 1970.

Cambridge University Press: *The Targums and Rabbinic Literature*, by J. Bowker, 1969.

Eerdmans: *The Epistle of Paul to the Galatians*, by Alan Cole, 1965.

InterVarsity: *Christ and the Bible*, by John W. Wenham, 1972. *Jesus and the Old Testament*, by R. T. France, 1971.

Multnomah: *The Prayer of Jabez*, by Bruce Wilkinson, 2000.

Yale University Press: *Validity in Interpretation*, by E. D. Hirsch, 1967.

Zondervan: *How to Read the Bible for All Its Worth: A Guide to Understanding the Bible*, by Gordon Fee and Douglas Stuart, 1993.

PREFACE

In the study of any subject there are four identifiable but overlapping developmental stages. The first stage involves the recognition of an area that is important and relevant but unexplored. Initial exploration involves identifying what is there. In the area of hermeneutics the primary question is, How do we understand the meaning of someone else's words?

In the second stage attempts are made to articulate certain broad principles characterizing the area of investigation. One set of conceptual categories is advanced, then others, as investigators try to develop conceptual systems that organize or explain the data cogently and coherently. For example, is the meaning of a text solely what the author intended it to mean, or does the meaning of a text change depending on what it means to each reader or hearer?

During the third stage the focus shifts from elucidation of broad principles to the investigation of more specific principles. Investigators with various theoretical orientations pursue the study of specific principles, although they may start with different presuppositions and may disagree about which set of broad principles yields the most accurate conceptual system.

In the fourth stage the principles elucidated in the second and third stages are translated into specific skills that can be easily taught and applied to the field being studied.

The majority of hermeneutics texts available today appear to have as their primary goal the elucidation of proper principles of biblical interpretation (third stage). It is in the fourth stage—the translation of hermeneutical theory into the practical steps needed to interpret a biblical passage—that we hope to make a contribution.

The goal of this text is to give the reader not only an understanding of the principles of proper biblical interpretation but also the ability to apply those principles in sermon preparation, personal Bible study, and/or in writing.

Past experience in teaching hermeneutics has suggested to us that if students are given seven rules for interpreting parables, five for interpreting allegories, and eight for interpreting prophecy, although they may well memorize these for a final examination, they may not be able to retain them for longer periods. For this reason we have attempted to develop a common six-step process that can be applied to all biblical literature, with memorization restricted to specific differentiating characteristics. To give practice in applying hermeneutical principles, we have included exegetical exercises drawn primarily from public sermons, books, or counseling situations. To make the exercises a better learning aid, the answers should be written out.

This textbook is intended for those who accept historical, evangelical presuppositions concerning the nature of revelation and inspiration. There are thoughtful Christians who study Scripture from other perspectives. These other views are presented briefly for comparison and contrast. Interested readers will find a brief bibliography of works in hermeneutics written from other perspectives in appendix A.

We can see as far as we do only because we build on the work of those who have gone before us. We acknowledge our debt to many careful scholars in the field—Milton S. Terry, Richard C. Trench, Bernard Ramm, Walter Kaiser Jr., A. Berkeley Mickelsen, Louis Berkhof, D. A. Carson, Gordon D. Fee, Douglas Stuart, John Feinberg, Paul Feinberg, Moisés Silva, William W. Klein, Craig L. Blomberg, Robert L. Hubbard Jr., I. Howard Marshall, Grant R. Osborne, Anthony C. Thiselton, Robert Stein, Kevin J. Vanhoozer, and Roy B. Zuck—to name just a few. The work of these scholars will be referred to repeatedly in the text, and there are undoubtedly instances when they should be cited and are not.

It is perhaps the height of audacity (or foolhardiness) to attempt to write a book outside one's major area of competence, which in the first author's case is the integration of theology and psychology. The first edition of this book was written because I could find no text by a theologian who translated hermeneutical principles into practical exegetical steps.[1] It was originally intended for limited distribution in the Christian counselor training program where I taught at the time and was offered

---

1. The late A. B. Mickelsen's *Interpreting the Bible* (Grand Rapids: Eerdmans, 1963) is a notable exception to this statement. However, he translated theory to practical exegesis only for certain literary forms.

to the broader field of theological students only after strong encouragement from several people.

God blessed the first edition of the text in ways far beyond my expectations, and it has been used and is presently being used in conservative Bible colleges and seminaries in the United States and around the world. It has been translated into eight languages.

Important advances in hermeneutical theory have been made in the last twenty-five years, and it became increasingly evident that the time had come to update the text to incorporate those refinements. Since this is an *introduction* to hermeneutics, its focus is on the most important contributions that have emerged in the last twenty-five years without including all the detail that can be found in advanced texts on the topic.

A second consideration for this second edition was the obvious importance of enlisting a person with advanced training in theology as a coauthor. Karelynne Ayayo graciously consented to serve as coauthor, and anyone familiar with the first edition of this book will see ample evidence of the fine contributions she has made.

While preserving continuity with the first edition, the second edition incorporates several changes: (1) an updated history (chap. 2) reflecting trends in the last quarter of the twentieth century; (2) a new section on computer-based resources for exegetical study (related to chap. 4 and included as appendix D); (3) significant rewriting of chapter 5 to reflect the ongoing discussions between dispensational and covenantal theologians; (4) a more nuanced theological discussion in many chapters, especially chapters 6 through 8; (5) increase in the number of exercises from sixty-eight to one hundred; and (6) the availability of an Instructor's Resource CD (see appendix E).

Henry A. Virkler
Karelynne Gerber Ayayo
Palm Beach Atlantic University
West Palm Beach, Florida

ONE

INTRODUCTION TO BIBLICAL HERMENEUTICS

After completing this chapter, you should be able to

1. Define the terms *hermeneutics*, *general hermeneutics*, and *special hermeneutics*.
2. Describe the various fields of biblical study (study of the canon, textual criticism, historical criticism, exegesis, biblical theology, systematic theology, practical theology) and their relationship to hermeneutics.
3. Explain the theoretical and biblical basis for the need for hermeneutics.
4. Identify three basic views of the doctrine of inspiration and explain the implications of these views for hermeneutics.
5. Identify five controversial issues in contemporary hermeneutics and explain each issue in a few sentences.

Some Basic Definitions

The word *hermeneutics* is said to have its origin in the name Hermes, the Greek god who served as messenger for the gods, transmitting and interpreting their communications to their fortunate, or often unfortunate, recipients. By the first century, the verb form *hermeneuo* was used to mean "explain," "interpret," or "translate." This verb appears three times in the New Testament, each time with the sense of translating from one language to another (John 1:42; 9:7; Heb. 7:2).

In its technical meaning, hermeneutics is often defined as *the science and art of biblical interpretation*. Hermeneutics is considered a science because it has rules, and these rules can be classified in an orderly system. It is considered an art because communication is flexible, and therefore a mechanical and rigid application of rules will sometimes distort the true meaning of a communication.[1] To be a good interpreter one must learn the rules of hermeneutics as well as the art of applying those rules.

Hermeneutical theory is sometimes divided into two subcategories: general and special hermeneutics. General hermeneutics is the study of those rules governing interpretation of the entire biblical text. It includes the topics of historical-cultural, contextual, lexical-syntactical, and theological analyses. Special hermeneutics is the study of those rules that apply to specific genres, such as parables, allegories, types, and prophecy. General hermeneutics is the focus of chapters 3 through 5, special hemeneutics the focus of chapters 6 and 7.

Relations of Hermeneutics to Other Fields of Biblical Study

Hermeneutics is not isolated from other fields of biblical study. It is related to study of the canon, textual criticism, historical criticism, exegesis, and biblical, systematic, and practical theology.[2]

Among these various fields of biblical study, the area that conceptually precedes all others is the study of canonicity, that is, the differentiation between those books that bear the stamp of divine inspiration and those that do not. The historical process by which certain books came to be placed in the canon and others excluded is a long and interesting one and can be found elsewhere.[3] Essentially the process of canonization was a

1. Bernard Ramm, *Protestant Biblical Interpretation*, 3rd rev. ed. (Grand Rapids: Baker, 1970), 1.

2. Ibid., 7–10. See also Richard A. Muller, *The Study of Theology: From Biblical Interpretation to Contemporary Formulation* (Grand Rapids: Zondervan, 1991), for an excellent argument for the unity of the theological disciplines.

3. Paul R. House, "Canon of the Old Testament," in *Foundations for Biblical Interpretation*, ed. David S. Dockery, Kenneth A. Mathews, and Robert B. Sloan (Nashville: Broadman & Holman, 1994), 134–55; Linda L. Belleville, "Canon of the New Testament," in *Foundations for Biblical Interpretation*, Dockery et al., 374–95. A more advanced treatment appears in F. F. Bruce, *The Canon of Scripture* (Downers Grove, IL: InterVarsity, 1988).

historical one in which the Holy Spirit guided the church to recognize that certain books bear the impress of divine authority.

The field of biblical study that conceptually follows the development of the canon is textual criticism, sometimes referred to as lower criticism. Textual criticism is the attempt to ascertain the original wording of a text. It is needed because we have no original manuscripts, only many copies of the originals, and these copies have variations among them. By carefully comparing one manuscript with another, textual critics perform an invaluable service by providing us with a biblical text that closely approximates the original writings given to Old and New Testament believers.[4] One of the world's most renowned New Testament scholars, F. F. Bruce, has said in this regard, "The variant readings about which any doubt remains among textual critics of the New Testament affect no material question of historic fact or of Christian faith and practice."[5]

A third field of biblical study is known as historical or higher criticism. Scholars in this field study the authorship and audience of a book, the date of its composition, the historical circumstances surrounding its composition, the authenticity of its contents, and its literary unity.[6]

Many scholars engaged in higher criticism have begun with presuppositions questioning the belief that Scripture is God's inspired Word to humanity. For this reason some conservative Christians have tended to equate historical criticism with liberalism. This need not be the case. It is possible to engage in historical criticism starting from presuppositions upholding biblical authority. The introductions to each book of the Bible found in the *NIV Study Bible*, in the *Scofield Reference Bible*, and in conservative commentaries are examples. Knowledge of the historical circumstances surrounding the composition of a book is crucial to a proper understanding of its meaning. Chapter 3 is devoted to this topic.

Only after a study of canonicity, textual criticism, and historical criticism is the scholar ready to do exegesis. In exegesis the reader of Scripture applies the principles of hermeneutics to arrive at a correct understanding of the text. The prefix *ex* ("out of" or "from") refers to the idea that the interpreter is attempting to derive understanding *from* the text, rather than reading meaning *into* the text (eisegesis).

4. The primary manuscripts for the Old Testament include the Masoretic Text, the Greek translation of the Old Testament known as the Septuagint (LXX), and the Dead Sea Scrolls. More than five thousand manuscripts exist recording the writings of the New Testament. Most English translations of Old and New Testament texts draw on the work of textual critics. It is noteworthy that the KJV and NKJV differ from other English translations in this regard.

5. F. F. Bruce, *The New Testament Documents: Are They Reliable?* 6th rev. ed. (Grand Rapids: Eerdmans, 1981), 14–15.

6. Ramm, *Protestant Biblical Interpretation*, 9.

Following exegesis are the twin fields of biblical theology and systematic theology. Biblical theology is the study of divine revelation as it was given through the Old and New Testaments. It asks the question, How did this specific revelation add to the knowledge that believers already possessed at that time? It attempts to show the development of theological knowledge during the Old and New Testament era.

In contrast to biblical theology, systematic theology organizes the biblical data in a logical rather than a historical manner. It attempts to place all the information on a given topic (e.g., the nature of God, the nature of the afterlife, the ministry of angels) together so that we can understand the totality of God's revelation on that topic. Biblical and systematic theology are complementary fields: together they give us greater understanding than either would alone.

The discipline of practical theology rounds out the fields of study related to hermeneutics.[7] Practical theology utilizes a three-step process that first describes and analyzes contemporary situations and practices. With the description of a particular situation in mind, practical theology dialogues with the work of the fields discussed above as well as with other social and natural sciences to arrive at a response to the contemporary situation. Practical theology completes its task by developing an effective strategy for Christian life and practice that speaks to the contemporary situation. Practical theology, as the final stage of the hermeneutical process, provides the necessary application of exegesis and theology to lived religious experience.

The diagram summarizes the previous discussion and shows the central role that hermeneutics plays in the development of a proper theology.

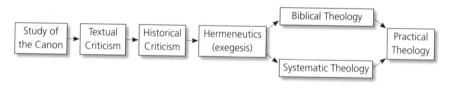

The Need for Hermeneutics

When we hear someone recite or read a text, our understanding of what we hear or read is usually spontaneous—the rules by which we interpret meaning occur automatically and unconsciously. When something blocks

7. For a more extensive introduction to this interdisciplinary field, see Don S. Browning, ed., *Practical Theology: The Emerging Field in Theology, Church, and World* (San Francisco: Harper & Row, 1983).

that spontaneous understanding, we become more aware of the processes we use to understand (for example, when translating from one language to another). Hermeneutics is essentially a codification of the processes we normally use at an unconscious level to understand the meaning of a communication. The more obstacles to spontaneous understanding, the more aware we must become of the process of interpretation and the need for hermeneutics.

When we interpret Scripture, we encounter several obstacles to a spontaneous understanding of the original meaning of the message.[8] There is a historical gap caused by the time separating the original writers and contemporary readers. Jonah's antipathy for the Ninevites, for example, takes on added meaning when we understand the extreme cruelty and sinfulness of the people of Nineveh in his time.

Second, a cultural gap results from the significant differences between the cultures of the ancient Hebrews or the first-century Mediterranean world and our contemporary one. Harold Garfinkel, the controversial UCLA sociologist and founder of ethnomethodology, suggests that it is impossible for an observer to be objective and dispassionate when studying a phenomenon (which in our case would be the study of Scripture). Each of us sees reality through eyes conditioned by our culture and a variety of other experiences. To use a favorite analogy of Garfinkel: it is impossible to study people or phenomena as if we were looking at fish in a goldfish bowl from a detached position outside the bowl; each of us is inside a bowl ourselves.[9]

Applied to hermeneutics, the analogy suggests that we are goldfish in one bowl (our own time and culture) looking at goldfish in another bowl (biblical times and culture). Failure to recognize either that cultural environment or our own, or the differences between the two, can result in serious misunderstanding of the meaning of biblical words and actions.[10] More will be said about this in chapters 3 and 8.

A third significant block is the philosophical gap. Views of life, of circumstances, of the nature of the universe differ among cultures. To transmit a message successfully from one culture to another, a translator or reader must be aware of both the similarities and the contrasts in worldviews.

A fourth block to spontaneous understanding of the biblical message is the linguistic gap. The Bible was written in three languages: the Old Testament contains both Hebrew and Aramaic, and the New Testament is in Greek. The structures and idioms of each of these three languages

8. Ramm, *Protestant Biblical Interpretation*, 4–7.
9. Harold Garfinkel, *Studies in Ethnomethodology* (Upper Saddle River, NJ: Prentice Hall, 1967).
10. Tim Tyler, "The Ethnomethodologist," *Human Behavior* 3 (April 1974): 56–61.

differ from one another as well as from our own language. Consider the distortion in meaning that resulted, for example, when Kentucky Fried Chicken attempted to translate its ad campaign for a Chinese market. Without recognizing the presence of idioms, the translators rendered "Finger lickin' good" as "Eat your fingers off." Similar problems can arise in translating from other languages if the reader is not aware that phrases such as "God hardened Pharaoh's heart" may contain Hebrew idioms that make the original meaning of this phrase something different from that conveyed by the literal English translation.

Hermeneutics is needed, then, because of the historical, cultural, philosophical, and linguistic gaps that block a spontaneous, accurate understanding of God's Word.

> **Exercise 1.** To be an informed citizen, you regularly read your local newspaper. Are you typically aware of the hermeneutical process you utilize to understand the articles? Why, or why not? Suppose you were to read Abraham Lincoln's Emancipation Proclamation, written in 1863. Are you likely to be more aware or less aware of your hermeneutical process? Consider the same question with regard to your reading of Shakespeare's *Macbeth*. Describe the additional barriers to understanding that exist for you when you read the Emancipation Proclamation and *Macbeth* that do not exist when you read today's newspaper.

Alternative Views of Inspiration

The view of inspiration that a biblical interpreter holds has direct implications for hermeneutics. This section offers only a very simplified introduction to the three main views of inspiration. There are several excellent discussions of the topic available elsewhere.[11]

A position on inspiration common to liberalism is that the biblical writers were inspired in somewhat the same sense as Shakespeare and other great writers. What they transcribed were primitive Hebrew reli-

11. Carl F. H. Henry, *Revelation and the Bible* (Grand Rapids: Baker, 1958); J. I. Packer, *"Fundamentalism" and the Word of God* (Grand Rapids: Eerdmans, 1958); J. I. Packer, "Revelation," in *The New Bible Dictionary* (Downers Grove, IL: InterVarsity, 1996), 1014–16; B. B. Warfield, *The Inspiration and Authority of the Bible* (Philadelphia: Presbyterian & Reformed, 1948); John M. Frame, "The Spirit and the Scriptures," in *Hermeneutics, Authority, and Canon*, ed. D. A. Carson and John D. Woodbridge (Grand Rapids: Zondervan, 1986), 217–35.

gious conceptions about God and his workings. This position emphasizes developing theories of how editors called redactors pieced the ancient manuscripts together from previous writings, and what these compilations reveal about the growing spiritual awareness of the compilers.

A second general position, one held by many neoorthodox scholars, maintains that God revealed himself only in mighty acts, not in words. The words of Scripture attributed to God reflect a human understanding of the significance of God's action, and the biblical stories are the attempt to record an encounter with God in human, culturally meaningful words. The Bible *becomes* the Word of God when individuals read it and the words acquire personal, existential significance for them. This view emphasizes the process of demythologizing, that is, removing the mythological packaging that has been used to convey the existential truth, so that the reader may have a personal encounter with that truth.

The third view of inspiration, the one traditionally held by historic Christianity, is that God worked through the personalities of the biblical writers in such a way that, without suspending their personal styles of expression or freedom, what they produced was literally "God-breathed" (2 Tim. 3:16; Greek: *theopneustos*). The emphasis of the 2 Timothy text is that Scripture itself, not the writers only, was inspired ("All Scripture is inspired by God," NASB). If it were only the writers themselves who were inspired, then one might argue that their writings were contaminated by the interaction of the message with their own primitive and idiosyncratic conceptions. The teaching in 2 Timothy 3:16, however, is that God guided the scriptural authors in such a way that their *writings* bear the impress of divine "inspiration."

Based on such verses as 2 Timothy 3:16 and 2 Peter 1:21, the traditional Christian view is that the Bible communicates objective, propositional truth.[12] Unlike the neoorthodox position, which conceives Scripture as becoming the Word of God when it acquires personal existential significance, the traditional position is that Scripture is and always will remain truth, whether or not we read and appropriate it personally. For those who hold this view of inspiration, then, hermeneutical skills possess great importance because they give us a means for discovering more accurately the truths we believe Scripture possesses.

---

12. To say that Scripture communicates propositional truth need not imply that it communicates only propositional truth. For further discussion, see Kevin J. Vanhoozer, "Lost in Interpretation? Truth, Scripture, and Hermeneutics," *Journal of the Evangelical Theological Society* 48, no. 1 (2005): 89–114; Kevin J. Vanhoozer, "The Semantics of Biblical Literature: Truth and Scripture's Diverse Literary Forms," in Carson and Woodbridge, *Hermeneutics, Authority, and Canon*, 49–104.

Controversial Issues in Contemporary Hermeneutics

Before looking at the history and the principles of biblical hermeneutics, we should first become acquainted with some of the pivotal
yet controversial issues in hermeneutics. Just as the view of inspiration
affects the reader's approach to exegesis, so also do these five issues affect hermeneutics.

Validity in Interpretation

Perhaps the most basic question in hermeneutics is, Is it possible to
say what constitutes *the* valid meaning of a text? Or are there multiple
valid meanings? If there are more than one, are some more valid than
others? In that case, what criteria can be used to distinguish the more
valid from less valid interpretations? To understand the important issues
raised by these questions, consider the Naphtunkian's problem.

Exercise 2. The Naphtunkian's Dilemma

Situation: You once wrote a letter to a close friend. En route to its
destination, the postal service lost your message, and it remained
lost for the next two thousand years, amid nuclear wars and other
historical transitions. One day it was discovered and reclaimed. Three
poets from the contemporary Naphtunkian society each translated
your letter and unfortunately arrived at three different meanings.
"What this means to me," said Tunky I, "is . . ." "I disagree," said
Tunky II. "What this means to me is . . ." "You are both wrong,"
claimed Tunky III. "My interpretation is the correct one."

Resolution: As a dispassionate observer viewing the controversy
from your celestial (we hope) perspective, what advice would you
give the Tunkies to resolve their differences? We will assume that
you are a fairly articulate writer.

a. Is it possible that your letter actually has more than one valid
   meaning? If your answer is yes, go to (b). If no, go to (c).

b. If your letter can have a variety of meanings, is there any limit on
   their number? If there is a limit, what criteria would you propose
   to differentiate between valid and invalid meanings?

c. If your letter has only one valid meaning, what criteria would you
   use to discern whether Tunky I, II, or III has the best interpretation?

If you conclude that Tunky II's interpretation is superior, how would
you justify this to Tunkies I and III?

If you have not spent at least fifteen minutes trying to help the Tunkies resolve their problem, go back and see what you can do to help them. The problem they are wrestling with is probably the most crucial issue in all of hermeneutics.

E. D. Hirsch, in his volume *Validity in Interpretation*, discusses the philosophy that has been gaining acceptance since the 1920s: the belief that "the meaning of a text is what it means to me." Whereas previously the prevailing belief had been that a text means what its author meant, T. S. Eliot and others contended that "the best poetry is impersonal, objective and autonomous; that it leads an afterlife of its own, totally cut off from the life of its author."[13]

Such a belief, fostered by the relativism of our contemporary culture, soon influenced literary criticism in areas other than poetry. The study of "what a text says" became the study of "what it says to an individual critic."[14] Such a belief was not without its difficulties, as Hirsch cogently points out:

> When critics deliberately banished the original author, they themselves usurped his place [*as the determiner of meaning*], and this led unerringly to some of our present-day theoretical confusions. Where before there had been but one author [*one determiner of meaning*], there now arose a multiplicity of them, each carrying as much authority as the next. To banish the original author as the determiner of meaning was to reject the only compelling normative principle that could lend validity to an interpretation. . . . For if the meaning of a text is not the author's, then no interpretation can possibly correspond to *the* meaning of text, since the text can have no determinate or determinable meaning.[15]

In the study of Scripture, the task of the exegete is to determine as closely as possible what God meant in a particular passage, rather than "what it means to me."[16] By accepting the view that the meaning of a text is what it means to me, God's Word can have as many meanings as it does readers. Such a position provides no basis for concluding that an orthodox interpretation of a passage is more valid than a heretical one: indeed, the distinction between orthodox and heretical interpretations is no longer meaningful.

13. T. S. Eliot, "Tradition and the Individual Talent," in *Selected Essays* (New York, 1932), cited in E. D. Hirsch, *Validity in Interpretation* (New Haven: Yale University Press, 1967), 1. The Hirsch volume is an excellent source for further discussion of this and other related topics.

14. Hirsch, *Validity in Interpretation*, 3.

15. Ibid., 5–6.

16. The benefits of such an author-centered hermeneutic will be argued more fully in chap. 2.

At this juncture it may be helpful to distinguish between interpretation and application or, to use the terminology of Hirsch and others, between meaning and significance.[17] To say that a text has one valid interpretation (the *author's* intended meaning) is not to say that his writing has only one possible application (significance for a reader in any given situation).[18] For example, the command in Ephesians 4:26–27 ("Do not let the sun go down while you are still angry, and do not give the devil a foothold") has one meaning but can have multiple applications depending on whether the reader is angry with his employer, his wife, or his child. Likewise the promise in Romans 8:39 that nothing can "separate us from the love of God" has one meaning but will have different applications (in this case, emotional significance), depending on the particular life situation a person is facing.

The position scholars take on the validity of interpretation influences their exegesis. It is thus a crucial issue in the study of hermeneutics.

Double Authorship and Sensus Plenior

A second controversy in hermeneutics is the double author issue. The orthodox view of Scripture is one of confluent authorship; that is, the divine author and the human authors worked together (flowed together) to produce the inspired text. This issue raises these important questions: What meaning did the human author intend? What meaning did the divine author intend? Did the intended meaning of the divine author exceed that of the human author?

The question of whether Scripture has a fuller sense (referred to as *sensus plenior*) than that intended by the human author has been debated for centuries. Donald A. Hagner notes the following concerning this issue:

17. Walter C. Kaiser and Moisés Silva, *An Introduction to Biblical Hermeneutics: The Search for Meaning* (Grand Rapids: Zondervan, 1994), 41–44. Even this terminology is not without its critics: "Rather than speak of single intent or single meaning with multiple applications or significances, however, it seems to us better to speak of fixed meaning with varying significances. Kaiser's language could wrongly suggest that certain passages originally intended to communicate only one idea when in fact several are present," William W. Klein, Craig L. Blomberg, and Robert L. Hubbard Jr., *Introduction to Biblical Interpretation* (Dallas: Word, 1993), 406.

18. Article VII of the Chicago Statement on Biblical Hermeneutics affirms this position: "WE AFFIRM that the meaning expressed in each biblical text is single, definite and fixed. WE DENY that the recognition of this single meaning eliminates the variety of its application." "The Chicago Statement on Biblical Hermeneutics," in *A Guide to Contemporary Hermeneutics: Major Trends in Biblical Interpretation*, ed. Donald K. McKim (Grand Rapids: Eerdmans, 1986), 21–26.

To be aware of *sensus plenior* is to realize that there is the possibility of more significance to an Old Testament passage than was consciously apparent to the original author, and more than can be gained by strict grammatico-historical exegesis. Such is the nature of divine inspiration that the authors of Scripture were themselves often not conscious of the fullest significance and final application of what they wrote. This fuller sense of the Old Testament can be seen only in retrospect and in the light of the New Testament fulfillment.[19]

Several arguments are used to support a *sensus plenior* position: (1) 1 Peter 1:10–12 seems to suggest that the Old Testament prophets did at times speak things they did not understand, (2) Daniel 12:8 seems to indicate that Daniel did not understand the meaning of all the prophetic visions that had been given to him, and (3) a number of prophecies seem unlikely to have had contemporaneous comprehension (e.g., Dan. 8:27; John 11:49–52).

Those who argue against a *sensus plenior* position make the following points: (1) accepting the idea of double meanings in Scripture may open the way for all sorts of eisegetical interpretations, (2) 1 Peter 1:10–12 can be understood to mean that the Old Testament prophets were ignorant only of the *time* of the fulfillment of their predictions but not of the *meaning* of their predictions, (3) in some instances prophets understood the meaning of their predictions but not their full implications (e.g., in John 11:50 Caiaphas *did* understand that it was better that one man die for the people than that the whole nation perish, but did not understand the full implications of his prophecy), and (4) in some instances the prophets may have understood the meaning of their prophecy but not its historical referent.

The *sensus plenior* controversy is one of those issues not likely to be settled before we enter eternity. The interpretation of prophecy will be discussed more fully in chapter 7. Perhaps a guiding canon on which the majority of those on both sides of the issue can agree is that any passage that seems to have a fuller meaning than is likely to have been comprehended by the human author should be so interpreted only when God has expressly declared the nature of his fuller meaning through later revelation.[20] A bibliography introducing many of the important writings on this subject can be found in appendix C.

19. Donald A. Hagner, "The Old Testament in the New Testament," in *Interpreting the Word of God*, ed. Samuel J. Schultz and Morris A. Inch (Chicago: Moody, 1976), 92.

20. J. Barton Payne, *Encyclopedia of Biblical Prophecy* (New York: Harper & Row, 1973), 5; Gordon D. Fee and Douglas Stuart, *How to Read the Bible for All Its Worth: A Guide to Understanding the Bible*, 3rd ed. (Grand Rapids: Zondervan, 2003), 202–3.

Literal, Figurative, and Symbolic Interpretations of Scripture

A third controversial issue in contemporary hermeneutics involves the literalness with which we interpret the words of Scripture. As Bernard Ramm points out, conservative Christians are sometimes accused of being "wooden-headed literalists" in their interpretations.[21] Their more theologically liberal brethren claim that incidents such as the fall, the flood, and the story of Jonah's undersea adventure should be understood as metaphors, symbols, and allegories rather than as actual historical events. Since all words are symbols representing ideas, say these liberal interpreters, we should not seek to apply these words in a strictly literal sense.

Conservative theologians agree that words can be used in literal, figurative, or symbolic senses. The following three sentences exemplify this point:

1. *Literal:* "I will stand there before you by the rock at Horeb. Strike the rock, and water will come out of it for the people to drink" (Exod. 17:6a).
2. *Figurative:* "The Lord is my rock, my fortress and my deliverer; my God is my rock, in whom I take refuge" (Ps. 18:2).
3. *Symbolic:* "They drank from the spiritual rock that accompanied them, and that rock was Christ" (1 Cor. 10:4).

The differences among the three uses of the word *rock* is not that one sense refers to actual historical events while the others do not. Literal and figurative expressions usually do refer to actual historical events. The relationship between the ideas expressed by the words and reality is direct, rather than symbolic. However, ideas conveyed in symbolic language (e.g., allegorical and apocalyptic literature) also frequently have historical referents. Thus the rock in 1 Corinthians 10:4 is described as signifying Christ.

Problems result when readers interpret statements in a mode other than the one intended by the author. As much distortion of the author's meaning results from interpreting a literal statement figuratively as from interpreting a figurative statement literally. If one believes God to be the large piece of limestone at the quarry and proceeds to worship it, idolatry will have replaced true worship. Likewise, had Moses overlooked the actual rock to which God directed him and instead sought out an individual who was solid and dependable, the blow from his staff would have resulted in blood rather than water!

21. Ramm, *Protestant Biblical Interpretation*, 122, 146.

If all words are in some sense symbols, how can we determine when they are to be understood literally, figuratively, or symbolically? The conservative theologian would reply that the same criterion for determining the valid interpretation of all other types of literature applies here, namely, that the words are to be interpreted according to the author's intention. If the author meant them to be interpreted literally, we err if we interpret them symbolically. If the author meant them to be interpreted symbolically, we err equally if we interpret them literally. The principle is easier to state than to apply; as we will show in later chapters, however, context and syntax provide important clues to intent and thus to meaning.

Spiritual Factors in the Perceptual Process

A fourth controversial issue in contemporary hermeneutics concerns whether spiritual factors affect our ability to accurately perceive the truths contained in Scripture. On the one hand, if Scripture is read like any other historical writing, two people who are equally prepared intellectually to do hermeneutics (educated in the original languages, history, culture, etc.) will be equally good interpreters.

On the other hand, Scripture itself teaches that spiritual commitment, or lack of it, influences ability to perceive spiritual truth. Romans 1:18–22 describes the result of a continuous suppression of the truth as a darkened understanding. First Corinthians 2:6–14 speaks of wisdom and gifts that are the potential possession of the believer but which the unregenerate person does not possess. Ephesians 4:17–24 describes the blindness to spiritual realities of a person living in the old nature and the new realities open to the believer. First John 2:11 declares that the man who harbors hatred experiences a blindness resulting from that hatred. Based on such passages as these, this view posits that spiritual blindness and darkened understanding hinder a person's ability to discern the truth regardless of one's knowledge and application of hermeneutical principles.

This issue is more important to hermeneutics than it might initially seem. If, as asserted earlier, the meaning of Scripture is to be found in a careful study of words and of the culture and history of its writers, then where do we look to find this added dimension of spiritual insight? If we rely on the spiritual intuitions of fellow believers for added insights, we soon end in a hopeless babble of confusion because we no longer have any normative principles for comparing the validity of one intuition with another. On the other hand, the alternative idea that the meaning of Scripture can be found by mastering the prerequisite exegetical knowledge and skills without regard to spiritual condition seems to contradict the verses cited above.

One attempt to resolve this dilemma is based on a definition of the term *know*. According to Scripture, persons do not truly possess knowledge unless they are living in the light of that knowledge. True faith is not only knowledge about God (which even the demons possess [James 2:19]) but knowledge acted on. The unbeliever can *know* (intellectually comprehend) many truths of Scripture using the same means of interpretation he would use with nonbiblical texts, but he cannot truly *know* (act on and appropriate) these truths as long as he remains in rebellion against God.

This hypothesis, however, needs a slight corrective. A common experience illustrates the point: We set our minds on a certain course of action and then use selective attention to focus on those data that support our decision and minimize those data that would argue against it. The same principle can apply to sin in a person's life. Scripture teaches that yielding to sin causes an individual to become enslaved to it and blind to righteousness (John 8:34; Rom. 1:18–22; 6:15–19; 1 Tim. 6:9; 2 Pet. 2:19). Thus the truth principles in Scripture, available through application of the same skills of textual interpretation used with nonbiblical texts, become progressively less clear to one who continually rejects those truths. Unbelievers do not *know* the full meaning of scriptural teaching, not because that meaning is unavailable to them in the words of the text, but because they refuse to act on and appropriate spiritual truths for their own lives. Furthermore, the psychological results of such refusal make them less able and willing to comprehend these truths.

In conclusion, this moderate viewpoint suggests that the meaning of God's Word is contained in the words he authored and that it is unnecessary to turn to spiritual intuitions not supported by an understanding of those words. Those who are indwelt by the Holy Spirit should not ignore this resource in pursuing biblical interpretation. Just as the inspiration of the biblical authors was the work of the Holy Spirit, another ministry of the Holy Spirit is the work of illumination, of helping believers understand the full meaning of the words of Scripture.

The concept of illumination need not extend beyond the Holy Spirit's enabling one to understand the full meaning of the text. Rather than giving new meaning, the Spirit will enable the original meaning in the text to speak with power and conviction to each reader in his or her own circumstances (John 16:8–15). Kevin Vanhoozer aptly expresses this idea, noting that the "Spirit may blow where, but not *what*, He wills."[22] In other

---

22. Kevin J. Vanhoozer, *Is There a Meaning in This Text? The Bible, the Reader, and the Morality of Literary Knowledge* (Grand Rapids: Zondervan, 1998), 429.

words, the Spirit works with the Word and cannot be set in opposition to it. Indeed, if we allow for illumination by the Spirit to include meaning that is disconnected from the Word, we have no logically coherent rationale for distinguishing the divinely intended meaning from the intuitions and additions of a thousand different interpreters.

Therefore, for the Christian believer, hermeneutics should not be a process that attempts to use only human faculties and education to discover the author's intended meaning, but neither should it be a process that ignores a disciplined approach. That is to say, hermeneutics should be methodical but not mechanical. In approaching a passage, the believer should be praying, "Holy Spirit, help me to understand the meaning you intended when you inspired human hands to write these words." Then, with an awareness of the Holy Spirit's working in us, we can do our hermeneutical studies.[23]

Exercise 3. While at a Bible study, you come across a word in the text whose meaning is unclear. One participant suggests, "We should look up the word and also find other places where it occurs in the Bible. That will help us to determine what the most likely meaning is." Another participant replies, "That sounds so academic! I don't know why we need to go through all those steps when we can pray and ask the Holy Spirit." How would you respond?

The Question of Inerrancy

Of all the controversial issues with implications for hermeneutics, one of the most important being debated by evangelicals today is the issue of biblical inerrancy.[24] The primary debate is between the stance of full inerrancy and that of limited inerrancy.[25] Full inerrancy affirms that the original manuscripts of Scripture are without error in the things they assert. Limited inerrancy affirms that Scripture is without error in matters of faith and practice but may include errors on matters such as history, geography, or science.

23. For further discussion of these matters, see Roy Zuck, "The Role of the Holy Spirit in Hermeneutics," *Bibliotheca Sacra* 141 (1984): 120–30.

24. Fuller discussions of inerrancy can be found in Millard J. Erickson, *Christian Theology,* 2nd ed. (Grand Rapids: Baker, 1998), 246–65; Wayne Grudem, *Systematic Theology: An Introduction to Biblical Doctrine* (Grand Rapids: Zondervan, 1994), 90–104.

25. An additional position known as absolute inerrancy, which treats the Bible as a text intent on conveying absolute precision in all matters discussed, is more rarely held. More liberal theologians often reject the sense of inerrancy on any level.

The inerrancy issue is important for evangelicals for a number of reasons. First, if the Bible errs when it speaks on matters not essential to salvation, then it may be in error whenever it speaks about the nature of human beings, interpersonal and family relationships, sexual lifestyles, the will and emotions, and a host of other issues related to Christian living. An errant Scripture may be only a reflection of ancient Hebrew philosophy and psychology, with little to offer us. Second, as church history has repeatedly shown,[26] groups that begin by questioning the validity of small details of Scripture eventually question larger doctrines as well. Many observers of contemporary American seminaries have seen this pattern repeated: acceptance of an errant Scripture in peripheral matters has soon been followed by the allegation that Scripture is errant in more central teachings as well.

The issue of inerrancy is also important in the field of hermeneutics. If we begin with the presupposition that Scripture does contain errors and then find an apparent discrepancy between two or more texts, we may decide that one or both of them contains errors. If we begin with the presupposition that Scripture does not contain errors, we are motivated to seek an exegetically justifiable way of resolving any seeming discrepancy. The different results of these presuppositional bases become most apparent in that part of hermeneutics called "theological analysis" (see chap. 5), which consists essentially in comparing a given text with all other texts on the same subject. Our approach to theological analysis will differ according to whether we assume that the teaching of the various texts, properly interpreted, represents a unity of thought, or that the texts may represent a diversity of thought occasioned by errors. Because this issue has such importance for hermeneutics, the final section of this chapter will examine the arguments in the inerrancy debate.

JESUS AND THE BIBLE

If Jesus Christ is, in fact, the Son of God, then his attitude toward Scripture will provide the best answer to the question of inerrancy. A full discussion can be found in John W. Wenham's *Christ and the Bible*. Several points are summarized here.

First, Jesus consistently treated the historical narratives of the Old Testament as straightforward records of fact. Wenham notes:

We have references [by Christ] to: Abel (Luke 11:51), Noah (Matt. 24:37–39; Luke 17:26–27), Abraham (John 8:56), the institution of circumcision (John 7:22; cf. Gen. 17:10–12; Lev. 12:3), Sodom and Gomorrah (Matt. 10:15; 11:23–24; Luke 10:12), Lot (Luke 17:28–32), Isaac and Jacob (Matt.

26. Harold Lindsell, *The Battle for the Bible* (Grand Rapids: Zondervan, 1976), 141–60.

30

8:11; Luke 13:28), the manna (John 6:31, 49, 58), the wilderness serpent (John 3:14), David eating the shewbread (Matt. 12:3–4; Mark 2:25–26; Luke 6:3–4) and as a psalm-writer (Matt. 22:43; Mark 12:36; Luke 20:42), Solomon (Matt. 6:29; 12:42; Luke 11:31; 12:27), Elijah (Luke 4:25–26), Elisha (Luke 4:27), Jonah (Matt. 12:39–41; Luke 11:29–30, 32), Zechariah (Luke 11:51). This last passage brings out his sense of the unity of history and his grasp of its wide sweep. His eye surveys the whole course of history from "the foundation of the world" to "this generation." There are repeated references to Moses as the giver of the law (Matt. 8:4; 19:8; Mark 1:44; 7:10; 10:5; 12:26; Luke 5:14; 20:37; John 5:46; 7:19); the sufferings of the prophets are also mentioned frequently (Matt. 5:12; 13:57; 21:34–36; 23:29–37; Mark 6:4 [cf. Luke 4:24; John 4:44]; 12:2–5; Luke 6:23; 11:47–51; 13:34; 20:10–12); and there is a reference to the popularity of the false prophets (Luke 6:26). He sets the stamp of his approval on passages in Genesis 1 and 2 (Matt. 19:4–5; Mark 10:6–8).

Although these quotations are taken by our Lord more or less at random from different parts of the Old Testament and some periods of the history are covered more fully than others, it is evident that he was familiar with most of our Old Testament and that he treated it all equally as history.[27]

Second, Jesus often chose as the basis of his teaching those very stories that most modern critics find unacceptable (e.g., Noah and the flood—Matt. 24:37–39; Luke 17:26–27; Sodom and Gomorrah—Matt. 10:15; 11:23–24; the story of Jonah—Matt. 12:39–41; Luke 11:29–32).

Third, Jesus consistently adduced the Old Testament Scriptures as the authoritative court of appeal in his controversies with the scribes and the Pharisees. His complaint with them was not that they gave too much credence to Scripture, but that they had, by their rabbinic casuistry (misleading technical distinctions), managed to circumvent the clear and authoritative teachings to be found in it.

Fourth, Jesus taught that nothing could pass from the law until all had been fulfilled (Matt. 5:17–20) and that Scripture could not be broken (John 10:35).

Finally, Jesus used Scripture in his rebuttal to each of Satan's temptations. It is noteworthy that both Jesus and Satan accepted the scriptural statements as arguments against which there was no further argument (Matt. 4:4–11; Luke 4:4–13).

Jesus does not seem to have made any distinction between the validity and accuracy of revelatory versus nonrevelatory (historical, incidental) matters. His attitude, as recorded in the Gospels, seems to be an unquestioning acceptance. Harold Lindsell points out that even liberal and

---

27. John W. Wenham, *Christ and the Bible* (Downers Grove, IL: InterVarsity, 1972), 12–13. Several ideas in the following pages are also borrowed or adapted from his book.

neoorthodox scholars, who themselves deny biblical inerrancy, agree that Jesus viewed the Scriptures as infallible.[28] Kenneth Kantzer, second dean of Trinity Evangelical Divinity School and former editor of *Christianity Today*, discussed the testimony of these liberal scholars:

> H. J. Cadbury, Harvard professor and one of the more extreme New Testament critics of the last generation, once declared that he was far more sure as a mere historical fact that Jesus held to the common Jewish view of an infallible Bible than that Jesus believed in His own messiahship. Adolph Harnack, greatest church historian of modern times, insists that Christ was one with His apostles, the Jews, and the entire early Church, in complete commitment to the infallible authority of the Bible. John Knox, author of what is perhaps the most highly regarded recent life of Christ, states that there can be no question that this view of the Bible was taught by our Lord himself.[29]

Harold Lindsell, another former *Christianity Today* editor, describes Rudolf Bultmann as "a radical antisupernaturalist but acknowledged by many to be the greatest New Testament scholar of modern times, [who] asserts that Jesus accepted the common notion of His day regarding the infallibility of Scripture."[30] Bultmann wrote:

> Jesus agreed always with the scribes of his time in accepting without question the authority of the [Old Testament] Law. When he was asked by the rich man, "What must I do to inherit eternal life?" he answered, "You know the commandments," and he repeated the well-known Old Testament Decalogue. . . . Jesus did not attack the Law but assumed its authority and interpreted it.[31]

The words of J. I. Packer summarize much of the discussion on this issue and place it in perspective:

> The fact we have to face is that Jesus Christ, the Son of God incarnate, who claimed divine authority for all that He did and taught, both confirmed the absolute authority of the Old Testament for others and submitted to it unreservedly Himself. . . . If we accept Christ's claims, therefore, we commit ourselves to believe all that He taught—on His authority. If we refuse

---

28. Lindsell, *Battle for the Bible*, 43–44.
29. Kenneth Kantzer, "Mission and the Church's Authority," in *The Church's Worldwide Mission: An Analysis of the Current State of Evangelical Missions, and a Strategy for Future Activity*, ed. Harold Lindsell (Waco: Word, 1966), 31, cited in Lindsell, *Battle for the Bible*, 43.
30. Lindsell, *Battle for the Bible*, 43.
31. Rudolf Bultmann, *Jesus and the Word* (New York: Scribner, 1934), 61–62.

to believe some part of what He taught, we are in effect denying Him to be the divine Messiah—on our own authority.[32]

OBJECTIONS AND ANSWERS

Even if the Gospel records portray Jesus as having unquestioning faith in the validity and authority of Scripture, many writers and theologians maintain that Christians need no longer accept this stance. Literature on this subject usually cites about nine major objections to a full-inerrancy view of Scripture. These objections are discussed briefly below. Fuller discussions can be found in the references noted and in the suggested readings at the end of this chapter.

Objection 1: It is possible that Jesus understood and used the Old Testament stories in a nonliteral fashion, meaning them to be understood as nonhistorical events used for illustrative purposes only.

Jesus certainly made use of stories to illustrate points as he spoke. However, in the majority of incidents he cites, the illustrations make more sense if understood as actual historical events. For example, in Matthew 12:41 Jesus is quoted as saying, "The men of Nineveh will arise at the judgment with this generation and condemn it; for they repented at the preaching of Jonah, and behold, something greater than Jonah is here" (RSV). T. T. Perowne comments: "Is it possible to understand a reference like this on the non-historic theory of the book of Jonah? . . . [Are we] to suppose him [Christ] to say that imaginary persons who at the imaginary preaching of an imaginary prophet repented in imagination, shall rise up in that day and condemn the actual impenitence of those his actual hearers?"[33]

The argument that Jesus used in his dispute with the Sadducees concerning the resurrection (Mark 12:18–27), for example, would carry no weight unless both he and his opponents understood that Abraham, Isaac, and Jacob were actual historical figures. Jesus' claim to deity, for which he was nearly stoned (John 8:56–59), contains an allusion to Abraham that could have meaning only if he and his opponents recognized Abraham as a historical figure. Wenham remarks that "as the matter is pursued the impression gains in strength that our Lord understood the Bible stories in a natural way and that his teaching should be taken quite straightforwardly."[34]

Objection 2: It is possible that Jesus knew there was error in Scripture but accommodated his teaching to the prescientific views of his time.

---

32. J. I. Packer, *"Fundamentalism" and the Word of God*, 55–59.
33. T. T. Perowne, *Obadiah and Jonah* (Cambridge: University Press, 1894), 51.
34. Wenham, *Christ and the Bible*, 14.

Jesus did not hesitate to refute other aspects of the Jewish religious tradition that were in error. He clearly repudiated nationalistic misconceptions about the Messiah, even to the point of the cross. He was not slow to reject Pharisaic traditionalism. If the Scriptures are a combination of divine truth and human error, it would hardly be in character for him not to repudiate the human error.[35]

Moreover, if Jesus knew that Scripture contained human error yet never made this fact known to his followers, misleading them rather by his insistently positive attitude toward it, he could hardly qualify as a great moral teacher and as the incarnate God of truth.

Objection 3: As part of his self-emptying, it is possible that Jesus also emptied himself of the knowledge that Scripture contains errors, and thus he became a product of his conditioning.

Christ's kenosis is undoubtedly the most beautiful love story of all time and eternity. Scripture tells us that when Christ left heaven to become a human being he gave up his riches and glory (2 Cor. 8:9; Phil. 2:7), his immunity from temptation and trials (Heb. 4:15; 5:7–8), his divine powers and prerogatives (Luke 2:40–52; John 17:4), and his perfect, unbroken relationship with the Father when he took our sins on himself (Matt. 27:46). However, although Christ did empty himself of his glory, his riches, and many of his divine prerogatives, his own words make it clear that this self-limitation did not include a concession to error. Jesus claimed complete truth and authority for his teaching (Matt. 7:24–26; Mark 8:38), including his teachings on Scripture (Matt. 5:17–20; John 10:35). He said, "Heaven and earth will pass away, but my words will not pass away" (Matt. 24:35; Mark 13:31; Luke 21:33 RSV).

Objection 4: The views expressed by Jesus, including his view of Scripture, really belong to the Gospel writers more than to Jesus himself.

Jesus' teaching on the authority of Scripture so pervades his entire ministry that if we were to develop a critical theory that would successfully remove Jesus' teaching on Scripture from the Gospels, application of this theory to the Synoptics would leave us unable to make *any* historical statements about the person Jesus Christ. Thus this objection denies the historical reliability of the Gospel writers and maintains that their theological commitments motivated them to create a Jesus consistent with their beliefs. Numerous criticisms exist within Gospel studies that, in one way or another, seek to distance the historical Jesus from the Jesus depicted by the evangelists.

But we must ask whether it is more likely that the earliest Christian communities arrived at their own theology and then attributed it to Jesus or that the theology of the earliest Christians was determined by

35. Ibid., 21.

the practice and teaching of Jesus, which they accurately remembered and recorded. In fact, many scholars argue that the Gospels are far more trustworthy in their presentation of Jesus than the last few centuries of Gospel studies would lead one to believe.[36]

Objection 5: Since inerrancy is claimed only for the autographs (original manuscripts) and none of these is available to us now, inerrancy is a moot question.

The careful work of the Jewish scribes in transmitting the text and the present work of textual critics combine to give us a text that reflects the wordings of the original with a very high degree of accuracy.[37] The vast majority of variant readings concern grammatical details that do not significantly affect the meaning of the text. The words of F. F. Bruce are worth repeating in this regard: "The variant readings about which any doubt remains among textual critics of the New Testament affect no material question of historic fact or of Christian faith and practice."[38] The question of the authority and veracity of the biblical texts as we have them today should be decided on bases other than the fact that we do not possess the autographs.

Objection 6: Inerrancy should be claimed for the gospel but not for all of Scripture; that is, Scripture has only a limited inerrancy. This objection asserts infallibility with regard to matters of faith and practice in spite of incidental errors of historical and other facts.

Daniel Fuller, as dean of Fuller Theological Seminary, became a noted proponent of this view. He believes that Scripture can be divided into two categories—the "revelational" (matters that make us wise unto salvation) and the "nonrevelational" (those matters of science, history, and culture that "facilitate the transmission of the revelational").[39] Fuller argues that the scriptural authors intended to convey truth about spiritual matters (2 Tim. 3:15–16), and therefore we should not claim freedom from errors in those areas that were only incidental to the author's primary interest.[40]

---

36. Further discussion of Jesus' use of the Old Testament can be found in Clark Pinnock, "The Inspiration of Scripture and the Authority of Jesus Christ," in *God's Inerrant Word: An International Symposium on the Trustworthiness of Scripture,* ed. John Warwick Montgomery, 201–18 (Minneapolis: Bethany, 1974). For a larger treatise related to the accuracy of the Gospels, see Craig Blomberg, *The Historical Reliability of the Gospels* (Downers Grove, IL: InterVarsity, 1987).

37. R. K. Harrison, *Introduction to the Old Testament* (Grand Rapids: Eerdmans, 1969), 249.

38. Bruce, *New Testament Documents,* 14–15.

39. Daniel Fuller, "Benjamin B. Warfield's View of Faith and History," *Bulletin of the Evangelical Theological Society* 11 (1968): 80–82.

40. A more recent defense of a similar position can be found in Jack B. Rogers and Donald K. McKim, *The Authority and Interpretation of the Bible: An Historical Approach* (Eugene, OR: Wipf & Stock, 1999).

Although 2 Timothy 3:15 does teach that the primary purpose of Scripture is to teach spiritual truth, this verse was certainly not intended to be used as a critical scalpel to divide between that which is inerrant and that which is not.[41] Verse 16 asserts that *"all* Scripture is God-breathed." No Old Testament prophet, nor Jesus Christ, nor any New Testament writer gives any support for the idea that the portions of Scripture concerning space-time events contain errors. Had Scripture originated with human beings alone, then we would certainly have to reckon with cultural conditioning and human error; however, Scripture affirms that "prophecy never had its origin in the will of man, but men spoke from God as they were carried along by the Holy Spirit" (2 Pet. 1:21). Adding to this the teaching of Numbers 23:19 ("God is not a man, that he should lie"), the conclusion seems inescapable that neither Christ nor Scripture makes a distinction between revelatory and nonrevelatory data. Francis Schaeffer argues that the medieval dichotomy between "upper and lower storey knowledge" is unbiblical.[42] John Warwick Montgomery's epistemological arguments on the unity of knowledge[43] are also appropriate to this issue for those who wish to study it from a philosophical perspective.

Objection 7: The important issue is to have a saving Christ, not to hold to an inerrant Scripture.

Many people prefer not to become involved in doctrinal and theological issues. For them the important issue is a saving relationship with Jesus Christ, and they neither see nor wish to be concerned with the relationship between Christology and other matters. Lindsell points out the close relationship between Christology and inerrancy: "If Jesus taught biblical inerrancy, either He knew inerrancy to be true, or He knew it to be false but catered to the ignorance of his hearers, or He was limited and held to something that was not true but He did not know it."[44]

Accepting either of the last two alternatives leads to a strange Christology. If Jesus knew inerrancy was false but taught otherwise, he was guilty of deception and could not have been a sinless being; therefore, he was unable to provide a sinless atonement for our sins. If Jesus' understanding of truth was limited to the point that he was teaching untruth, then we have no assurance that his teaching on other matters such as salvation avoids untruth. The only alternative that leaves our

41. Clark Pinnock, "Limited Inerrancy: A Critical Appraisal and Constructive Alternative," in Montgomery, *God's Inerrant Word*, 149.

42. Francis Schaeffer, *Escape from Reason* (Downers Grove, IL: InterVarsity, 1968).

43. John Warwick Montgomery, "Biblical Inerrancy: What Is at Stake?" in Montgomery, *God's Inerrant Word*, 23–28.

44. Lindsell, *Battle for the Bible*, 45.

Christology intact is that Jesus knew the Scripture to be inerrant and his knowledge was correct.[45]

Objection 8: Some biblical passages seem to contradict each other or to be contradicted by modern science.

Probably every believer has been confronted with texts that seem difficult to reconcile either with other texts or with scientific discoveries. Those who hold to an errant Scripture are fond of searching out such texts and holding them up to prove their position. As our knowledge of proper principles of interpretation, of archaeology, and of ancient languages and cultures has grown, however, these seeming discrepancies have been steadily resolved. One of the experiences that can most build one's faith in the accuracy of Scripture is to read several examples of how difficult texts have, with the aid of continuing scientific investigation, been shown to be correct.

The following books are helpful in this regard:

Gleason L. Archer. *Encyclopedia of Bible Difficulties.* Grand Rapids: Zondervan, 1982.

J. W. Haley. *An Examination of the Alleged Discrepancies of the Bible.* Grand Rapids: Baker, 1977.

K. A. Kitchen. *Ancient Orient and Old Testament.* Downers Grove, IL: InterVarsity, 1966.

Harold Lindsell. *The Battle for the Bible.* Grand Rapids: Zondervan, 1976. (Chap. 9 explores the resolution of several difficult scriptural passages.)

Bernard Ramm. *Protestant Biblical Interpretation.* 3rd rev. ed. Grand Rapids: Baker, 1970. (See chap. 8, "The Problem of Inerrancy and Secular Science in Relation to Hermeneutics.")

Raymond Surburg. *How Dependable Is the Bible?* Philadelphia: Lippincott, 1972.

Edwin Thiele. *The Mysterious Numbers of the Hebrew Kings.* Rev. ed. Grand Rapids: Eerdmans, 1965. (This book discusses the ancient Hebrew manner of dating kingship reigns, reconciling the chronologies of 2 Samuel, 1 and 2 Kings, and 1 and 2 Chronicles, a feat once considered impossible by those who hold an errant Scripture position.)

Objection 9: Inerrancy is proved by a circular argument. Inerrantists start with the assumption that Scripture is infallible, proceed to show

45. Ibid.

(based on Scripture's own testimony) that both Jesus and the writers considered it to be infallible, and then conclude that it is infallible.

Although some have used an argument very similar to this objection to support their belief in infallibility, R. C. Sproul has suggested that a more rigorous logical rationale for belief in scriptural infallibility can be made. An adaptation of Sproul's reasoning is given here:

Premise A: The Bible is a basically reliable and trustworthy document (cf. C. K. Barrett, *Luke the Historian in Recent Study* [London: Epworth, 1961]; James Martin, *The Reliability of the Gospels* [London: Hodder & Stoughton, 1959]; F. F. Bruce, *The New Testament Documents: Are They Reliable?* 6th rev. ed. [Grand Rapids: Eerdmans, 1981]).

Premise B: On the basis of this reliable document we have sufficient evidence to believe confidently that (1) Jesus Christ claimed to be the Son of God (John 1:14, 29, 36, 41, 49; 4:42; 20:28) and (2) that he provided adequate proof to substantiate that claim (John 2:1–11; 4:46–54; 5:1–18; 6:5–13, 16–21; 9:1–7; 11:1–45; 20:30–31).

Premise C: Jesus Christ, being the Son of God, is a completely trustworthy (i.e., infallible) authority.

Premise D: Jesus Christ teaches that the Bible is the very Word of God.

Premise E: The Word of God is completely trustworthy because God is completely trustworthy.

Conclusion: On the basis of the authority of Jesus Christ, the church believes the Bible to be utterly trustworthy.[46]

A CONCLUSION TO THE MATTER

When we affirm that God's Word is without error, we should understand this statement in the same way that we would the statement that a particular report or analysis is accurate and without error. It is important to distinguish *levels of intended precision*. For example, most of us would agree with the statement that the population of the United States is 300 million, even though this figure may actually be incorrect by several

---

46. Adapted from R. C. Sproul, "The Case for Infallibility: A Methodological Analysis," in Montgomery, *God's Inerrant Word*, 242–61. An alternative way of avoiding circular reasoning is to start with the hypothesis of the truth of the Bible as revelation from God and test this hypothesis in terms of the coherence criterion of truth: its internal consistency and fitting of all the facts, including the historicity of the Bible, the person of Jesus, his works, his teachings, his claims, his resurrection, personal conversion experiences of believers, etc. For a development of this approach, see Gordon Lewis, *Testing Christianity's Truth Claims* (Chicago: Moody, 1976), chaps. 7–11.

million people. However, both the speaker and the hearer recognize that this figure is intended to be an approximation and that when understood within its intended level of precision it is a true statement.

The same principle must be applied when understanding the affirmations of Scripture: they should be understood within the parameters of precision intended by their authors. Specific principles for interpretation include the following:

1. Numbers are often given approximately, a frequent practice in popular communication (Acts 2:41).
2. Speeches and quotations may be paraphrased rather than reproduced verbatim, a usual practice when summarizing someone else's words (Acts 7:2–3).
3. The world may be described in phenomenological terms (how events appear to human viewers) (Judg. 19:14).
4. Speeches made by humans or Satan are recorded or paraphrased accurately without implying that what these persons affirmed was correct (Job 11:1–2).
5. Sources were sometimes used by a writer to make a point without implying divine affirmation of everything else that the source said (Jude 9).

These qualifications are so universal that we apply them to all natural communication usually without even being aware that we are doing so. A statement is considered accurate when it meets the level of precision intended by the writer and expected by his audience. A technical scientific article may be much more detailed and precise than an article written for the general public, yet both are accurate when understood within the context of their intended purpose. Thus the affirmation that God is accurate and truthful in all that he says in Scripture should be understood within the context of the level of precision that he intended to communicate.

The hermeneutical principles discussed in the following chapters are relevant regardless of the position one takes regarding Scripture's inerrancy. The process of determining the author's intended meaning is similar for both groups. Differences, when they emerge, are likely to concern the *validity* of the author's teaching rather than the *content* of his teaching. For example, those who differ on inerrancy may have a high level of agreement regarding what Paul intended to teach, but they may disagree regarding the validity of what he taught. Thus while we do hold to a position of full inerrancy, the hermeneutical principles found in the following chapters are also relevant for those who adopt a less conservative view of Scripture.

Chapter Summary

Hermeneutics is the science and art of biblical interpretation. General hermeneutics is the study of those rules that govern interpretation of the entire biblical text. Special hermeneutics is the study of those rules that govern the interpretation of specific literary forms such as parables, types, and prophecy.

Hermeneutics (applied exegesis) plays an integral role in the process of theological study. The study of canonicity attempts to determine which books bear the stamp of divine inspiration and which do not. Textual criticism attempts to ascertain the original wording of a text. Historical criticism studies the contemporaneous circumstances surrounding the composition of a particular book.

Exegesis applies the principles of hermeneutics to understand the author's intended meaning. Biblical theology organizes those meanings in a historical manner, systematic theology arranges them in a logical fashion, and practical theology explores their significance and application for specific contemporary contexts.

Hermeneutics is essentially a codification of those processes we normally use at an unconscious level to understand the intended meaning of another person. Only when something blocks our spontaneous understanding of another person's message do we recognize the need for some method of understanding what the person intended. Blocks to such spontaneous understanding arise when there are differences in history, culture, language, or philosophy between ourselves and the speaker.

Several issues affect how one will "do" hermeneutics. We must decide whether Scripture represents the religious theorizing of the ancient Hebrews, the divinely guided but not infallible writings of men, or the divinely guided and infallible writings recorded by men but initiated and superintended by God.

We must also decide whether there is a single valid meaning of a text or whether each reader's individual understanding of a text represents a valid meaning. As you probably experienced in exercise 2, once we leave the premise that the meaning of a text is the author's intended meaning, we have no normatively compelling criterion for determining that an orthodox interpretation of a passage is more valid than any number of heretical ones.

Other issues affecting how a person does hermeneutics include: (1) whether one believes that God's intended meaning can include a fuller sense than the human author's; (2) how one determines when a passage is to be interpreted literally, figuratively, or symbolically; and (3) how one's spiritual commitment affects one's ability to understand spiritual truth.

The following chapter discusses some ways interpreters of the Bible have answered these questions throughout history.

A bibliography including books cited in this volume and others relating to hermeneutics from a variety of theological viewpoints may be found in appendix A. Those interested in further study on the topic of revelation, inspiration, and inerrancy will find a number of resources in appendix B. Those interested in further reading on the *sensus plenior* issue will find material in appendix C.

Resources for Further Reading

Norman Geisler. "The Relation of Purpose and Meaning in Interpreting Scripture." *Grace Theological Journal* 5, no. 2 (Fall 1984): 229–45.

Elliot Johnson. "Dual Authorship and the Single Intended Meaning of Scripture." *Bibliotheca Sacra* 143 (July 1986): 218–27.

Walter C. Kaiser Jr. "The Single Intent of Scripture." In *Evangelical Roots: A Tribute to Wilbur Smith*, edited by Kenneth Kantzer, 123–41. Nashville: Nelson, 1978.

I. Howard Marshall. "The Holy Spirit and the Interpretation of Scripture." *Theological Review* (February 1979): 2–8. Reprinted in *Rightly Divided: Readings in Biblical Hermeneutics*, edited by Roy Zuck, 66–74. Grand Rapids: Kregel, 1996.

Robert H. Stein. *Playing by the Rules: A Basic Guide to Interpreting the Bible.* Grand Rapids: Baker, 1994.

Moses Stuart. "Interpreting the Bible like a Book." In *Rightly Divided*, edited by Roy Zuck, 53–65.

Roy Zuck. Chapter 1 in *Basic Biblical Interpretation: A Practical Guide to Discovering Biblical Truth.* Colorado Springs: Victor Books, 1991.

TWO

THE HISTORY OF BIBLICAL INTERPRETATION

After completing this chapter, you should be able to identify the most important exegetical presuppositions and principles found in each of the following periods of biblical interpretation.

1. Ancient Jewish Exegesis
2. New Testament Use of the Old Testament
3. Patristic Exegesis
4. Medieval Exegesis
5. Reformation Exegesis
6. Post-Reformation Exegesis
7. Modern Hermeneutics
8. Hermeneutics in the Mid-Twentieth Century and Beyond

Why a Historical Overview?

Throughout the centuries since God revealed the Scriptures, there have been a number of approaches to the study of God's Word. More orthodox

43

interpreters have emphasized the importance of a literal interpretation, by which they mean interpreting God's Word the way one interprets normal human communication. Others have practiced an allegorical approach, and still others have looked at individual letters and words as having secret significance that needs to be deciphered. More recently some interpreters have questioned who or what controls the entire hermeneutical enterprise and whether it is even possible to determine meaning.

A historical overview of these practices will enable us to overcome the temptation to believe that our system of interpretation is the *only* system that has ever existed. An understanding of the presuppositions of other methods provides a more balanced perspective and a capacity for more meaningful dialogue with those who believe differently.

By observing the practices of those who have preceded us, we can identify their successes and be more aware of possible dangers when we ourselves are similarly tempted. Santayana's adage that the one who does not learn from history is bound to repeat it is as applicable to the field of interpretation as it is to any other field.

Furthermore, as we study the history of interpretation, we will see that many great Christians (e.g., Origen, Augustine, Luther) understood and prescribed better hermeneutical principles than they practiced. We may thus be reminded that knowledge of a principle must also be accompanied by its application to our study of the Word.

This historical survey makes use of material found in classic works on hermeneutics, to which the reader is referred for more extensive coverage. Sources are listed at the end of the chapter.

Ancient Jewish Exegesis

A discussion of the history of biblical interpretation usually begins with the work of Ezra. On their return from the Babylonian exile, the people of Israel requested that Ezra read to them from the Pentateuch. Nehemiah 8:8 recalls: "They [Ezra and the Levites] read from the Book of the Law of God, making it clear and giving the meaning so that the people could understand what was being read."

Since the Israelites had probably lost their understanding of Hebrew during the exilic period, most biblical scholars assume that Ezra and his helpers translated the Hebrew text and read it aloud in Aramaic, adding explanations to make the meaning clear. Thus began the science and art of biblical interpretation.[1]

---

1. Adherents of redaction criticism suggest that the interpretation of Scripture began considerably before Ezra.

The scribes that followed took great care in copying the Scriptures, believing every letter of the text to be the inspired Word of God. This profound reverence for the scriptural text had both advantages and disadvantages. A chief advantage was that the texts were carefully preserved in their transmission across the centuries. A major disadvantage was that the rabbis soon began interpreting Scripture by methods other than the ways in which communication is normally interpreted. The rabbis presupposed that since God is the author of Scripture, the interpreter could expect numerous meanings in a given text, and every incidental detail of the text possessed spiritual significance. Rabbi Akiba, in the first century AD, eventually extended this approach to maintain that every repetition, figure of speech, parallelism, synonym, word, letter, and even the shapes of letters had hidden meanings.[2] This letterism (excessive focus on the *letters* from which the words of Scripture were composed) was often carried to such an extent that the human author's intended meaning was overlooked and fantastic speculation introduced in its place.

At the time of Christ, Jewish exegesis could be classified into four main types: literal, midrashic, *pesher*, and allegorical.[3] The *literal method* of interpretation, referred to as *peshat*, apparently served as the basis for other types of interpretation. Richard Longenecker, citing Adolf Löwy, suggests that the reason for the relative infrequency of literalistic interpretations in Talmudic literature is "that this type of commentary was expected to be known by everyone; and since there were no disputations about it, it was not recorded."[4]

Midrash comes from the Hebrew verb *darash* meaning to search. Midrash, then, speaks of an inquiry or an exposition. *Midrashic interpretation* included a variety of hermeneutical devices that had developed considerably by the time of Christ and continued to develop for several centuries thereafter. The primary goal of midrash was to highlight and explain the relevance of scriptural teaching in new and changing circumstances.

Rabbi Hillel, whose life precedes the rise of Christianity by a generation or so, is credited with developing the basic rules of rabbinic exegesis, which emphasized the comparison of ideas, words, or phrases found in more than one text, the relationship of general principles to particular instances, and the importance of context in interpretation.[5]

2. Milton S. Terry, *Biblical Hermeneutics* (1890; repr., Grand Rapids: Zondervan, 1974), 609.
3. Richard Longenecker, *Biblical Exegesis in the Apostolic Period* (Grand Rapids: Eerdmans, 1975), 28–50.
4. Ibid., 29.
5. For a fuller discussion of Rabbi Hillel's rules, see C. A. Evans, "Midrash," in *Dictionary of Jesus and the Gospels*, ed. Joel B. Green, Scot McKnight, and I. Howard Marshall

The trend toward more fanciful rather than conservative exposition continued, however; the result was an exegesis that (1) gave meaning to texts, phrases, and words without regard to the context in which they were meant to apply; (2) combined texts that contained similar words or phrases whether or not such texts were referring to the same idea; and (3) bestowed interpretive significance on incidental aspects of grammar.[6] Much of this midrashic interpretation is recorded in the Mishnah, a collection of rabbinic commentaries compiled around AD 200, and in the Babylonian and Palestinian Talmuds, topically arranged works offering commentary on the Mishnah. The following example from the Mishnah demonstrates midrashic interpretation defending certain agricultural practices:

> Whence do we learn of a garden-bed, six handbreadths square, that five kinds of seed may be sown therein, four on the sides and one in the middle? Because it is written, *For as the earth bringeth forth her bud and as the garden causeth the seeds sown in it to spring forth* [Isa 61:11]. It is not written, *Its seed*, but the *seeds sown in it*.

> R. Judah said: "The earth bringeth forth her bud"; "bringeth forth"—one; "her bud"—one; making two. "Seeds sown" means (at least) two more; making four; "causeth to spring forth"—one; making five in all.[7]

By focusing on the identification of hidden meanings, midrashic exegesis often lost sight of the literal meaning of the text.

Pesher interpretation was practiced particularly among the Qumran community. This form borrowed extensively from midrashic practices but included a significant eschatological (end-time) focus. The community believed that everything the ancient prophets wrote had a veiled prophetic meaning that was to be imminently fulfilled through their covenant community.[8] Apocalyptic interpretation (see chap. 7) was common, together with the idea that through the Teacher of Righteousness, God had revealed the meaning of the prophecies that had formerly been shrouded in mystery. *Pesher* interpretation was often denoted by the phrase "this

---

(Downers Grove, IL: InterVarsity, 1992), 544–48; and Longenecker, *Biblical Exegesis in the Apostolic Period*, 34–35.

6. Longenecker, *Biblical Exegesis in the Apostolic Period*, 35.

7. Shabbat 9.2 (from Danby, *The Mishnah*, 108, including n. 8), cited in William W. Klein, Craig L. Blomberg, and Robert L. Hubbard Jr., *Introduction to Biblical Interpretation* (Dallas: Word, 1993), 25.

8. W. H. Brownlee, "Biblical Interpretation among the Sectaries of the Dead Sea Scrolls," *Biblical Archaeologist* 14 (1951): 60–62, cited in Longenecker, *Biblical Exegesis in the Apostolic Period*, 39. See also Geza Vermes, *The Dead Sea Scrolls in English* (New York: Penguin Books, 1997), 67–72.

is that," indicating that "*this* present phenomenon is a fulfillment of *that* ancient prophecy." Thus the Dead Sea Scrolls' commentary on Habakkuk interprets Habakkuk 1:13 by saying, "Interpreted this concerns the House of Absalom and the members of its council who were silent at the time of the chastisement of the Teacher of Righteousness and gave him no help against the Liar who flouted the Law in the midst of their whole [congregation] (1QpHab IV.10)."[9]

Allegorical exegesis was based on the idea that beneath the literal meaning of Scripture lay the true meaning.[10] Historically, allegory had been developed by the Greeks to resolve the tension between their mythological religious tradition and their philosophical heritage.[11] Because the religious myths contained much that was immoral or otherwise unacceptable, Greek philosophers allegorized these stories; that is, the myths were to be understood not literally but as stories whose real truth lay at a deeper level. At the time of Christ, Jews who wished to remain faithful to the Mosaic tradition and yet adopt Greek philosophy were faced with a similar tension. Some Jews resolved this by allegorizing the Mosaic tradition. Philo (ca. 20 BC–AD 50) is well known in this regard.

Philo believed that the literal meaning of Scripture represented an immature level of understanding; the allegorical meaning was for the mature reader. The allegorical interpretation should be used (1) if the literal meaning seems to say something unworthy of God, (2) if the statement seems to contradict some other statement in Scripture, (3) if the record claims to be an allegory, (4) if expressions are doubled or superfluous words are used, (5) if something already known is repeated, (6) if an expression is varied, (7) if synonyms are employed, (8) if a play on words is possible, (9) if there is anything abnormal in number or tense, or (10) if symbols are present.[12]

As can be seen, criteria (3) and (10) are valid indications that the author intended his writing to be understood allegorically, in which case allegorical interpretation is not only warranted but also required. However, the allegorizing of Philo and his contemporaries went far beyond this, often reaching fantastic proportions. Ramm cites this example: "Abraham's trek to Palestine is *really* the story of a Stoic philosopher who leaves Chaldea (sensual understanding) and stops at Haran, which means 'holes,' and signifies the emptiness of knowing things by the holes, that is the senses.

9. Vermes, *Dead Sea Scrolls in English*, 481.
10. Bernard Ramm, *Protestant Biblical Interpretation*, 3rd rev. ed. (Grand Rapids: Baker, 1970), 24.
11. Ibid., 26.
12. Ibid., 27–28. F. W. Farrar, *History of Interpretation*, 149–51, cited in A. Berkeley Mickelsen, *Interpreting the Bible* (Grand Rapids: Eerdmans, 1963), 29.

When he becomes Abraham he becomes a truly enlightened philosopher. To marry Sarah is to marry abstract wisdom."[13]

During the first century AD, then, Jewish interpreters agreed that Scripture represents the words of God and that these words are full of meaning for believers. Literal interpretation was employed in the areas of judicial and practical concerns. Most interpreters employed midrashic practices, particularly the rules developed by Hillel, and most used moderate amounts of allegorical exegesis. Within the Jewish community, however, some groups went in separate directions. The Pharisees continued to develop midrashic exegesis in order to tie their oral tradition more closely to Scripture. The Qumran community, believing themselves to be the faithful remnant and recipients of the prophetic mysteries, continued to use midrashic and *pesher* methods to interpret Scripture. And Philo and those who desired to reconcile Jewish Scripture with Greek philosophy continued to develop allegorical exegetical methods.[14]

New Testament Use of the Old Testament

Approximately 10 percent of the New Testament consists of direct quotations, paraphrases, or allusions to the Old Testament. Of the thirty-nine books of the Old Testament, only nine are not expressly referred to in the New Testament.[15] Consequently, there is a significant body of literature illustrating the interpretive methods of Jesus and the New Testament writers.[16]

Several general conclusions can be drawn from an examination of Jesus' use of the Old Testament, as noted in chapter 1. Jesus consistently treated the historical narratives as straightforward records of fact.[17] The allusions to Abel, Noah, Abraham, Isaac, Jacob, and David, for example, all seem to be intended and were understood as references to actual people and historical events. When Jesus applied the historical record, he drew it from the literal, as opposed to the allegorical, meaning of the text. He showed no tendency to divide scriptural truth into levels—a superficial level based on the literal meaning of the text and a deeper

13. Ramm, *Protestant Biblical Interpretation*, 28.

14. Longenecker, *Biblical Exegesis in the Apostolic Period*, 48–50.

15. Roger Nicole, "Old Testament Quotations in the New Testament," in *Hermeneutics*, ed. Bernard Ramm (Grand Rapids: Baker, 1971), 41–42.

16. There is also a significant body of literature about their methods. See D. A. Carson and H. G. M. Williamson, eds., *It Is Written: Scripture Citing Scripture* (Cambridge: University Press, 1988); J. Kugel and R. Greer, *Early Biblical Interpretation* (Philadelphia: Westminster, 1986); R. B. Hays, *Echoes of Scripture in the Letters of Paul* (New Haven: Yale University Press, 1989).

17. John Wenham, *Christ and the Bible* (Downers Grove, IL: InterVarsity, 1972), 12.

truth based on some derived mystical level. Finally, Jesus even denounced the casuistic methods of certain religious leaders that set aside the very Word of God they claimed to be interpreting and replaced it with their own traditions (Matt. 15:1–9; Mark 7:6–13).

The apostles followed their Lord in regarding the Old Testament as the inspired Word of God (2 Tim. 3:16; 2 Pet. 1:21). In at least fifty-six instances God is explicitly referred to as the author of the biblical text.[18] Like Christ, they accepted the historical accuracy of the Old Testament (e.g., Acts 7:9–50; 13:16–22; Heb. 11). As Roger Nicole observes:

> They appeal to Scripture when in debate; they appeal to it when requested to answer questions, whether serious or captious; they appeal to it in connection with their teaching even to those who would not be inclined to press them for other authorities than their own word; they appeal to it to indicate the purpose of some of their own actions or their insight into God's purpose in relation to contemporary developments; and they appeal to it in their prayers.[19]

The high esteem with which the New Testament writers regarded the Old Testament strongly suggests that they would not consciously or intentionally have misinterpreted the words that they believed God himself had spoken.

While it is evident that the New Testament authors, the majority of whom were first-century Jews, overwhelmingly utilized *peshat* in their interaction with the Old Testament, the question remains whether they also employed the other contemporary methods such as midrash and allegorical interpretation. Is it accurate to claim that the Old Testament quotations in the New Testament are inexact? Do the evangelists incorrectly identify fulfillments of prophetic texts? Does Paul allegorize the Scriptures? These are the issues we must address.

In some places where the New Testament authors quote the Old Testament, they modify the original wording. Three considerations are relevant here. *First*, there were several Hebrew, Aramaic, and Greek versions of the biblical text circulating in Palestine at the time of Christ, not all of which had the same wording.[20] Although a given quotation from one of these versions might not have the same wording as the texts from which our present English translations are made, they still represent

---

18. Nicole, "Old Testament Quotations," 44.
19. Ibid., 46–47.
20. Longenecker, *Biblical Exegesis in the Apostolic Period*, 64. See also Donald A. Hagner, "The Old Testament in the New Testament," in *Interpreting the Word of God*, ed. Samuel J. Schultz and Morris A. Inch (Chicago: Moody, 1976), 78–104.

a faithful interpretation of the biblical text available to the New Testament writer.

Second, as Wenham notes, it was not necessary for the writers to quote Old Testament passages word for word unless they claimed to be quoting verbatim, particularly since they were writing in a language different from that of the original Old Testament texts.[21]

Third, in ordinary life, freedom from quotation is usually a sign of mastery of one's material; the more sure a speaker is that he understands an author's meaning, the less afraid he is to expound those ideas in words that are not exactly those of the author.[22] Hence the fact that the New Testament writers sometimes paraphrased or quoted indirectly from the Old Testament in no way indicates that they were using inaccurate or illegitimate interpretive methods.

The New Testament usage of the Old Testament that probably raises the most questions with regard to hermeneutical legitimacy involves the fulfillment passages. To the English reader it may seem that the New Testament writer is giving an interpretation to these verses different from the original intention of the Old Testament author.[23] For instance, Matthew 2:14–15 presents Jesus' childhood in Egypt in terms of fulfillment of Hosea 11:1 ("Out of Egypt I called my son"), a text that speaks of God's redemption of Israel at the exodus.

Many believe that, rather than being an illegitimate interpretation, this approach reflects a typological interpretation of the Old Testament.[24] Beginning with a belief that God is consistent in his interaction with his people, typology, as an interpretive method, views texts about God's past involvement as historical but also as a foreshadowing of ways that God will act in the future.[25] When the fulfillment passages are typological, the New Testament writers present the typology not as the meaning of the Old Testament text but as a contemporary event analogous to God's past actions.

Finally, a handful of New Testament passages are regularly cited as evidence of the New Testament writers' allegorical or unnatural, and

---

21. Wenham, *Christ and the Bible*, 92.

22. Ibid., 93.

23. The issue is a complex one and relates to the matter of *sensus plenior* discussed in chap. 1. Chap. 7 includes a detailed discussion of the Hebrew conceptions of historical, prophetic, and typological fulfillment.

24. Craig Blomberg, *The Historical Reliability of the Gospels* (Downers Grove, IL: InterVarsity, 1987), 52.

25. Such typological interpretations may have similarities to the *pesher* practiced at Qumran. The earliest Christians were thoroughly eschatological in their mind-set, believing that Jesus, as the Messiah, ushered in the last days. With Jesus himself as the lens through which they interpreted the Old Testament and with the view of their own times as the end times, much of their typological correspondence is eschatological in nature.

thus illegitimate, handling of an Old Testament passage (1 Cor. 10:4; Gal. 3:16; 4:22–31). Although each text must be considered in its own context, only an overview of the issues that arise in Paul's discussion of the word *seed* in Galatians 3:16 will be offered here.

The promise had been given to Abraham that through him all the nations of the world would be blessed (Gen. 12:3; Gal. 3:8). Galatians 3:16 says, "The promises were spoken to Abraham and to his seed. The Scripture does not say 'and to seeds,' meaning many people, but 'and to your seed,' meaning one person, who is Christ." Some scholars have assumed that in this instance Paul borrowed from illegitimate rabbinic methods to make his point, since it seems impossible that a word could simultaneously have both a singular and a plural referent.

However, even in English, *seed* (or *offspring*, RSV) can have a collective sense in the singular. Paul is saying that although the promises were given to Abraham and to his offspring, their ultimate fulfillment is found only in Christ.[26] In the Hebrew culture of that time, the idea of corporate identity (a "complex of thought in which there is an oscillation between the individual and the group—family, tribe or nation—to which he belongs"[27]) was even stronger than in the collective sense expressed by the idea of offspring. There was frequent oscillation between the king or some representative figure within the nation, on the one hand, and the elect remnant or the Messiah, on the other. The nature of the relationship is not exactly translatable into modern categories but was readily understood by Paul and his audience.

In conclusion, the vast majority of the New Testament references to the Old Testament interpret it literally; that is, they interpret it according to the commonly accepted norms for interpreting all types of communication—history as history, poetry as poetry, and symbols as symbols. There is no attempt to separate the message into literal and allegorical levels.[28] The few cases where the New Testament writers seem to interpret the Old Testament unnaturally can usually be resolved as we understand more fully the interpretive methods of biblical times. Thus the New Testament itself lays the basis for the grammatical-historical method of modern evangelical hermeneutics.

Exercise 4. Several New Testament scholars claim that Jesus and the New Testament writers borrowed both legitimate and illegitimate hermeneutical methods from their contemporaries.

26. Alan Cole, *The Epistle of Paul to the Galatians* (Grand Rapids; Eerdmans, 1965), 102–3.
27. Longenecker, *Biblical Exegesis in the Apostolic Period*, 93–94.
28. See chap. 6 for a discussion of Paul's allegory in Galatians 4.

a. How would you define an illegitimate hermeneutical method?

b. Do you agree that Jesus and the New Testament writers borrowed illegitimate hermeneutical methods from their contemporaries? Why, or why not?

c. How do your conclusions relate to the doctrine of inspiration?

d. How do your conclusions relate to your Christology?

Patristic Exegesis (AD 100–600)

In the centuries following the apostolic period, several schools of thought developed with regard to the interpretation of Scripture. The Alexandrian school is associated primarily with allegorical interpretation, while the school of Antioch maintained that the spiritual sense of a text cannot be separated from its literal sense. The Western school occupied a more eclectic position containing elements of both Alexandrian and Antiochian method.

The School of Alexandria

A well-known patristic exegete, Clement of Alexandria (ca. 150–215), believed that Scriptures hide their true meaning so that we might be inquisitive and because it is not suitable for everyone to understand. He theorized that Scripture has both a literal and a spiritual meaning, with the deepest riches available only to those who understand the deeper, spiritual sense. His exegesis of Genesis 22:1–4 (Abraham's journey to Moriah to sacrifice Isaac) gives the flavor of his writings:

Abraham, when he came to the place which God told him of on the third day, looking up, saw the place afar off. For the first day is that which is constituted by the sight of good things; and the second is the soul's best desire; on the third the mind perceives spiritual things, the eyes of the understanding being opened by the teacher who rose on the third day. The three days may be a mystery of the seal (baptism) in which God is really believed. It is, consequently, afar off that he perceives the place. For the reign of God is hard to attain, which Plato calls the reign of ideas, having learned from Moses that it was a place that contained all things universally. But it is seen by Abraham afar off, rightly, because of his being in the realms of generation, and he is forthwith initiated by the angel. Thence says the apostle, "Now we see through a glass, but then face to face," by those sole pure and incorporeal applications of the intellect.[29]

29. Cited in Terry, *Biblical Hermeneutics*, 639.

Origen (185–254) was the noted successor of Clement. He believed that Scripture is one vast allegory in which every detail is symbolic,[30] and he made much of 1 Corinthians 2:6–7 ("We speak the wisdom of God in a mystery," KJV).

Origen believed that even as human beings consist of three parts—body, soul, and spirit (1 Thess. 5:23)—so too Scripture possesses three senses. The body is the literal sense, the soul the moral or ethical sense, and the spirit the allegorical or mystical sense. In practice Origen typically disparaged the literal sense, rarely referred to the moral sense, and constantly employed allegory, since only allegory yielded true knowledge.[31]

This allegorization of the school of Alexandria sprang from a proper motive: the desire to understand the Old Testament as a Christian document. However, the allegorical method as practiced by the church fathers often completely neglected the author's intended meaning and the literal understanding of a text in developing speculations the author himself never would have recognized. Once the author's intended meaning, as expressed through his words and syntax, was abandoned, there remained no regulative principle to govern exegesis.[32]

The Syrian School of Antioch

A group of scholars at Antioch in Syria attempted to avoid both the letterism of the Jews and the allegorism of the Alexandrians.[33] They, and particularly one of their number, Theodore of Mopsuestia (ca. 350–428), staunchly defended the principle of grammatical-historical interpretation, that is, that a text should be interpreted according to the rules of grammar and the facts of history. They avoided dogmatic exegesis, asserting instead that an interpretation be justified by a study of its grammatical and historical context rather than by an appeal to authority. They criticized the allegorists for casting into doubt the historicity of much of the Old Testament.

The Antiochian view of history differed from that of the Alexandrians. According to the allegorists, another, more spiritual, meaning hovered above the historical meaning of the Old Testament events. The Antiochians, in contrast, believed that the spiritual meaning of a historical event was implicit within the event itself.[34] For example, according to the

---

30. Jean Daniélou, *Origen*, 184, cited in Ramm, *Protestant Biblical Interpretation*, 32.
31. Louis Berkhof, *Principles of Biblical Interpretation* (Grand Rapids: Baker, 1950), 20.
32. K. Fullerton, *Prophecy and Authority*, 81, cited in Ramm, *Protestant Biblical Interpretation*, 31.
33. Ramm, *Protestant Biblical Interpretation*, 48.
34. Ibid., 49–50.

allegorists, Abraham's departure from Haran signified his rejection of knowing things by means of the senses; to the Antiochians, Abraham's departure from Haran represented an act of faith and trust as he followed God's call to go from the historical city of Haran to the land of Canaan.

The exegetical principles of the Antiochian school laid the groundwork for modern evangelical hermeneutics. Unfortunately, one of Theodore's students, Nestorius, became involved in a major heresy concerning the person of Christ, and his association with the school, together with other historical circumstances, led to the eventual demise of this promising school of thought.

The Western School

In terms of originality and genius, Augustine (354–430) was by far the greatest man of his age, and he serves as an example of the Western hermeneutic. In his book on Christian doctrine, he laid down a number of rules for the exposition of Scripture, some of which remain in use today. His rules include the following, summarized from Ramm:

1. The interpreter must possess a genuine Christian faith.
2. The literal and historical meaning of Scripture should be held in high regard.
3. Scripture has more than one meaning, and therefore the allegorical method is a proper one.
4. Significance inheres in biblical numbers.
5. The Old Testament is a Christian document because Christ is pictured throughout it.
6. The task of the expositor is to understand the meaning of the author, not to bring his own meaning to the text.
7. The interpreter must consult the true orthodox creed.
8. A verse should be studied in its context, not in isolation from the verses around it.
9. If the meaning of a text is unclear, nothing in the passage can be made a matter of orthodox faith.
10. The Holy Spirit is not a substitute for the necessary learning to understand Scripture. The interpreter should know Hebrew, Greek, geography, and other subjects.
11. The obscure passage must yield to the clear passage.
12. The expositor should take into account that revelation is progressive.[35]

35. Ibid., 36–37.

In practice Augustine forsook most of his own principles and tended toward excessive allegorizing; this practice makes his exegetical commentaries some of the least valuable of his writings. He justified his allegorical interpretations from 2 Corinthians 3:6 ("For the letter kills, but the Spirit gives life"), which he interpreted to mean that a literal interpretation of the Bible kills, but an allegorical or spiritual interpretation gives life.[36]

Augustine believed that Scripture had a fourfold sense: historical, etiological, analogical, allegorical. His view became the predominant view of the Middle Ages.[37] Thus Augustine's influence on the development of a scientific exegesis was mixed: in theory he articulated many of the principles of sound exegesis, but in practice he often failed to apply those principles in his own biblical study, and he employed the "rule of faith," a practice of interpretation that made Scripture yield to the authority of the church and established doctrines.

Medieval Exegesis (600–1500)

Little original scholarship was done during the Middle Ages; students of Scripture devoted themselves to studying and compiling the works of the earlier fathers. Interpretation was bound by tradition, and the allegorical method was prominent.

The fourfold sense of Scripture articulated by Augustine was the norm for biblical interpretation. These four levels of meaning, expressed in the following verse that circulated during this period, were believed to exist in every biblical passage:

The *letter* shows us what God and our fathers did;

The *allegory* shows us where our faith is hid;

The *moral* meaning gives us rules of daily life;

The *anagogy* shows us where we end our strife.[38]

The city of Jerusalem can be used to illustrate this idea. Literally, Jerusalem refers to the historical city itself; allegorically, it refers to the church of Christ; morally, it indicates the human soul; and anagogically (eschatologically), it points to the heavenly Jerusalem.[39]

36. Ibid., 35.
37. Berkhof, *Principles of Biblical Interpretation*, 22.
38. Robert M. Grant, *A Short History of the Interpretation of the Bible*, rev. ed. (New York: Macmillan, 1963), 119.
39. Ibid., 119–20.

During this period the principle was generally accepted that any interpretation of a biblical text must adapt itself to the tradition and doctrine of the church. The source of dogmatic theology was not the Bible alone but the Bible as interpreted by church tradition.[40]

Although the fourfold method of interpretation was predominant, other strains of exegesis were still being developed. Throughout the late medieval period, the Kabbalists in Europe and Palestine continued in the tradition of earlier Jewish mysticism. They carried the practice of letterism to the extreme, believing that every letter, and even every possible transposition or substitution of letters, had supernatural significance. Attempting to unlock divine mysteries, they resorted to substituting one biblical word for another that had the same numerical value; adding to the text by regarding each individual letter of a word as the initial letter of other words; and introducing new words into a text by interchanging some of the letters of the original words.[41]

Among some groups, however, a more scientific method of interpretation was in use. The Spanish Jews of the twelfth to fifteenth centuries sparked a return to a grammatical-historical method of interpretation. The Victorines at the Abbey of Saint Victor in Paris maintained that the meaning of Scripture is to be found in its literal rather than allegorical exposition. Exegesis should result in doctrine rather than make the meaning of a text coincide with previous ecclesiastical teaching.

One individual who had a significant impact on the return to literal interpretation was Nicolas of Lyra (1270?–1340?). Although he agreed that there are four senses to Scripture, he gave decided preference to the literal and urged that the other senses be founded firmly on the literal. He complained that other senses were often used to choke the literal and asserted that only the literal should be used as a basis for doctrine.[42] Nicolas of Lyra's work affected Martin Luther profoundly, and there are many who believe that without his influence, Luther would not have sparked the Reformation.

Reformation Exegesis (1500s)

In the fourteenth and fifteenth centuries, dense ignorance prevailed concerning the content of Scripture: some doctors of divinity had never read the Bible in its entirety.[43] The Renaissance called attention to the

40. George Eldon Ladd, *A Theology of the New Testament* (Grand Rapids: Eerdmans, 1974), 13.

41. Berkhof, *Principles of Biblical Interpretation*, 17.

42. Ibid., 25.

43. Ibid.

necessity of knowing the original languages in order to understand the Bible. Erasmus facilitated this study by publishing the first critical edition of the Greek New Testament and Reuchlin by translating a Hebrew grammar and lexicon. The fourfold sense of Scripture was gradually abandoned and replaced with the principle that Scripture has but a single sense.[44]

Luther (1484–1546)

Luther believed that faith and the Spirit's illumination were prerequisites for an interpreter of the Bible. He asserted that the Bible should be viewed with eyes wholly different from those with which we view other literary productions.[45]

Luther also challenged the prevailing "rule of faith," maintaining that rather than the church determining what the Scriptures teach, Scripture itself should determine what the church teaches. He also believed that the Bible is a clear book (the perspicuity of Scripture), in opposition to the Roman Catholic dogma that the Scriptures are so obscure that only the church can uncover their true meaning.

He rejected the allegorical method of interpreting Scripture, calling it "dirt," "scum," and "obsolete loose rags." According to Luther, a proper interpretation of Scripture must come from a literal understanding of the text. The interpreter should consider historical conditions, grammar, and context in the process of exegesis.

By abandoning the allegorical method, which had so long served as a means of making the Old Testament a Christian book, Luther was forced to find another way of explaining its relevance to New Testament believers. He did so by maintaining that all of the Old and the New Testament points to Christ. This organizing principle, which in reality became a hermeneutical principle, caused Luther to see Christ in many places (such as some of the psalms that he designated as messianic) where later interpreters failed to find christological references. Whether or not all of Luther's designations are convincing, his christological principle did enable him to show the unity of Scripture without recourse to mystical interpretations of the Old Testament text.

One of Luther's major hermeneutical principles was that one must carefully distinguish between law and gospel. For Luther, law refers to God in his wrath, his judgment, and his hatred of sin; gospel refers to God in his grace, his love, and his salvation. Repudiation of the law was wrong, according to Luther, for that leads to lawlessness. Fusion of law

44. Ibid., 25–26.
45. The materials on Luther and Calvin have been summarized from Ramm, *Protestant Biblical Interpretation*, 53–59.

and gospel was also wrong, for that leads to the heresy of adding works to faith. Thus Luther believed that recognition and careful maintenance of the law-gospel distinction was crucial to proper biblical understanding. (See chap. 5 for a further discussion of law and gospel.)

Melanchthon, Luther's companion in exegesis, continued the application of Luther's hermeneutical principles in his own expositions of the biblical text, sustaining and augmenting the impetus of Luther's work.

Calvin (1509–64)

Probably the greatest exegete of the Reformation was John Calvin, who agreed in general with the principles articulated by Luther. He too believed that spiritual illumination is necessary and regarded allegorical interpretation as a contrivance of Satan to obscure the sense of Scripture.

"Scripture interprets Scripture" was a favorite phrase of Calvin, which alluded to the importance he placed on studying the context, grammar, words, and parallel passages rather than importing one's own meaning into the text. In one famous sentence he stated that "it is the first business of an interpreter to let the author say what he does say, instead of attributing to him what we think he ought to say."[46]

Calvin probably surpassed Luther in aligning his exegetical practices with his theory. He did not share the opinion of Luther that Christ is to be found everywhere in Scripture (e.g., he differed from Luther on the number of psalms that are legitimately messianic). In spite of some differences, the hermeneutical principles articulated by these Reformers were to become the guiding principles for modern orthodox Protestant interpretation.

Post-Reformation Exegesis (1550–1800)

Confessionalism

The Council of Trent, which met at various times from 1545 through 1563, drew up a list of decrees setting forth the dogmas of the Roman Catholic Church and criticizing Protestantism. In response, Protestants began developing creeds to define their own position. At one point nearly every important city had its own favorite creed, with bitter theological controversies prevailing. Hermeneutical methods were often poor during this time, for exegesis became the handmaid of dogmatics and often degenerated into mere proof-texting.[47] F. W. Farrar describes theologians

46. Cited in Frederic W. Farrar, *History of Interpretation* (1885; repr., Grand Rapids: Baker, 1961), 347.
47. Berkhof, *Principles of Biblical Interpretation*, 29.

of that day as reading "the Bible by the unnatural glare of theological hatred."[48]

Pietism

Pietism arose as a reaction to the dogmatic and often bitter exegesis of the confessional period. Philipp Jakob Spener (1635–1705) is considered to be the leader of the Pietist revival. In a tract titled *Pious Longings*, he called for an end to needless controversy, a return to mutual Christian concern and good works, better Bible knowledge on the part of all Christians, and better spiritual training for ministers.

A. H. Francke exemplified many of the qualities called for in Spener's tract. In addition to being a scholar, linguist, and exegete, he was active in forming many institutions for the care of the destitute and the sick. He was also involved in developing mission work to India.

Pietism made significant contributions to the study of Scripture but was not immune from criticism as well. Although the Pietists combined a deep desire to understand the Word of God and appropriate it for their lives, on the one hand, with a fine appreciation of grammatical-historical interpretation, on the other, many later Pietists discarded the grammatical-historical basis of interpretation and depended instead on an "inward light" or "an unction from the Holy One." These expositions, based on subjective impressions and pious reflections, often resulted in self-contradictory interpretations that had little relationship to the author's intended meaning.

Rationalism

Rationalism, the philosophical position of accepting reason as the only authority for determining one's opinions or course of action, emerged as an important position during this period and was soon to have a profound effect on theology and hermeneutics.

For several centuries before this time, the church had emphasized the reasonableness of faith. Although revelation was considered superior to reason as a means of understanding truth, revelational truth itself was considered to be inherently reasonable.

Luther made a distinction between the magisterial and the ministerial use of reason. By ministerial use of reason, he meant the use of human reason to help us understand and obey God's Word more fully. Magisterial use of reason referred to the use of human reason to stand

48. Farrar, *History of Interpretation*, 363–64, cited in Ramm, *Protestant Biblical Interpretation*, 60.

in judgment *over* God's Word. Luther clearly affirmed the former and disapproved of the latter.

During the period following the Reformation, the magisterial use of reason began to emerge more strongly. Empiricism, the belief that the only valid knowledge we can possess is that which can be obtained through the five senses, emerged and joined hands with rationalism. The result was that many noted thinkers began insisting that reason rather than revelation was to guide our thinking and actions and that reason would determine which parts of revelation were acceptable (which came to include only those parts subject to natural physical laws and empirical verification).

Modern Hermeneutics (1800 to the Mid-Twentieth Century)

Liberalism and the Historical-Critical Method

Rationalism in philosophy laid the basis for liberalism in theology, which expressed itself by means of the historical-critical method of exegesis. Whereas in previous centuries revelation had determined what reason ought to think, by the late 1800s reason determined what parts of revelation (if any) were to be accepted as true. In previous centuries the divine authorship of Scripture had been emphasized; during this period its human authorship was the focus. Some authors suggested that various parts of Scripture possessed various *degrees* of inspiration, with the material characterized by lower degrees (such as historical details) being capable of error. Other writers, such as Schleiermacher, even totally denied the supernatural character of inspiration. For many *inspiration* no longer referred to the process whereby God guided the human authors to produce a scriptural product that was his truth. Rather, *inspiration* referred to the (humanly produced) Bible's ability to inspire religious experience.

A rigorous naturalism was also applied to the Bible. The rationalists claimed that whatever was not in conformity with the "educated mentality" was to be rejected. This included biblical records of supernatural events and such doctrines as human depravity, hell, the virgin birth, and frequently even Christ's vicarious atonement. Miracles and other examples of divine interventions were regularly explained away as examples of precritical thinking.[49] Influenced by the thinking of both Darwin and Hegel, a history-of-religions school viewed the Bible as a record of the evolutionary development of Israel's (and later the church's) religious consciousness, rather than as God's revelation of himself to man.

49. Ramm, *Protestant Biblical Interpretation*, 63–69.

Each of these presuppositions profoundly influenced the credibility that interpreters accorded the biblical text and thus had important implications for interpretive methods. Frequently the interpretive focus itself changed: The scholars' question was no longer What is God saying in the text? or even What is the human author saying in this text? but rather What sources does this text incorporate? or What does the text tell me about the developing religious consciousness of this primitive Hebrew cult?

The techniques of source criticism and form criticism were developed during this time as scholars sought to answer these questions about the history behind the biblical text. Source critics treat the biblical texts as the final products of a lengthy process of compilation. Their primary interest is to identify when and where the biblical authors used both oral and written sources in their work. It is source criticism that posits the documentary hypothesis to explain the composition of the Pentateuch and that proposes "Q" as a source for the Gospel writers. Form critics focus specifically on the oral tradition behind the written texts. By analyzing the literary form of small portions of biblical texts, they attempt to determine the original life situation in which the material arose.

Neoorthodoxy

Neoorthodoxy is a twentieth-century phenomenon. In some respects, it occupies a position midway between the liberal and the orthodox view of Scripture. It breaks with the liberal view that Scripture is only a product of humanity's deepening religious awareness but stops short of the orthodox view of revelation.

Rudolf Bultmann and others within neoorthodox circles generally believe that Scripture is humankind's witness to God's revelation of himself. They maintain that God reveals himself not in words but only by his presence. When a person reads the words of Scripture and responds to God's presence in faith, revelation occurs. Revelation is not considered to be something that happened at a historical point in time that is now transmitted to us in the biblical texts but rather is a present experience that must be accompanied by a personal existential response.

Neoorthodox positions on several issues differ from traditional orthodox ones. Infallibility or inerrancy has no place in the neoorthodox vocabulary. Scripture is seen as a compendium of sometimes conflicting theological systems accompanied by a number of factual errors. Bible stories about the interaction between the supernatural and the natural are considered myths—not in the same sense as pagan myths but in the sense that they do not teach literal history. Biblical "myths" (such as the creation, the fall, the resurrection) introduce theological truths as historical incidents that speak to a particular audience. In neoorthodox interpretation, the fall, for example, "informs us that man inevitably corrupts his moral nature." The incarnation and the cross show us that we cannot achieve our own salvation but that it "must come from beyond as an act of God's grace."[50] The major task of the interpreter, then, is to "demythologize" Scripture—to divest the myth of its historical wrappings in order to discover the existential truth contained within.

Hermeneutics in the Mid-Twentieth Century and Beyond

In the twentieth century, the field of hermeneutics underwent a tremendous paradigm shift. Prior to this time theologians were by no means monolithic in their approaches to Scripture. As we have seen, significant debates existed regarding whether the biblical writings were a product of divine and human hands or human hands alone. Biblical scholars held different beliefs about whether the Bible is best understood as history, theology, or myth. However, even as their decisions about authorship and purpose differed, they nonetheless approached the Bible to determine what its author(s) intended to convey. In other words, they were united in their belief that the meaning was controlled by the historical author(s) and that interpretation was author-centered. The paradigm shift brought that view into question, proposing a model that highlighted the biblical texts as literary documents freed from their authors to take on a life of their own not bound by the time or circumstances of their historical composition. The new paradigm integrates linguistic, philosophical, and sociological perspectives into the interpretive enterprise. Often this combination results in highly complex theories and technical vocabulary that make it exceedingly challenging to present a brief overview. What follows attempts to preserve enough complexity to reflect the theories adequately but also enough simplicity to be accessible to the beginning student. Some students may prefer to skip this section and resume reading with the section "Hermeneutics within Orthodox Christianity (p. 73)."

The "New Hermeneutic"

The "new hermeneutic" has been primarily a European development since World War II.[51] It emerged basically from the work of Bultmann

50. Ibid., 70–79.
51. This movement in many ways parallels the "new criticism" prominent within literary circles from 1940 to 1960. Much within the new hermeneutic can also be categorized as a moderate reader-response hermeneutic as discussed below.

and was carried further by Ernst Fuchs and Gerhard Ebeling. The new hermeneutic differs from previous movements in that it does not seek to delineate a method of interpretation. Instead it asks the larger metacritical question about how understanding itself takes place.

Much of what has been said regarding the neoorthodox position applies to this category of interpretation as well. Building on the work of the philosopher Martin Heidegger, Fuchs and Ebeling assert that Bultmann did not go far enough. Language, they maintain, is not reality but only a personal interpretation of reality. One's use of language, then, is a hermeneutic—an interpretation. Hermeneutics for them is no longer the science of stating principles whereby texts can be understood but rather is an investigation of the hermeneutical function of speech as such and thus has a much wider and more profound scope.[52]

Two important assertions arise within the new hermeneutic. First, it claims that the author of the text is inaccessible to the reader; therefore hermeneutics should not, and actually cannot, attempt to arrive at the author's intended meaning. What is available to the reader is the text. For the new hermeneutic, the text, now distanced but not divorced from its author, creates a speech event that invites the reader to encounter the subject of the text.[53] In this sense, the new hermeneutic differentiates between the repetition of words and the reproduction of the event that the words were meant to produce.[54]

Second, within the new hermeneutic the reader is identified not as an objective outsider but as a contributor to the interpretive process. Philosopher Hans-Georg Gadamer argues that readers rightly bring their preunderstanding into dialogue with the text to produce a "fusion of horizons," which is the merging of the text with the reader's perspective as the text challenges and interprets the reader. Such fusion of horizons is identified as the goal of interpretation.

In the last sixty years of the twentieth century, both psychology and theology have increasingly recognized that people view neither the world nor the biblical text as it actually is but rather through eyes that have been affected by previous experiences and by the attitudes adopted as a result of those experiences. In the field of psychology this phenomenon is

52. Ernst Fuchs, "The New Testament and the Hermeneutical Problem," in *The New Hermeneutic*, ed. James M. Robinson and John B. Cobb (New York: Harper & Row, 1964), 125. Cited in Ramm, *Protestant Biblical Interpretation*, 83–92.

53. Much of this work has appeared in studies of the New Testament Gospels and specifically the parables. For further discussion and an evaluation of the strengths and weaknesses of this approach, see Blomberg, *Historical Reliability of the Gospels*, 54–58.

54. As A. C. Thiselton argues, there is a difference between understanding the concept of joy and preaching so that joy is actually experienced. See Thiselton, "The New Hermeneutic," in *New Testament Interpretation: Essays on Principles and Methods*, ed. I. H. Marshall (Grand Rapids: Eerdmans, 1991), 308–33.

studied in the subdiscipline called perception, and in the field of hermeneutics it is studied under the discussion of preunderstanding.

Infants are born with various sense organs and a brain that has the capacity to begin making deductions about what the sense data mean. Over the first few years of life children learn, through the environment in which they live and through cause-and-effect experimentation, to interpret the various sensory data they experience. For example, children who are brought up in harsh, unpredictable family environments may come to believe that the world is a dangerous place, and they must always be on guard in order to avoid pain. Children brought up in loving families with consistent rules may develop a very different set of presuppositions about the world.

These early presuppositions, often called core beliefs, provide the answers to many of life's basic questions, for example, (1) Am I lovable? (2) Am I significant? (3) Are other people trustworthy or untrustworthy? (4) Is there a God? (5) If there is a God, what is he like? (6) How does God feel about me? and so on. These core beliefs often function without being consciously articulated (at least by young children), and they gradually produce a set of intermediate beliefs (e.g., assumptions, attitudes, expectations). Core beliefs and intermediate beliefs together produce our automatic thoughts, those automatically occurring, sometimes subconscious thoughts that affect how we respond to the events of everyday life.

The process by which we perceive everyday life is thus not an objective reflection of what is actually out there but is instead affected by the core beliefs, intermediate beliefs, and automatic thoughts resulting from our life experience and the conclusions we have drawn (often unconsciously) from that life experience. Some people, especially those who have grown up in families characterized by high levels of love and stability, are more likely to interpret reality with a minimum of distortion. Those who have grown up in situations characterized by high levels of abuse and unpredictability are likely to have developed core beliefs, intermediate beliefs, and automatic thoughts that reflect the reality that they have experienced. Those core beliefs and attitudes may cause them to interpret all reality as abusive and unpredictable, even when they are in relationships that are not harsh or exploitive.

Core beliefs, intermediate beliefs, and automatic thoughts also affect how we interpret a text, including the Bible. For example, people who have experienced abuse or abandonment from an earthly father may have difficulty accepting and internalizing passages that tell them that they have a loving, caring heavenly Father. Just as earlier experiences can affect our psychological perceptions of people and relationships, those experiences can also affect our theological perceptions of the biblical text. The beliefs that we learn through our theological training may affect how we interpret various passages of Scripture. For example, someone brought up in a strongly Calvinist environment may interpret passages dealing with human choice differently than someone brought up in an Arminian environment. Or someone who has adopted the assumption of philosophical naturalism (i.e., that everything that exists is within the natural world) will view the miracles differently than someone who believes that both the natural and the supernatural world exist.

The point is that none of us looks at reality, including the biblical text, with totally objective perception. We are all influenced to some extent by the core beliefs, intermediate beliefs, and automatic thoughts that we have developed since birth. This helps to explain why two people can study the same passage and sometimes draw very different conclusions from it.

Does this mean that our preunderstandings inevitably *determine* how we interpret God's Word? Many people would say no.[55] If we fail to recognize that we have preunderstandings that could affect our understandings of God's Word, our interpretations are more likely to be determined by those preunderstandings. However, if we are willing to identify our preunderstandings, recognize that they are theories (hypotheses), and then are willing to reconsider our hypotheses if the data seem to warrant it, then our preunderstandings will serve as *influences* rather than *determinants* of our interpretations. If we are unwilling to identify our preunderstandings, recognize that they are theories, and change them even when the data suggest that they need to be modified, then in those areas our preunderstandings will lock us into a rigid, unbending (and sometimes unbiblical) stance.

Structuralism

Consistent with the rationalistic emphasis on reason and objectivity begun within modernity, many within the field of literary studies desired to establish a "scientific" way to study texts and literature. One result was structuralist interpretation, which appeared in the mid-1900s.[56] For the structuralist, meaning is not found in the author's intentions in writing a text. Instead, structuralism draws on linguistic theory in concluding that all language and all writing function as signs of something else and follow certain rules. Structuralists therefore believe that just as one must use the conventions of English grammar to write a sentence in English,

55. Adherents of a radical reader-response hermeneutic would disagree. See the discussion below.
56. In literary circles Russian formalism laid the groundwork for much structuralist thought.

authors must follow the conventions of literature to write a text at all. Structuralism is interested in this universal "grammar," that is, in the cross-cultural deep structures[57] that exist and determine how all people process data and text. These embedded patterns control human thinking and communication regardless of the author's awareness or ignorance of them. Thus, for structuralists, it is quite possible that a text's author may not have even been aware of the true "meaning" of the text he or she composed.

Structuralism views the text as an arbitrary system of signs that have to be decoded in order to arrive at meaning. Interpreters look at the literary structure, the narrative units, the syntax, and other codes embedded in a text in order to determine the configuration behind the structure. Reconstructing these codes is the goal of interpretation.

Many structuralist interpreters employ a method known as actantial analysis of narrative texts to discover how a plot is developed. The "actants" they wish to identify include sender, subject, helper, opponent, object, and receiver.[58] They believe that these six actants exist in all completed stories and interact with one another in predictable ways. Actantial analysis of the biblical account of Esther, for example, identifies that "the *subject*, Esther, is assisted by a *helper*, Mordecai, and hindered by an *opponent*, Haman, in the quest for the *object* of deliverance, in relation to which the Jews stand as *receiver*."[59] Such is the underlying code or structure, and thus the meaning, of the text.

A second popular method within structuralism utilized by adherents such as Claude Lévi-Strauss is paradigmatic analysis. This method views the biblical text as a myth that seeks to address opposition or conflict. Through an analysis of structure (repetition, binary opposites, metaphor and metonymy, diachronic/synchronic study), the paradigm of a text becomes apparent and reveals the underlying literary myth in which the meaning resides. By this method Edmund Leach produced an analysis of the beginning chapters of Genesis summarized here.

> Leach provides an elaborate diagram intended to summarize the binary distinctions and mediations of the Creation myth, which following the principle of redundancy, appears in three permutations (the two Creation stories and the Cain-Abel sequence). Genesis 1 divides into two three-day periods, the first characterized by the creation of the static or "dead" world, the second by the creation of the moving, sexual, "live" world. Just as the

57. Deep structures are contrasted with surface structures such as characters and plot.

58. Klein, Blomberg, and Hubbard, *Introduction to Biblical Interpretation*, 429.

59. Anthony C. Thiselton, *New Horizons in Hermeneutics: The Theory and Practice of Transforming Biblical Reading* (Grand Rapids: Zondervan, 1992), 572.

static triad of grass, cereals, and fruit-trees is created on the third day, the triad of domestic and wild animals and creeping things appear on the sixth, "but only the grass is allocated to the animals. Everything else, including the meat of the animals, is for Man's use." Finally, man and woman are created simultaneously and commanded to be fruitful and multiply, "but the problems of Life versus Death, and Incest versus Procreation are not faced at all."[60]

Although structuralism's methods can help to define the various literary features of a text, structuralism's contributions end with mere analysis and lack an interest in actually understanding the text. Structuralist hermeneutical theory has been critiqued properly as esoteric, deterministic, and atheistic.[61] One beneficial result, however, is an increased literary awareness among those who continue to use the historical-critical method. The fields of rhetorical and narrative criticism, for instance, are refreshing in their willingness to treat the biblical compositions as completed products with literary features.[62]

Reader Response

Previous hermeneutical methods have focused on the place of the author or the place of the text in determining meaning. Stanley Fish is the major proponent of another interpretive scheme that positions the reader at the center of hermeneutics. Such reader-centered approaches can be separated into moderate reader response and radical reader response, depending on whether the reader merely contributes to meaning or is the sole producer of the meaning of a text.

Within moderate reader response, the reader is believed to derive meaning through his or her interaction with the text. For adherents of this theory, it is self-evident that different readers may read the same text in different ways. What it means to one reader is not necessarily the same as what it means to another. It is the recognition of readers' preunderstandings—that is, their view of the world, assumptions, attitudes, and biases, which are established by their social location (race,

60. Cited in Richard Jacobson, "The Structuralists and the Bible," in *A Guide to Contemporary Hermeneutics: Major Trends in Biblical Interpretation*, ed. Donald K. McKim (Grand Rapids: Eerdmans, 1986), 284. Additional examples of structuralist methods applied to the biblical text appear in *Semeia 2* (1974).

61. Blomberg, *Historical Reliability of the Gospels*, 59; Grant R. Osborne, *The Hermeneutical Spiral: A Comprehensive Introduction to Biblical Interpretation* (Downers Grove, IL: InterVarsity, 1991), 373; Tremper Longman III, *Literary Approaches to Biblical Interpretation* (Grand Rapids: Zondervan, 1987), 37.

62. The position that sees literary and historical approaches as compatible rather than competing is presented well in Longman, *Literary Approaches to Biblical Interpretation*.

class, gender, etc.)—that lead readers to ask certain questions of a text while leaving other questions unasked. Readers' preunderstandings make them sensitive to seeing certain truths in a text while blind spots persist with regard to other details.

Moderate reader response maintains that a text is incomplete until the individual reader participates in it. In fact, texts themselves invite such reader participation. Until the reader reads, meaning is only potential, not actual, but the actualized meaning is what was potentially there in the text. Thus although multiple interpretations (polysemy) are possible, valid interpretations are nonetheless constrained by the text in some way. The act of reading itself is where meaning resides because only in the act of reading is there dialogue between the text and the reader, a conversation that allows the horizons of both text and reader to come together. Thus with the move to a reader-response approach, meaning lies in front of rather than behind a text. The "new hermeneutic" discussed above can appropriately be classified as moderate reader response.

While moderate reader response argues that the reader has a *partial* role in determining meaning, radical reader response postulates that the reader *alone* determines meaning. Thus Fish declares that the "reader's response is not *to* the meaning; it *is* the meaning."[63] With this move, readers in effect become authors who are invited to use the text in whatever manner they desire. Radical reader response begins with the belief that objective reading is impossible and that preunderstanding *determines* interpretation. As a result, proponents argue that ethical readers can and should embrace their own commitments and interpret the text in a way that furthers their own, often political, agenda. Thus a reading strategy that posits human experience as the center of the interpretive enterprise—a hermeneutics of experience—reigns. In effect, what a reader finds in a text is a result of what he or she brings to it.

In this context the term *reader* has been redefined. Whereas moderate reader response spoke of individual readers, radical reader response is interested in "reading communities" whose members share historically conditioned expectations on the basis of common race, class, gender, religion, age, sexuality, and so on, with each combination of variants comprising a separate reading community. Each community defines what constitutes valid reading for it, establishing localized rather than universal norms for interpretation. Thus constraints on interpretation exist for individuals within a community, while across reading communities all externally imposed interpretive norms are denied.

Liberation theology, feminist theology, and black theology demonstrate radical reader-response hermeneutics. What these various sociocritical

63. Cited in Thiselton, *New Horizons in Hermeneutics*, 539.

schools share is a commitment to critiquing the ideological stance of a text and its ability to manipulate and control any who submit to its ideology. In other words, all texts project a worldview and seek to draw the reader into an acceptance of that worldview. Sociocritical interpreters approach texts with a hermeneutic of suspicion, an adversarial attitude of skepticism rather than trust toward the ideology of a text. The hermeneutic of suspicion aims to unmask the worldview of a text, which is suspected of supporting the powerful and oppressing the powerless, and to evaluate it based on their community norms. They also employ a hermeneutics of proclamation, which grants authority to those texts that can be evaluated as emancipatory, in order to harness the text as a tool for societal change. The validity of interpretation is measured pragmatically in terms of how well it fits the expressed interpretive goal.[64]

Although each reading community has its own unique characteristics,[65] an example from feminist liberationist hermeneutics models the kinds of methods put forward by each group. Feminist liberationist approaches[66] suspect (hermeneutics of suspicion) that the worldview of the Bible is patriarchal, bolstering an illegitimate domination of women by men. Even texts that are not overtly patriarchal have been interpreted in male-centered cultures to perpetuate the oppression of women. So interpretation begins by asking whether a text, its interpretation, or its application in any way supports patriarchal interests or functions in the interests of domination.

In evaluating a text, feminist liberationist hermeneutics upholds women's experience as a normative standard by which to critique and evaluate (hermeneutics of critical evaluation) the patriarchal ideology of the biblical cultures and texts. Any text determined to fall short of the goal of "women's self-affirmation, power and liberation from all patriarchal alienation, marginalization, and oppression"[67] is not granted authority within the reading community. Such texts are said to reflect only the word of man/men and not the Word of God as it is present in the biblical traditions.

64. Kevin J. Vanhoozer, *Is There a Meaning in This Text? The Bible, the Reader, and the Morality of Literary Knowledge* (Grand Rapids: Zondervan, 1998), 102.

65. There are multiple approaches even under the umbrella of feminist hermeneutics. See Carolyn Osiek, "The Feminist and the Bible: Hermeneutical Alternatives," in *Feminist Perspectives on Biblical Scholarship*, ed. A. Yarbro Collins (Atlanta: Scholars Press, 1985), 98–104.

66. This discussion of method draws heavily on the work of Elisabeth Schüssler Fiorenza, *But She Said: Feminist Practices of Biblical Interpretation* (Boston: Beacon, 1992).

67. Elisabeth Schüssler Fiorenza, "The Will to Choose or Reject: Continuing Our Critical Work," in *Feminist Interpretation of the Bible*, ed. Letty M. Russell (Philadelphia: Westminster, 1985), 125–36.

Feminist interpreters do combine reconstructive methods with these deconstructive tools. Some texts are evaluated positively and are proclaimed (hermeneutics of proclamation) as representative of the true, liberative core of Scripture that is to be upheld. Other texts that had been deemed patriarchal are given new interpretations to make them liberative. Texts and traditions that attest to the existence of women's leadership roles are remembered (hermeneutics of remembrance) as are texts that record the abuse of women.[68] The act of bringing to the forefront the women who have suffered abuse, both by the historical events that occurred and at the hand of the author who recorded them, can be offered up *in memoriam*. Women gain a voice and a presence insofar as the abuse against them is named and critiqued.

Finally, feminist liberationist readings seek to actualize and dramatize their interpretations through song, art, drama, and ritual (hermeneutics of ritualization). By means of creative imagination and ritual, the interpreter can present visions of the ideal of liberation yet to be realized and in presenting that vision, enable others to imagine the possibilities; once imagined, there is increased potential that they might be realized.

This combination of methods is well illustrated by the following interpretation of 2 Kings 22:14–20.[69] Employing a hermeneutics of suspicion toward both the text and its interpreters, Johanna Bos cites patriarchal elements in the text. She observes the unexpectedness of Huldah's appearance and the naturalness with which the text records the presence of a female authority figure who speaks God's Word for overcoming "the temple of patriarchy," a structure of oppressive ideology. But even as the story introduces Huldah as a prophet of God, Bos shows how Huldah's identity as a woman is cloaked under patriarchal influence as she is identified by her profession and by the names of three male relatives. Although Huldah is overlooked by most commentators, Bos celebrates her as a woman with a word from God, who has a crucial role in biblical history, and who serves as an example of survival, perseverance, reimagining, and ecclesial (church) subversion, even though she functioned outside the recognized authority structure of her day. Bos says that the temple remained "an entirely male enterprise and perhaps [Huldah] was not entirely unhappy to call out its disastrous future" and the judgment on the entire community that failed to exercise God's justice and service for the poor and oppressed. On the basis of her interpretation, Bos proclaims that for women today who recognize the pit of patriarchy in the church, "it may not be enough to clean it all up. The old has got to

---

68. See, for instance, Phyllis Trible, *Texts of Terror: Literary-Feminist Readings of Biblical Narratives* (Philadelphia: Fortress, 1984).

69. Johanna W. H. Bos, "Re-imagining Language-Word" (paper presented at "Re-imagining ... God ... the Community... the Church," Minneapolis, November 4–7, 1993).

come down before the new community can begin"; her concluding rally cry, "We will not give up the fight, we have only started," commissioned her audience to the task.

Although the feminist hermeneutic of remembrance that proclaims the stories of women in the Bible serves as a valuable corrective to an area where Christians throughout history have often fallen short, it becomes suspect when it glorifies women in the Bible uncritically, assuming the innocence and wisdom of their actions. Similarly, if we consider the Bible to be the true revelation of God and the authority for the Christian faith, we cannot apply a hermeneutic of suspicion to the scriptural texts themselves, although doing so might be appropriate when we evaluate suggested interpretations. Suspicion toward interpretations is valid because of the pervasiveness of human sinfulness. The biblical text as divine revelation, however, warrants not an approach characterized by suspicion but one characterized by discernment and understanding, with a willingness to learn and obey. Finally, the belief that women's experience is equivalent to or an even greater authority than the written Word of God must also be rejected. The opinions of no person, male or female, are on par with Scripture. Nonetheless, we should affirm that women can and should be actively engaged in reading the Scriptures and applying the biblical teachings in their lives and work.

Deconstructionism

Finally, the most recently proposed hermeneutical framework is deconstructionism. Advanced by Frenchman Jacques Derrida, deconstructionism rejects the ability of a text to refer to anything outside itself, that is, to anything in the external world.[70] Language is metaphorical rather than referential. If we have a written text, it means that we do not have the actual presence of the author. The very act of writing frees the text from its author's control and points to the author's absence.

Deconstructionist hermeneutics makes much out of the fact that texts can be repeated. Although they were produced in one context, they might be read in another. Iterability—the ability of a text to be repeated—is, for the deconstructionist, evidence that meaning cannot be fixed, for when a text is repeated, the reader is unable to determine the significance that belongs to the original context and that which belongs to the new.[71] Therefore, interpretation becomes play.[72] Just as a musical score (a text) played by the musician produces slightly different results in each performance, so too each time a text is uttered, it is uttered differently.

70. Thiselton, *New Horizons in Hermeneutics*, 108.
71. Vanhoozer, *Is There a Meaning in This Text?* 78–79.
72. Osborne, *Hermeneutical Spiral*, 382.

Deconstructionists maintain that the notion of authorial intention is inadequate for stabilizing meaning;[73] with no stable point outside a text or language, meaning is variable, and eventually all texts will lapse into contradiction or ambiguity. Thus the interpreter is invited to enjoy the play and "celebrate interpretive creativity."[74]

Deconstructionism is thoroughly postmodern in its rejection of all overarching systems of meaning or worldviews. Since there is no authorial control over meaning, all texts are open to multiple interpretations. Therefore, the interpretive approach of deconstructionists is to object to any authoritative voice.[75] Arguments in favor of one interpretation over another amount to nothing more than power struggles,[76] but since all interpretations are equally valid, the deconstructionist expresses a moral imperative to withstand any attempt to postulate a single version of reality as normative.[77] Thus, when interpreting biblical texts, deconstructionists seek to unmask the subtle contradictions and ambiguities that they believe demonstrate the impossibility of fixed meaning,[78] and they attempt to negate, reverse, or contradict any claims to knowledge or truth while emphasizing areas "where the text fails to cohere."[79]

J. D. Crossan and Stephen Moore are among the few scholars who have tried to apply this hermeneutical approach to the biblical text. Anthony Thiselton provides helpful summaries of Crossan's work with Matthew 13:44:

> In rabbinic parables the two acts of selling/buying and finding follow the sequence: (i) transference of ownership, (ii) finding treasure. But Jesus transposes the sequence, making the series of actions dubious from a moral viewpoint. The Jewish parable has a didactic content about value of work-ethics which leads to discovery. According to Crossan, the point of Jesus's utterance is that it simply points to a present opportunity which remains unspecified. Obtaining the field procures the space for discovery; but the content remains hidden. The parable therefore shows us how language fails to refer beyond itself: "I will tell you, it says, what the Kingdom of God is like. Watch carefully how, and as I *fail* to do so and learn that *it cannot be done* . . . the more magnificent my failure, the greater my success."[80]

73. Vanhoozer, *Is There a Meaning in This Text?* 80.
74. Ibid., 50.
75. Ibid., 88.
76. Ibid., 119.
77. Ibid., 183.
78. Klein, Blomberg, and Hubbard, *Introduction to Biblical Interpretation*, 441.
79. Vanhoozer, *Is There a Meaning in This Text?* 39, 111.
80. Thiselton, *New Horizons in Hermeneutics*, 118.

Although some scholars have affirmed deconstructionism insofar as it stands as a corrective to interpretive pride and maintains a high respect for otherness,[81] it is difficult if not impossible to reconcile it with a theistic worldview. Engaging in deconstructionism is a countertheological task. When one rejects signs as communicators of reality, one must object to Jesus as a sign that effectively communicates God's presence and being.[82] The orthodox Christian reader will find little use for this approach.

Hermeneutics within Orthodox Christianity

During the last two hundred years, some interpreters have continued to believe that Scripture represents God's revelation of himself—his words and his actions—to humanity. The task of the interpreter, according to this group, is to understand more fully the intended meaning of the original author.[83] Studies of the surrounding history, culture, language, and theological understanding of the original recipients are undertaken in order to understand what the scriptural revelation meant to its original recipients. Important scholars within this general tradition (and this list is by no means exhaustive) include E. W. Hengstenberg, Carl F. Keil, Franz Delitzsch, H. A. W. Meyer, J. P. Lange, F. Godet, Henry Alford, Charles Ellicott, J. B. Lightfoot, B. F. Westcott, F. J. A. Hort, Charles Hodge, John A. Broadus, and Theodore B. Zahn.[84] Hermeneutical manuals within this tradition have included those by C. A. G. Keil, A. B. Davidson, Patrick Fairbairn, A. Immer, Milton S. Terry, Louis Berkhof, A. Berkeley Mickelsen, and Bernard Ramm.

Nonetheless, the hermeneutical approach that seeks the fixed meaning an author intended in a text has been labeled by opponents as the "intentional fallacy." Several objections are raised against it:

1. Some authors publicly repudiate things they have written earlier, proving that the meaning of a text is changeable.

81. Vanhoozer, *Is There a Meaning in This Text?* 184–85.
82. Ibid., 86.
83. The consensus among conservative evangelical scholars during this time is that the ideal goal of hermeneutics is to understand the author's intended meaning. However, in recent years some authors have stated that we cannot ascertain the author's intended meaning since he is no longer available to us and that we must accept that we can recover only as much of the author's intention as is mediated by the text. We believe that this is an unnecessary dichotomy for the following reason: If one accepts the traditional doctrine of inspiration (as we do), we believe that God so guided the human authors that what he intended them to communicate is encoded in the words of the biblical text. Therefore by attempting to understand the meaning of the words encoded in the text, we are at the same time attempting to understand the author's intended meaning.
84. This list is from Mickelsen, *Interpreting the Bible*, 47–48.

2. It is impossible to reproduce the meaning experience that an author had when first writing a text.

3. Sometimes other people understand an author's meaning better than the author.

E. D. Hirsch provides a convincing response to each of these objections:

1. Responding to the accusation that the meaning of a text changes, even for the author, Hirsch argues:

> When critics assert that the author's understanding of his text changes, they refer to the experience that everybody has when he rereads his own work. His response to it is different. . . . These examples do not show the meaning of the work has changed, but precisely the opposite. If the work's meaning had changed (instead of the author himself and his attitudes), then the author would not have needed to repudiate his meaning and could have spared himself the discomfort of a public re-cantation. No doubt the *significance* of the work to the author had changed a great deal, but its meaning had not changed at all. . . . Even though the author has indeed changed his mind about the meaning he wants to convey by his words, he has not managed to change his earlier meaning. This is very easily proved by his own report. He could report a change in his understanding only if he were able to compare his earlier construction of his meaning with his later construction.[85]

2. Responding to the criticism that one cannot reproduce the exact meaning experience that an author had when he or she first wrote a text, Hirsch argues that it is important to distinguish between meaning and meaning experience. Meaning (what I intended to convey by certain signs and symbols) is reproducible. Meaning experience (meaning plus psychological significance to me at the time I wrote it) is not necessarily reproducible, nor does it need to be.[86]

3. Responding to the argument that in some situations another person understands the text better than the author, Hirsch argues that it is more accurate to say either that a later writer may understand the subject matter better than an earlier author (but this is not the same as saying that the later writer understood the original author's

---

85. E. D. Hirsch Jr., *Validity in Interpretation* (New Haven: Yale University Press, 1967), 7–9.
86. Ibid., 14–18.

meaning better than did the original author) or that a later writer may understand the *implications* of what an earlier author wrote more fully than the original author understood the implications. Again, this does not mean that the later writer understood the original author's meaning better.[87]

Although today's interpreter obviously faces a plethora of interpretive schemes, there are both pragmatic and theological reasons to employ an author-centered hermeneutic. Robert Stein asserts that "the greatest argument in favor of understanding the author as the determiner of a text's meaning is that it is the common sense approach to all communication. . . . Communication between two people can only take place if both parties seek to understand what the other person means by their words."[88]

No one likes to have his or her words taken out of context and portrayed in a manner that misunderstands one's intentions. Such is the stuff of slander and lawsuits. Or consider the grade you can expect on a paper if you deliberately misrepresent a source. All authors expect the courtesy of being understood and thus quoted and interpreted in context and with an eye for accuracy. One would expect this courtesy to be extended to the biblical authors as well. Even those who adhere to a radical reader-response hermeneutic have been known to object to interpreters "bent on reading my text against my clearly expressed intentions"![89]

Some have argued, however, that the biblical texts are "literature," which takes on a life of its own as "art," and therefore typical rules of communication fail to apply. But who defines what constitutes literature (as opposed to writing not necessarily intended as art)? Consider Paul's letter to the Romans. Certainly it was written as a natural means of communicating with them. If Paul's letter to the Romans was communication to them, how is it literature to us? Such a question demonstrates that the line between communication and literature cannot be drawn easily if at all. The biblical text is not a special sort of literature free of the rules that reign over all communication.

There are also theological grounds for preferring an author-centered hermeneutic. As Vanhoozer asserts, "Beliefs about human authors are tied to beliefs about God."[90] Orthodox Christianity believes in a

87. Ibid., 20–21.
88. Robert H. Stein, "The Benefits of an Author-Oriented Approach to Hermeneutics," *Journal of the Evangelical Theological Society* 44, no. 3 (2001): 455.
89. Elisabeth Schüssler Fiorenza, *Jesus and the Politics of Interpretation* (New York: Continuum, 2000), 119.
90. Vanhoozer, *Is There a Meaning in This Text?* 71.

sovereign creator God, that is, a God who authored reality. God, as author and authority, has the right to institute the rules of behavior for what he created. Theologian Millard Erickson puts it this way: "In the ultimate sense, if there is a supreme being higher than humans or anything else in the created order, he has the right to determine what we are to believe and how we are to live. From the Christian standpoint, God is the authority in these matters because of who he is."[91] The idea of a sovereign creator God speaks of God's freedom, transcendence, and otherness but also particularly of God's power to be and to act independent of external constraints. Conversely, this means that we as the creatures are utterly dependent upon our Creator, our author, for meaning. So, too, with human authors of texts. The author controls the meaning of his creation, the text receives meaning from the author, and the reader rightly seeks the author's intentions as mediated by the shared text.

The theological position that views God as author offers additional theological reasons for interpreting or understanding Scripture's literal meaning rather than evaluating it according to human reason, experience, or desires. Consider the emphasis on preunderstanding within reader-response hermeneutics. With a proper view of God as author, the reader's race, class, gender, age, country of origin, and so on are of no consequence in biblical interpretation because God's Word originates in a context divorced from human differences: its origin is God himself. God's revelation continually attests to an unalterable, unchanging message. What its author sought to communicate to the original human audience, it seeks to communicate now, and biblical interpretation rightly discerns the same message that was delivered to the original audience.

Chapter Summary

This chapter has attempted to provide a brief overview of some of the major trends in the historical development of hermeneutics. More complete discussions may be found in the books listed below, and the reader with access to and interest in them is encouraged to develop further historical understanding than this brief discussion provides.

Throughout history we can see the gradual emergence of the presuppositions and practices now known as the grammatical-historical method of interpretation. This method suggests that the meaning of

91. Millard J. Erickson, *Christian Theology*, 2nd ed. (Grand Rapids: Baker, 1998), 270.

a text is the author's intended meaning and that the author's intention can be derived most accurately by observing the facts of history and the rules of grammar as they apply to the text being studied. Major contributions to the development of the grammatical-historical method include (1) the predominant use of literal exegesis by Christ and the New Testament writers; (2) the theoretical principles (but not the practice) of Augustine; (3) the Syrian school of Antioch; (4) the Spanish Jews of the twelfth to fifteenth centuries; (5) the work of Nicolas of Lyra, Erasmus, and Reuchlin; (6) the work of Luther and Calvin; and (7) those scholars named in the last section.

Throughout history a second set of presuppositions and methods has been manifested in a variety of ways. The basic premise has been that the meaning of a text is discoverable, not by the methods usually used to understand communication between persons but by the use of some special interpretive key. The result of the use of most of these interpretive keys has been to impart the reader's meaning to the text (*eisegesis*) rather than to read the author's meaning from the text (*exegesis*). Examples of such interpretive keys include (1) Jewish and Christian allegorism, (2) the fourfold medieval exegesis, and (3) the letterism and numerology of the Kabbalists. Post-Reformation liberalism and neoorthodoxy have supplied interpretive keys derived from their presuppositions about the origin and nature of Scripture.

Finally, recent trends in hermeneutics have raised fundamental challenges to the location of meaning. Examples include (1) the new hermeneutic's introduction of discussions on preunderstanding and fusion of horizons, (2) structuralism's search for deep structures, (3) reader response's insistence on the plurality of meaning and a hermeneutics of experience and suspicion, and (4) deconstruction's denial of meaningful communication.

Resources for Further Reading

Louis Berkhof. Chapters 2 and 3 in *Principles of Biblical Interpretation*. Grand Rapids: Baker, 1950.

Darrell Bock. "Evangelicals and the Use of the Old Testament, Part I." *Bibliotheca Sacra* 142 (July 1985): 209–23.

———. "Evangelicals and the Use of the Old Testament, Part II." *Bibliotheca Sacra* 142 (October 1985): 306–19.

Gerald Bray. *Biblical Interpretation: Past and Present*. Downers Grove, IL: InterVarsity, 1996.

F. F. Bruce. "The History of New Testament Study." In *New Testament Interpretation: Essays on Principles and Methods*, edited by I. Howard Marshall, 21–59. Grand Rapids: Eerdmans, 1991.

Frederic W. Farrar. *History of Interpretation*. 1885. Reprint, Grand Rapids: Baker, 1961.

K. Fullerton. *Prophecy and Authority: A Study in the History of the Doctrine and Interpretation of Scripture*. New York: Macmillan, 1919.

Robert M. Grant. *A Short History of the Interpretation of the Bible*. Rev. ed. New York: Macmillan, 1963.

James D. Hernando. Chapters 2, 3, and 4 in *Dictionary of Hermeneutics: A Concise Guide to Terms, Names, Methods, and Expressions*. Springfield, MO: Gospel Publishing House, 2005.

Walter C. Kaiser and Moisés Silva. Chapters 12 and 13 in *An Introduction to Biblical Hermeneutics: The Search for Meaning*. Grand Rapids: Zondervan, 1994.

William W. Klein, Craig L. Blomberg, and Robert L. Hubbard Jr. Chapter 2 and appendix in *Introduction to Biblical Interpretation*. Dallas: Word, 1993.

Richard N. Longenecker. *Biblical Exegesis in the Apostolic Period*. Grand Rapids: Eerdmans, 1975.

Donald K. McKim, ed. Part 4 in A *Guide to Contemporary Hermeneutics: Major Trends in Biblical Interpretation*. Grand Rapids: Eerdmans, 1986.

———, ed. Parts 5 and 6 in *Historical Handbook of Major Biblical Interpreters*. Downers Grove, IL: InterVarsity, 1998.

A. Berkeley Mickelsen. Chapter 2 in *Interpreting the Bible*. Grand Rapids: Eerdmans, 1963.

Roger Nicole. "New Testament Use of the Old Testament." In *Revelation and the Bible: Contemporary Evangelical Thought*, edited by Carl Henry, 135–51. Grand Rapids: Baker, 1958.

Grant R. Osborne. Appendix 1 in *The Hermeneutical Spiral: A Comprehensive Introduction to Biblical Interpretation*. 2nd ed. Downers Grove, IL: InterVarsity, 2006.

Bernard Ramm. Chapters 3, 6, and 9 in *Hermeneutics*. Grand Rapids: Baker, 1971.

———. Chapter 2 in *Protestant Biblical Interpretation*. 3rd rev. ed. Grand Rapids: Baker, 1970.

Milton S. Terry. Part 3 in *Biblical Hermeneutics*. 1883. Reprint, Grand Rapids: Zondervan, 1974.

Ronald Youngblood. "Old Testament Quotations in the New Testament." In *The NIV: The Making of a Contemporary Translation*, edited by Kenneth L. Barker, 111–18. Grand Rapids: Academie Books, 1986.

THREE

HISTORICAL-CULTURAL
AND CONTEXTUAL ANALYSIS

After completing this chapter, you should be able to

1. Define the following terms:
   a. Historical-cultural analysis
   b. Contextual analysis
   c. Lexical-syntactical analysis
   d. Theological analysis
   e. Literary analysis
2. Describe a six-step model that can be used to interpret any biblical text.
3. List and describe three basic steps involved in historical-cultural and contextual analysis.
4. Identify three ways of discerning an author's intention in writing a specific book.
5. List six important secondary steps involved in contextual analysis.
6. Apply the above principles to identify misinterpretations of selected biblical texts and advance more accurate interpretations of them.

Introductory Comments

The preceding chapters discussed the principle that, based on the assumption that an author is an articulate communicator (as we believe God inspired the biblical authors to be), the primary presupposition of hermeneutical theory must be that *the meaning of a text is the author's intended meaning*, rather than the meanings we may wish to ascribe to his words. If we abandon this principle, there remains no normative, compelling criterion for discriminating between valid and invalid interpretations.

Chapter 2 specifically surveyed historical trends in interpretation, observing that some interpreters have followed normal principles of communication while others have fallen into vagaries of interpretation through development of unusual hermeneutical principles.

Chapters 3 through 8 present the principles of hermeneutics and show how to apply them to the interpretation of scriptural texts. The complex skill of biblical interpretation and application is divided into six steps:

1. *Historical-cultural analysis* considers the historical-cultural milieu in which an author wrote in order to understand his allusions, references, and purpose. *Contextual analysis* considers the relationship of a given passage to the entire passage surrounding it, since a better understanding of an author's intended meaning results from an acquaintance with the larger context.
2. *Lexical-syntactical analysis* develops an understanding of the definitions of words (lexicology) and their relationship to one another (syntax) in order to understand more accurately the meaning the author intended to convey.
3. *Theological analysis* studies the level of theological understanding at the time a revelation was given in order to ascertain the meaning of the text for its original recipients. It also takes into account related Scriptures, whether given before or after the passage being studied.
4. *Literary (genre) analysis* identifies the literary form or method used in a given passage, such as historical narrative, letters, doctrinal exposition, poetry, or apocalyptic. Each has its unique mode of expression and interpretation.
5. *Comparison with other interpreters* compares the tentative interpretation derived from the four steps above with the work of other interpreters.
6. *Application* is the important step of translating the meaning a biblical text had for its original hearers into the significance it has for believers in a different time and culture. In some instances the

transmission is accomplished fairly easily; in other instances, such as biblical commands that were obviously influenced by cultural factors (e.g., greeting with the holy kiss), the translation across cultures becomes more complex.

In this six-step procedure steps 1 through 3 belong to general hermeneutics. Step 4 constitutes special hermeneutics. Step 6—transmission and application of the biblical message from one time and culture to another—is not always considered to be an integral part of hermeneutics per se but is included in this text because of its obvious relevance for the twenty-first-century believer so widely separated by both time and culture from the original recipients of Scripture.[1]

Historical-Cultural and Contextual Analysis

The meaning of a text cannot be interpreted with any degree of certainty without historical-cultural and contextual analysis. The following two exercises show the importance of such analysis.

Exercise 5. Proverbs 22:28 commands: "Do not move an ancient boundary stone set up by your forefathers." Which of the following sentences best conveys the true intent and meaning of this verse in its context?

a. Do not make changes from the way we have always done things.

b. Do not steal.

c. Do not remove the guideposts that direct travelers from town to town.

d. None of the above.

e. All of the above.

Exercise 6. Hebrews 4:12 affirms: "For the word of God is living and active. Sharper than any double-edged sword, it penetrates even to dividing soul and spirit, joints and marrow; it judges the thoughts and attitudes of the heart." Does this verse

1. Most historical critics would forego this step entirely as being irrelevant to their purposes. On the other hand, some interpreters reserve the term *hermeneutics* for this step alone; Gordon D. Fee and Douglas Stuart, *How to Read the Bible for All Its Worth: A Guide to Understanding the Bible*, 3rd ed. (Grand Rapids: Zondervan, 2003), 29.

a. Teach that man is trichotomous, since it speaks of a body, soul, and spirit?

b. Teach that the truth contained in God's Word is dynamic and changing rather than dead and static?

c. Give a warning to professing believers?

d. Encourage Christians to use the Word of God aggressively in their witnessing and counseling?

e. None of the above.

The answer to exercise 5 is (b). If you answered either (a) or (c), it is likely that you came to the text subconsciously asking, What does this text mean to me? The important question, however, is What did this text mean to the original writer and his audience? In this instance the ancient landmark refers to the boundary marker that separated one man's land from his neighbor's. Without modern surveying techniques, it was a relatively easy matter to increase one's acreage by moving such markers late in the evening. The prohibition is directed against a specific type of stealing.

The solution to exercise 6 will become clearer by the end of the chapter. The point of these exercises is to demonstrate that without knowledge of the writer's background, supplied through historical-cultural and contextual analysis, our tendency is to interpret his writings by asking, What does this mean to me? rather than, What did this mean to the original author? Until we can answer the latter question with some degree of certainty, we have no basis for claiming validity for our interpretation.

Historical-cultural and contextual analysis can be done by asking three basic questions, each more specific than the previous one. The three questions are

1. What is the general historical milieu in which the writer speaks?
2. What is the specific historical-cultural context and purpose of this book?
3. What is the immediate context of the passage under consideration?

Each of these general questions or steps is further subdivided in the following discussion.

Determining the General Historical-Cultural Context

Three secondary questions are important in determining the historical-cultural context. *First, what is the general historical situation facing the author and his audience?* What were the political, economic, and social situations? What was the main source of livelihood? What were the major threats and concerns? Knowledge of the historical-cultural context is crucial for answering basic questions about a text, such as What is happening to the author of Lamentations? Is he suffering from a "nervous breakdown" or from a normal grief reaction? Or, Why was Jonah so unwilling to obey God's command to preach to the people of Nineveh?

Second, knowledge of what customs will clarify the meaning of given actions? Suppose someone unfamiliar with American culture were to witness a young boy in a cowboy hat knock on the door of a stranger's home, wave a gun, and make a demand. Even more bizarre, the home-owner appears unfazed by the child's clothing, gives the child what he demands, and sends him to the house next door, where the scenario repeats itself. The awareness that this event occurred on Halloween along with an explanation of "trick or treating" would be necessary to prevent the bewildered observer from calling the police. Today's readers are similarly outsiders to the biblical cultures and need to develop awareness of cultural practices to avoid equally misguided interpretations.

In Mark 7, for example, Jesus soundly upbraids the Pharisees for their concept of corban. In the practice of corban a man could declare that all his money would go to the temple treasury when he died, and that, since his money belonged to God, he was therefore no longer responsible for financially supporting his aging parents. Jesus argues that men were using this Pharisaic tradition to render God's command (the fifth commandment) of no account. Without knowledge of the cultural practice of corban, we would be unable to understand this passage.

Other examples of the advantages an understanding of cultural customs brings may be easily found. Consider the account of Jacob's wedding in Genesis 29. The text describes a feast during the day in celebration and then says that when it was time for the wedding night, Laban gave Leah to Jacob instead of Rachel. And in the morning, surprise! "When morning came, there was Leah" (Gen. 29:25). We might wonder how it was possible for Laban to switch sisters without Jacob realizing it. Learning that at that time the bride would have been escorted to a tent set up for the married couple and that she would have remained veiled and the tent kept in darkness until after the marriage was consummated helps explain the comparative ease with which Laban was able to substitute Leah for Rachel.

Or consider the ritual recorded in Genesis 15:9–21. As God promises Abram both land and descendants, Abram sacrifices animals, arranges their halved bodies, and witnesses a smoking firepot that passes between the pieces of the animals. It is unlikely that today's readers have experienced such an event. In Abram's time two parties making a legal agreement in a covenant would sacrifice animals and cut them in two. Often the weaker partner in a covenant made between a suzerain (leader) and a vassal would pass between the two halves as a means of saying that if he should fail to keep his end of the treaty, this—being cut in two—is what should happen to him. But what is striking about this passage? The smoking firepot, which is the visible manifestation of God in this passage, passes between the animal pieces. It is the Lord who passes between the pieces, and an accurate interpretation of the text would highlight how this act communicates that the Lord is the one who agrees to take on the punishment if Abram should break the covenant! Again, an awareness of cultural details alerts us to the significance of actions that could escape our understanding otherwise.

Third, what was the spiritual disposition of the audience? Many of the biblical books were written at times when the recipients' level of commitment was low because of carnality, discouragement, or temptation from unbelievers or apostates. The meaning of the text cannot be understood properly if divorced from a knowledge of these factors. How, for example, should we understand a person who intentionally marries a prostitute, has three children by her and gives them bizarre names, mourns for her when she continues her prostitution and unfaithfulness, finds her after she has left him and become a slave prostitute, buys her back, then talks to her as if in a mentally dissociated state? Is this person suffering from an overly active "rescuer complex," or is he blatantly psychotic? Neither, of course, as we find when we examine the context of the life of Hosea, within which these actions take on powerful meaning and significance.

In summary, then, an important first step in properly understanding any biblical passage is to study the historical-cultural milieu in which the author wrote. Good exegetical commentaries often supply such information as part of their introductions, study Bibles provide such information in highly condensed form, and Bible handbooks and Bible dictionaries can answer many cultural questions. Several resource books are listed at the end of this chapter.

Determining the Specific Historical-Cultural Context and Purpose of a Book

A second, more specific step is to determine the specific purpose(s) of a book. Several secondary questions are helpful guides:

1. Who was the writer? What was his spiritual background and experience?

2. To whom was he writing (e.g., believers, unbelievers, apostates, believers who were in danger of becoming apostates, those he knew well, strangers, an individual, a group)?
3. Does the writer explicitly or implicitly state his purpose (intention) in writing this particular book?

The author and his recipients can usually be determined from internal (textual) data or external (historical) data. In some instances the evidence seems fairly conclusive; in other instances the best that can be derived is an educated hypothesis. An example is the book of Hebrews. The book itself contains no direct evidence regarding its recipients or its author. It was given its name, *To the Hebrews*, on the basis of deductive evidence. The epistle contains numerous allusions to the Old Testament that would not be meaningful to the average non-Hebrew. It constantly contrasts the Mosaic covenant to the Christian one, showing the superiority of the new to the old, a line of reasoning that would not be meaningful to those who had no loyalty to the Hebrew faith. For these and a number of other reasons, we can be certain that the book was written primarily to Jews rather than Gentiles, and that the name *To the Hebrews* is therefore appropriate.

The authorship of Hebrews is entirely another matter. We can say with considerable certainty that it was probably not Paul because the literary expression, thought forms, and attitudes toward the Mosaic law found in this book differ significantly from those found in books of known Pauline authorship. However, beyond this we have little solid evidence of its exact author. Most hypotheses offered are conjectures unsupported by hard evidence. For practical purposes the question of the book's exact authorship is not as important as the fact that the early church recognized its divine inspiration and authority and thus included it in the canon.[2]

2. At this point we should consider the relationship between historical criticism and historical-cultural analysis. Some evangelical Christians may be concerned with the procedural similarity between the two. As mentioned in chap. 1, historical criticism studies the authorship of a book, the date, and historical circumstances surrounding its composition, the authenticity of its contents, and its literary unity. Historical-cultural analysis also engages in these tasks in an attempt to understand the author's meanings. Thus the two terms significantly overlap.

Historical criticism, however, starts with positivistic presuppositions and concludes with statements contrary to the orthodox Christian faith. (Positivism is the philosophical position that people can have knowledge of nothing but observable phenomena and therefore should reject all speculation about ultimate origins or causes.) Historical-cultural analysis begins with orthodox biblical presuppositions, a position that radically differs from historical criticism. To affirm the value of historical-cultural analysis is not to affirm the validity of historical criticism.

After study has revealed the specific historical-cultural context within which a book was written, the author's purpose should be determined. There are three basic ways[3] to do so.

First, note the author's explicit statement or his repetition of certain phrases. For example, Luke 1:1–4 and Acts 1:1 tell us that Luke's purpose in writing was to present an orderly account of the beginning of the Christian era. In John 20:31 John tells us that his purpose was to present an account of Christ's ministry so that we might believe. First Peter is an exhortation to stand fast amid persecution (5:12). The tenfold repetition of the phrase "these are the generations of" in the book of Genesis suggests that the purpose of this book is to record the earliest development of humankind and God's initial intervention in human history.

Second, observe the paraenetic (hortatory) part of this writing. Since the exhortations flow from the purpose, they often give an important clue regarding the author's intentions. The book of Hebrews, for example, is interspersed with exhortations and warnings, so there is little doubt that the author's purpose was to persuade Jewish believers undergoing persecution (10:32–35) not to return to Judaism but to stay true to their new profession of faith (10:19–23; 12:1–3). The Pauline books likewise are filled with theological facts immediately followed by a "therefore" and an exhortation. If the meaning of the theological fact is uncertain, the nature of the exhortation will often be valuable in understanding its meaning.

Third, observe the author's selectivity, that is, points omitted or issues emphasized. The writer of 1 and 2 Chronicles, for example, does not give a complete history of all national events during Solomon's reign and the divided kingdom. He selects events illustrating that Israel can endure only if the nation and its leadership remain faithful to God's commandments and his covenant. For instance, we see that he frequently uses the phrase "_____ did what was evil [or right] in the sight of the LORD."

A good check on whether you understand the author's purpose(s) is to summarize his purpose(s) in a single sentence. Beware of interpreting any passage without first understanding the author's intention in writing the entire work that contains it.

Developing an Understanding of the Immediate Context

Proof-texting is generally disparaged as a method of Bible study because it misses this important step: it interprets verses without paying

3. Walter C. Kaiser Jr., notes given in a hermeneutics class at Trinity Evangelical Divinity School, Spring 1974.

proper attention to their context. Several secondary questions help us understand a text in its immediate context.

First, what are the major blocks of material and how do they fit together into a whole? Alternatively, what is the outline of the book? Outlines should take into account the fact that some biblical writers were more organized than others. It is important that outlines of biblical books not be imposed on the text but be developed by study of the text itself. There is, however, some valid subjectivity in the outlining process. While Mark's Gospel could be outlined geographically or chronologically, it is far more enlightening to outline it thematically, in a way that demonstrates Mark's unique presentation of Jesus' life and ministry. Furthermore, chapter breaks were not part of the original text written by the biblical authors but were added later to aid readers in finding and referencing particular sections. Sometimes the breaks between chapters coincide with transitions between blocks of material in the text, but decisions about this should always be made by a careful reading of the text rather than by an observation of chapter breaks alone.

Second, how does the passage under consideration contribute to the flow of the author's argument? Alternatively, what is the connection between the passage under study and the blocks of material immediately preceding and following it? There is usually a logical and/or theological connection between any two adjacent passages. The collection of Psalms and parts of the book of Proverbs might be considered exceptions, but even there, logical groups of ideas may be evident.

Third, what is the perspective of the author? Authors sometimes write as if looking through the eyes of God (as spokesmen for God), particularly in moral matters, while in narrative sections they frequently describe things the way they appear from a human perspective (as reporters speaking phenomenologically). We speak of the sun's setting, a phenomenological metaphor for the more cumbersome description of a section of the earth rotating out of the path of the sun's direct rays. For an accurate understanding of his meaning, it is important to distinguish the author's intention to be understood as a direct spokesman for God from his intention to speak as a human reporter describing an event phenomenologically.

As an example of the importance of this principle, consider the question of whether the flood was universal or local. It is difficult to determine from the context whether the language in Genesis 6–9 was intended to be understood noumenologically (from God's perspective) or phenomenologically (from a human's perspective). If the phrases "all flesh died" (7:21 KJV) and "all the high hills . . . were covered" (7:19 KJV) are understood noumenologically, a universal flood is implied. If these same phrases are understood phenomenologically, they could mean "all the animals that I could observe died," and "all the high hills that I could observe were covered." A phenomenological description could then imply either a universal or a local flood.

The traditional interpretation of these verses has been noumeno-logical.[4] On the other hand, interpreters such as Milton Terry believe that the flood description should be understood phenomenologically. He states:

> The narrative of the flood is probably the account of an eyewitness. Its vividness of description and minuteness of details contain the strongest evidence that it is such. It was probably a tradition handed down from Shem to his descendants until it was finally incorporated in the Books of Moses. The terms "all flesh," "all the high hills," and "all the heavens," denote simply all those known to the observer.[5]

From the standpoint of hermeneutics, the important principle is that scriptural writers sometimes intended to write from a noumenological perspective and sometimes from a phenomenological one. Our interpretation of their meaning may err if we fail to make this distinction.

Fourth, is the passage stating descriptive or prescriptive truth? Descriptive passages relate what was said or what happened at a particular time without necessarily commenting on the veracity of the statement or the appropriateness of the action. What God says is true; what humans say may or may not be true; what Satan says usually mixes truth and error. When Scripture describes human actions without comment, it should not necessarily be assumed that those actions are approved by God.

When Scripture describes an action of God with respect to human beings in a narrative passage, it should not be assumed that this is the way he will always work in believers' lives at every point in history. Although God's character is immutable, his actions are not. The methods God used in the Gospels or the book of Acts are often wrongly asserted to be his methods in all believers' lives. Throughout biblical history, God responded in various ways to different people.

Prescriptive passages of Scripture claim to articulate normative principles. The Epistles are primarily prescriptive, but occasionally they contain instances of individual rather than universal prescriptions (e.g., the variety of church governments that seem to have prevailed in the early church communities; Paul's request that Timothy bring him his

4. For a detailed overview of the issues that favor noumenological interpretation, see Gleason Archer, *A Survey of Old Testament Introduction* (Chicago: Moody, 1975), 202–11.

5. Milton S. Terry, *Biblical Hermeneutics* (1883; repr., Grand Rapids: Zondervan, 1974), 543.

cloak and parchments [2 Tim. 4:13]). Differences between various prescriptive passages suggest that one should not universalize any of them uncritically but apply each one as appropriate. When there is only one prescriptive passage on an issue or when the various prescriptive passages concur with one another, the teaching of the passage is generally considered to be normative. Contextual analysis is the most valid way of differentiating descriptive from prescriptive passages.

Fifth, what constitutes the teaching focus of the passage, and what represents incidental detail only? Some of the major heresies of church history have been supported by exegesis that failed to maintain this distinction. For example, a major teaching of the allegory of Christ as the vine (John 15) is that we derive the power to live spiritual lives from Christ, not from ourselves. Using an incidental detail as a teaching focus, one group of early theologians (later branded heretics) declared that since Christ is the vine, and vines are part of the created order, it follows that Christ is part of the created order. The Pelagians of the early fifth century dealt similarly with the story of the prodigal son, arguing that since the prodigal son repented and returned to his father without the aid of a mediator, it follows that we do not need a mediator.

A contemporary example of the failure to make a distinction between incidental details and the teaching focus of a passage was given by a Christian educator in a classroom lecture a few years ago. The discussion centered around 1 Corinthians 3:16: "You yourselves are God's temple." Paul's central point in this verse is the sacredness of Christ's body, the church. Focusing on an incidental detail (the structure of the Old Testament temple), this educator concluded that since the temple had three parts (an outer court, an inner court, and a holy of holies) and since Christians are called temples, it therefore follows that humans have three parts: body, soul, and spirit!

Finally, who is being addressed in this passage? A popular statement claims: "Every promise in the Book is mine." Pious though it sounds, the concept is hermeneutically invalid. Certainly we would not want to claim *all* the promises of Scripture (e.g., Rev. 3:16)! Nor would we want to claim all the commands given to believers, such as the command to Abraham to sacrifice his son (Gen. 22:3). The humorous anecdote of the young man who was searching frantically for God's will and decided to follow the lead of whatever Scripture he opened to is well known: the first passage that fell open was Matthew 27:5 ("Judas . . . went away and hanged himself"); the second passage was Luke 10:37 ("Go and do likewise"); and the third, John 13:27 ("What you are about to do, do quickly").

Though we smile at the folly of applying a text without regard to its context, a significant number of Christians use this method to determine

God's will for their lives. A more valid hermeneutical procedure is to ask the questions discussed above: Who is speaking? Is the teaching normative or intended for specific individuals? To whom is the passage directed?

Promises and commands are usually directed to one of three groups: national Israel, Old Testament believers, or New Testament believers. Normative promises and commands directed to New Testament believers are those most likely to apply to contemporary Christians. Some of the promises and commands directed to Old Testament believers also apply, depending on context and content (see chap. 5). Some commentators "spiritualize" the physical promises and commands made to national Israel and then apply them also to contemporary settings, but this practice is difficult to justify since it violates authorial intent.

Chapter Summary

The following steps are involved in historical-cultural and contextual analysis:

1. Determine the general historical and cultural milieu of the writer and his audience.
   a. Determine the general historical circumstances.
   b. Be aware of cultural circumstances and norms that add meaning to given actions.
   c. Discern the spiritual disposition of the audience.
2. Determine the purpose(s) the author had in writing a book.
   a. Note explicit statements or repeated phrases.
   b. Observe paraenetic or hortatory sections.
   c. Observe issues that are omitted or emphasized.
3. Understand how the passage fits into its immediate context.
   a. Identify the major blocks of material in the book and show how they fit into a coherent whole.
   b. Show how the passage fits into the flow of the author's argument.
   c. Determine the perspective that the author intends to communicate—noumenological (the way things really are) or phenomenological (the way things appear).
   d. Distinguish between descriptive and prescriptive truth.
   e. Distinguish between incidental details and the teaching focus of a passage.
   f. Identify the person or category of persons for whom the particular passage is intended.

Resources for Further Information

Paul Achtemeier, Roger Boraas, and Michael Fishbane, eds. *The HarperCollins Bible Dictionary*. San Francisco: HarperSanFrancisco, 1996.

J. McKee Adams. *Biblical Backgrounds*. Nashville: Broadman, 1934.

T. Desmond Alexander and David W. Baker, eds. *Dictionary of the Old Testament: Pentateuch*. Downers Grove, IL: InterVarsity, 2003.

Bill Arnold and Bryan Beyer. *Encountering the Old Testament: A Christian Survey*. Grand Rapids: Baker, 1999.

Bill Arnold and H. G. M. Williamson, eds. *Dictionary of the Old Testament: Historical Books*. Downers Grove, IL: InterVarsity, 2005.

Denis A. Baly. *The Geography of the Bible*. New rev. ed. New York: Harper & Row, 1974.

Charles K. Barrett, ed. *The New Testament Background: Selected Documents*. New York: Harper & Row, 1961.

Barry Beitzel. *The Moody Atlas of Bible Lands*. Chicago: Moody, 1985.

Geoffrey W. Bromiley, ed. *International Standard Bible Encyclopedia*. 4 vols. Grand Rapids: Eerdmans, 1979–88.

D. A. Carson and Douglas Moo. *An Introduction to the New Testament*. 2nd ed. Grand Rapids: Zondervan, 2005.

Adrian Curtis, ed. *Oxford Bible Atlas*. 4th rev. ed. New York: Oxford University Press, 2007.

David DeSilva. *Honor, Patronage, Kinship and Purity: Unlocking New Testament Culture*. Downers Grove, IL: InterVarsity, 2000.

Roland DeVaux. *Ancient Israel*. 2 vols. New York: McGraw, 1965.

Raymond Dillard and Tremper Longman III. *An Introduction to the Old Testament*. Grand Rapids: Zondervan, 1994.

J. D. Douglas and Merrill Tenney, eds. *New International Dictionary of the Bible*. Grand Rapids: Regency Reference Library, Zondervan, 1987.

Alfred Edersheim. *The Life and Times of Jesus the Messiah*. 1883. Reprint, Grand Rapids: Eerdmans, 1972.

Walter A. Elwell, ed. *Baker Encyclopedia of the Bible*. Grand Rapids: Baker, 1988.

Walter Elwell and Robert Yarbrough. *Encountering the New Testament: A Historical and Theological Survey*. 2nd ed. Grand Rapids: Baker, 2005.

Craig A. Evans and Stanley E. Porter, eds. *Dictionary of New Testament Background*. Downers Grove, IL: InterVarsity, 2000.

David Noel Freedman, ed. *The Anchor Bible Dictionary*. 6 vols. New York: Doubleday, 1992.

James Freeman and Harold Chadwick. *The New Manners and Customs of the Bible*. Gainsville, FL: Bridge-Logos, 1998.

Joel Green, Scot McKnight, and I. Howard Marshall, eds. *Dictionary of Jesus and the Gospels*. Downers Grove, IL: InterVarsity, 1992.

Donald Guthrie. *New Testament Introduction*. 4th rev. ed. Downers Grove, IL: InterVarsity, 1990.

Roland K. Harrison. *A History of Old Testament Times*. Grand Rapids: Zondervan, 1957.

Gerald F. Hawthorne, Ralph P. Martin, and Daniel G. Reid, eds. *Dictionary of Paul and His Letters*. Downers Grove, IL: InterVarsity, 1993.

E. W. Heaton. *Everyday Life in Old Testament Times*. New York: Scribner, 1956.

Andrew Hill and John Walton. *A Survey of the Old Testament*. 2nd ed. Grand Rapids: Zondervan, 2000.

William Sanford LaSor, David Alan Hubbard, and Frederic W. Bush. *Old Testament Survey*. 2nd ed. Grand Rapids: Eerdmans, 1996.

I. Howard Marshall, A. R. Millard, J. I. Packer, and D. J. Wiseman, eds. *New Bible Dictionary*. 3rd ed. Downers Grove, IL: InterVarsity, 1996.

Ralph Martin and Peter Davids, eds. *Dictionary of the Later New Testament and Its Development*. Downers Grove, IL: InterVarsity, 1997.

Victor H. Matthews. *Manners and Customs in the Bible: An Illustrated Guide to Daily Life in Bible Times*. 3rd ed. Peabody, MA: Hendrickson, 2006.

Martin Noth. *The Old Testament World*. Translated by Victor I. Gruhn. Philadelphia: Fortress, 1966.

Charles F. Pfeiffer, ed. *The Biblical World: A Dictionary of Biblical Archaeology*. Grand Rapids: Baker, 1994.

James B. Pritchard, ed. *The Ancient Near East in Pictures Relating to the Old Testament*. Princeton, NJ: Princeton University Press, 1954.

———, ed. *The Ancient Near Eastern Texts Relating to the Old Testament*. 3rd ed., with suppl. Princeton, NJ: Princeton University Press, 1969.

Daniel G. Reid, ed. *The IVP Dictionary of the New Testament: A One-Volume Compendium of Contemporary Biblical Scholarship*. Downers Grove, IL: InterVarsity, 2004.

Merrill C. Tenney. *New Testament Times*. Grand Rapids: Eerdmans, 1965.

John Arthur Thompson. *The Bible and Archaeology*. Grand Rapids: Eerdmans, 1962.

William M. Thomson. *The Land and the Book*. 2 vols. New York: Harper, 1858.

Howard Vos. *Nelson's New Illustrated Bible Manners and Customs: How the People of the Bible Really Lived*. Nashville: Thomas Nelson, 1999.

Edwin Yamauchi. *The Stones and the Scriptures*. Philadelphia: Holman, 1977.

For several examples of good contextual and historical-cultural analysis, see

Walter C. Kaiser, ed. *Classical Evangelical Essays in Old Testament Interpretation*. Grand Rapids: Baker, 1972.

Exercises

By now you have the knowledge necessary to know how to find the correct answer to Exercise 6 posed earlier in the chapter. See what you can do.

7. Do you see a relationship between the Jewish hermeneutical fallacy of letterism and interpretation that fails to distinguish between teaching focus and incidental detail? If you do, describe the nature of this similarity.

8. Among Christian counselors, there are differences of opinion regarding the meaning and usefulness of dreams in counseling. Ecclesiastes 5:7 says that "much dreaming and many words are meaningless." Use your knowledge of hermeneutics to discern as accurately as you can the meaning of this verse and then discuss the implications of the meaning of that verse for your use of dreams in counseling.

9. A Christian author, discussing the way to discover God's will for one's life, made the point that inner peace was an important indicator. The sole verse he used to anchor his argument was Colossians 3:15 ("Let the peace of Christ rule in your hearts"). Would you agree with his use of this verse to make this point? Why, or why not?

10. You are discussing with a person the need for a personal relationship with Jesus Christ as the only means of salvation. He claims that living a moral life is what God expects of us and shows you Micah 6:8 to validate this point:

> He has showed you, O man, what is good.
>
> And what does the LORD require of you?
>
> To act justly and to love mercy,
>
> and to walk humbly with your God.

Will you argue that this verse is consistent with your point of view, and if so, how will you do it? If you take the point of view that in the Old Testament salvation was by works (as this verse seems to suggest), how will you reconcile this with Paul's statement in Galatians 2:16 that "by observing the law no one will be justified"?

11. A popular Christian counselor, talking about some people's inclination to say yes when they mean no and then to explode in anger because of all the pent-up frustration, said:

> Always being Mr. Nice-Guy and then turning your real feelings into stomach acid is self-defeating. You may get what you want—for the moment—by lathering others, but you don't like yourself for it.

Consider putting out what you're feeling in simple honesty. As Jesus put it, "Let your yes be a clear yes, and your no, no." Anything else spells trouble.[6]

Do you agree with this author's use of Scripture (paraphrase of Matt. 5:33–37) to make this point? Why, or why not?

12. A Christian man lost his job due to company downsizing. He and his wife interpreted Romans 8:28 ("All things work together for good," NRSV) to mean that he lost his job so that God might give him a better-paying one. Consequently he turned down several lower- or equal-paying job opportunities and remained on unemployment for over two years before returning to work. Do you agree with his way of interpreting this verse? Why, or why not?

class

13. Hebrews 10:26–27 states: "If we deliberately keep on sinning after we have received the knowledge of the truth, no sacrifice for sins is left, but only a fearful expectation of judgment and of raging fire that will consume the enemies of God." A person comes to you extremely depressed. A week ago she deliberately stole some merchandise from a local store, and now on the basis of the above verses she believes that there is no possibility of repentance and forgiveness. How would you counsel her?

14. A favorite verse used in Christmas carols and some sympathy cards is Isaiah 26:3 ("You will keep him in perfect peace, whose mind is stayed on You," NKJV). Are these valid uses of this Scripture?

online

15. A woman comes to you at the request of her husband. She says she has had a vision that instructed her to leave her husband and family and go to Bulgaria as a missionary. Her husband has tried to reason with her that this vision must have some explanation other than being sent from God since (1) her children and husband need her, (2) God has not given the rest of the family a similar call, (3) she has no financial support, and (4) the mission boards to whom she has applied have not accepted her. Her continuing response to all this is to quote Proverbs 3:5–6 ("Trust in the Lord with all your heart and lean not on your own understanding; in all your ways acknowledge him, and he will make your paths straight"). How would you counsel her, particularly regarding this verse, since it seems to be a mainstay of her belief?

16. You have just finished telling someone that you do not agree with the oracular use of Scripture (consulting the Bible by opening it and applying the first words one reads as God's instructions to him), because it generally interprets words without regard to their

6. David Augsburger, *Caring Enough to Confront* (Glendale: Regal, 1974), 32.

94

context. This person argues that God has often used just this method to bring him comfort and guidance. How would you reply?

17. Judges 6:36–40 describes Gideon's response when God calls him to lead Israel in battle. Gideon twice requests a sign from God to prove that God will fulfill his promise to save Israel through Gideon. Gideon lays out a fleece overnight and in the morning finds it wet although the ground around it is dry. He requests a confirmation, and this time the fleece is dry when the ground around it is wet. Does this text teach that those who doubt God should request a sign from him? Does it teach that God will honor requests for a sign? Why, or why not?

18. In a discussion about vegetarianism, a college student cites Romans 14:2–3, where she read, "One man's faith allows him to eat everything, but another man, whose faith is weak, eats only vegetables. The man who eats everything must not look down on him who does not, and the man who does not eat everything must not condemn the man who does, for God has accepted him." On the basis of these verses she has determined that God allows Christians to be either vegetarians or meat eaters but that those who are vegetarians have weaker faith. Would you agree with this use of Romans 14? Why, or why not?

FOUR

LEXICAL-SYNTACTICAL ANALYSIS

After completing this chapter, you should be able to

1. Identify two major reasons why lexical-syntactical analysis is important.
2. Recall seven steps involved in lexical-syntactical analysis.
3. Identify three methods of determining the meanings of ancient words and compare the validity of each method.
4. Recall five methods of determining which one of the several possible meanings of a word was actually intended by an author in a given context.
5. Identify and describe the three major types of parallelism found in Hebrew poetry.
6. Explain the difference between verbal parallels and real parallels.
7. Define the following terms: *lexical-syntactical analysis, syntax, lexicology, denotation, connotation,* and *figures of speech.*
8. Explain the usage of and be able to use the following lexical tools:
   a. Hebrew, Greek, and English concordances
   b. Lexicons

c. Theological wordbooks
d. E. W. Bullinger's *Figures of Speech Used in the Bible*
e. Interlinear Bible
f. Analytical lexicons
g. Hebrew and Greek grammars

Definition and Presuppositions

Lexical-syntactical analysis is the study of the meaning of individual words (lexicology) and the way those words are combined (syntax) in order to determine more accurately the author's intended meaning. It is necessary because the biblical author's intended meaning is communicated through words arranged in a particular way.

Lexical-syntactical analysis does not encourage blind literalism: it recognizes when an author intends his words to be understood literally, when figuratively, and when symbolically, and then interprets them accordingly. Thus when Jesus said, "I am the door" (John 10:9 NASB), "I am the true vine" (John 15:1), and "I am the bread of life" (John 6:35, 48), we understand these expressions to be metaphors, as he intended. When he said, "Be on your guard against the yeast of the Pharisees and Sadducees," he intended *yeast* to be symbolic of the teaching of those groups (Matt. 16:5–12). When he said to the paralytic, "Get up, take your mat and go home," he expected the paralyzed man to literally obey his command, which the man did (Matt. 9:6–7).

Lexical-syntactical analysis is founded on the premise that, although words may take on a variety of meanings in different contexts, they generally have but one intended meaning in any given context.[1] Thus, if I were to say "She had a ball," those words might mean that (1) she possessed a spherical object used for playing a sport, (2) she hosted a formal dance, or (3) she had a good time. Although the word *ball* could mean any of these three things, the context usually will indicate which of these ideas I wish to communicate. When "She had a ball" is followed by "She kicked it to her teammate," definition 1 is clearly in mind. Lexical-syntactical analysis helps the interpreter determine the variety of meanings that a word or group of words might possess and then decide that meaning X is more likely to be the author's intention in this specific passage than meaning Y or Z.

---

1. A pun is a notable exception in which the play between two possible definitions of a word is intended by the author as part of his meaning.

The Need for Lexical-Syntactical Analysis

The need for this type of analysis is demonstrated in the following quotations from two well-known theologians. Alexander Carson has aptly said:

> No man has a right to say, as some are in the habit of saying, "The Spirit tells me that such or such is the meaning of a passage." How is he assured that it is the Holy Spirit, and not a spirit of delusion, except from the evidence that the interpretation is the legitimate meaning of the words?[2]

John A. Broadus, a noted commentator, notes:

> It is a mournful fact that Universalists . . . [and] Mormons can find an apparent support for their heresies in Scripture, without interpreting more loosely, without doing greater violence to the meaning and connection of the Sacred Text than is sometimes done by orthodox, devout, and even intelligent men.[3]

Lexical-syntactical analysis is necessary because without it we have no valid assurance that our interpretation is the meaning God intended to convey through the words of the biblical author, nor do we have grounds for saying that our interpretations of Scripture are more valid than those of heretical groups.

Steps in Lexical-Syntactical Analysis

Lexical-syntactical analysis is sometimes difficult, but it often yields exciting and meaningful results. This complex process is somewhat easier to understand if organized into a seven-step procedure:

1. *Identify the general literary form.* The literary form an author uses (prose, poetry, etc.) influences the way he intends his words to be understood.
2. *Trace the development of the author's theme and show how the passage under consideration fits into the context.* This step, already begun as part of contextual analysis, provides a necessary perspective for determining the meaning of words and syntax.

2. Alexander Carson, *Examination of the Principles of Biblical Interpretation*, cited in Bernard Ramm, *Protestant Biblical Interpretation*, 3rd rev. ed. (Grand Rapids: Baker, 1970), x–xi.
3. John A. Broadus, *A Treatise on the Preparation and Delivery of Sermons*, 30th ed. (New York: Hoddard & Stoughton, 1899), 33.

3. *Identify the natural divisions of the text.* The main conceptual units and transitional statements reveal the author's thought process and therefore help clarify his meaning.

4. *Identify the connecting words within the paragraphs and sentences.* Connecting words (conjunctions, prepositions, relative pronouns) show the logical relationship between two or more thoughts.

5. *Determine what the individual words mean.* Any word that survives long in a language begins to take on a variety of meanings. Thus it is necessary to identify the various possible meanings of ancient words at the time the biblical author used them and then to determine which of the several possible meanings is the one the author intended to convey in a specific context.

6. *Analyze the syntax.* The relationship of words to one another is expressed through their grammatical forms and arrangement.

7. *Put the results of your lexical-syntactical analysis into nontechnical, easily understood words that clearly convey the author's meaning to the English reader.* Creating your own paraphrase requires that you both commit to and state clearly your interpretive decisions.

The General Literary Form

The literary form of a writing influences the way an author meant it to be interpreted. A writer composing poetry does not use words in the same way that he does when writing prose. This fact takes on significance when we recognize that *one-third* of the Old Testament is written in the form of Hebrew poetry. Interpreting these passages as if they were prose, a common practice, is to misinterpret their meaning.

For purposes of our analysis at this point, it is sufficient to speak of three general literary forms: prose, poetry, and apocalyptic literature (other genres will be discussed in later chapters).[4] Apocalyptic writing, found most obviously in the visionary passages of Daniel and Revelation, frequently uses words symbolically. Prose and poetry use words in literal and figurative ways: in prose the literal usage predominates; in poetry figurative language is used most often.

Discriminating between Hebrew poetry and prose is difficult for the English reader, particularly since Hebrew poetry is characterized by rhythm of ideas rather than rhythm of sound (more about this later in the

4. Gordon Fee and Douglas Stuart, *How to Read the Bible for All Its Worth*, 3rd ed. (Grand Rapids: Zondervan, 2003), provide an excellent general presentation of the various biblical genres such as narrative, law, psalms, wisdom literature, prophecy, gospels, parables, epistles, and apocalyptic literature. With the discussion of each genre, they address unique challenges for interpretation. See also parts 4 and 5 in J. Scott Duvall and J. Daniel Hays, *Grasping God's Word*, 2nd ed. (Grand Rapids: Zondervan, 2005).

chapter). For this reason the newer biblical translations place poetry in verse form so that it can be easily distinguished from prose, a format that offers an important interpretive advantage over older translations.

Development of the Author's Theme

This step, already begun as part of contextual analysis, is important for two reasons. First, the context is the best source of data for determining which of several possible meanings of a word the author intended. Second, unless a passage is put into the perspective of its context, one risks becoming so involved in the technicalities of a grammatical analysis that one loses sight of the primary idea(s) the words actually convey. The "hermeneutical circle" is a term for the recognition that one cannot accurately interpret the smaller parts of communication (such as words and grammar) without understanding the larger whole (such as entire writings and genres) of which they are a part and yet one cannot accurately interpret the whole without an understanding of the parts.

The Natural Divisions of the Text

Remember that the biblical chapter-and-verse divisions, which are so much a part of our thinking today, were not an original part of the Scriptures; these divisions were added many centuries after the Bible was written as an aid in locating passages for easy reference. Although verse divisions serve this purpose well, the standard verse-by-verse division of the text may have the disadvantage of dividing the author's thought unnaturally.

In modern prose style we are accustomed to the division of thoughts into conceptual units through the use of sentences and paragraphs. The first sentence in a paragraph serves either as a transition from one concept to the next or as a thesis that is elaborated in subsequent sentences. Since we are accustomed to understanding written concepts in this way, several of the newer translations have retained the verse numbers but placed the ideas in sentence and paragraph structure, making it easier for the modern reader to follow the flow of the author's conceptual process. Many newer translations also add topical headings to the text for the same reason, even though these clues to thematic arrangement were not part of the original author's writing.

Today's reader should remember that although these paragraph breaks and headings may provide helpful clues for interpretation, they are not inspired but reflect interpretive decisions that editors have made. The various translations of Scripture even differ on these matters. Therefore, it might be enlightening to compare the arrangements found among the translations. Some students may even prefer to access a copy of the biblical text that is free from chapter and verse numbers, paragraph breaks, and topic headings so that through a careful reading they themselves can determine where they think the natural divisions occur before comparing their decisions with those made in the standard translations. The multiplicity of electronic versions of Scripture available today makes it easy to find (or use the delete key to create) such paragraph-free versions.

Exercise 19. The NIV identifies seven paragraphs in Genesis 17 while the NRSV identifies four. Access a version of Genesis 17 with no paragraph breaks. Read this passage carefully and consider where natural divisions fall. Now indicate where you would divide this passage into paragraphs and explain why you split the text where you did.

Connecting Words within Paragraphs and Sentences

Connecting words, such as conjunctions, prepositions, relative pronouns, and so on, often aid in following the author's progression of thought. When a pronoun is used, it is important to ask, What is the noun being discussed? The word *therefore* often provides the connecting link between a theoretical argument and the practical applications of that argument. The word *if* may indicate that one portion of a sentence is conditional on another. *Because* suggests that one element of the argument is the grounds on which a conclusion stands.

By way of illustration, Galatians 5:1 says: "Stand firm, then, and do not let yourselves be burdened again by a yoke of slavery." Taken by itself the verse could have any one of several meanings: it could refer to human slavery, political slavery, slavery to sin, and so on. The "then" indicates, however, that this verse is a resulting application of a point Paul makes in the previous chapter. A reading of Paul's arguments (Gal. 3:1–4:30) and his conclusion (4:31) clarifies the meaning of the potentially ambiguous 5:1. Paul is encouraging the Galatians not to become enslaved again to the bonds of legalism (i.e., by trying to win salvation through good works).

Word Meanings

Most words that survive long in a language acquire many denotations (specific meanings) and connotations (additional implications often including the emotions associated with those specific meanings).

Words may have both technical and popular denotations, that is, usages found in ordinary conversation. For example, when typical laypersons say that a person is obsessive, they usually mean he or she is overly concerned with details. When counselors use the same word as part of the phrase "Obsessive Compulsive Disorder" they have a different meaning in mind. Consider also a few of the popular designations of the word *done*.

"I'm done," meaning "I've completed some work."

"I'm done in," meaning "I'm completely tired out."

"The cake is done," meaning "The cake is thoroughly baked."

Literal denotations may eventually lead to metaphoric denotations. When used literally, *green* designates a color; used metaphorically, its meaning can be extended from the literal color of an unripe apple to the idea of an immature or inexperienced person.

Words also have connotations, implied emotional meanings not explicitly stated. To say that someone is incorrigible does not have the same connotation as to say that he has the courage of his convictions. Incorrigibility carries with it an unstated (but undeniably present) negative connotation; to have the courage of one's convictions has a more positive, or at least a neutral, connotation.

A word that has more than one denotation may also have more than one connotation. When *green* is used as a color, it has relatively neutral connotations for most people; when used metaphorically, it has a pejorative cast to it.

METHODS OF DISCOVERING THE DENOTATIONS OF ANCIENT WORDS

To discover the semantic range of a word, that is, the variety of meanings a word is known to have, an interpreter may utilize three methods. One method is to study synonyms, looking for points of comparison as well as contrast. Earlier students of lexicology often drew up fairly rigid distinctions between words that had similar but not exactly equivalent meanings. For instance, the beginning Greek student is often taught to distinguish between two Greek words for love: *agapaō* and *phileō*. Many scholars have maintained that *agapaō* always speaks of a good, divine, perfect love, while *phileō* is reserved to speak of human, brotherly love. Thus, when analyzing John 21:15–17, some have observed that when Jesus twice asks Peter if he loves him, using the verb *agapaō*, Peter responds that he loves him with the verb *phileō*. In the third exchange, both use the verb *phileō*. More than one preacher has presented this passage, arguing that Peter was unable to love (*agapaō*) Jesus with a perfect, godly love but could only love (*phileō*) him with a lesser human

This is not necessarily true ↗

affection. D. A. Carson, however, skillfully argues that although two synonymous words such as these do not have an identical range of meaning, they do have considerable semantic overlap, and one should take great caution before building an interpretation based solely on contrasts between synonyms.[5]

A second method for determining word meanings is to study etymology, that is, to consider the historical roots of the word. Extensive etymological studies are used less frequently today than previously because of two disadvantages: the historical roots of words are often conjectural, and the meanings of words often change radically with the passage of time, so that little or no apparent connection remains between the original meaning of the root word and its meaning a few hundred years later.

Several examples from the English language illustrate this change. The English word *enthusiasm* originally meant "possessed by a god" and was so used until the early 1800s. When I pick a dandelion from my lawn, I am not literally picking a "lion's tooth," although this is the meaning of the French phrase (*dent de lion*) from which the word is derived. When I describe someone as nice, I do not mean that he is ignorant, even though this is the meaning of the Latin word *nescius*, from which the word *nice* has developed.

Thus an author may have had no intention of conveying the meaning that a word possessed two hundred years prior to his time; in fact, he probably was unaware of these former denotations. Hence an exegesis that depends heavily on etymological derivations possesses questionable validity; as a result, etymological derivations are used less than in previous centuries and are best limited to words that do not occur with sufficient frequency in ancient literature to allow for more traditional word studies.

A related expository method of even less hermeneutical value than expositions based on etymological derivations of Hebrew or Greek words are expositions based on etymological discussions of the English words into which those Greek or Hebrew words have been translated. For example, one occasionally hears a sermon on a text that includes the word *holy* in which the preacher does an etymological exposition of the Anglo-Saxon roots of the word *holy*. Similar expositions are sometimes done with the word *dynamis* and its historical connections with our English word *dynamite*. Obviously, such expositions have dubious validity because, interesting though they may be, they often import meaning into the text that the non-English-speaking author did not and could

---

5. See D. A. Carson, *Exegetical Fallacies*, 2nd ed. (Grand Rapids: Baker, 1996), 52–53. In this specific example, Carson concludes that John intended no distinction between *agapaō* and *phileō*. It is also noteworthy that although many have emphasized the distinction between the words for love in John 21, few give similar attention to the synonymous words for sheep/lamb (*probaton/arnion*) that also appear in that text.

not intend. The most valid method of determining word meanings is to discover the various denotations a word possessed at the time it was used by the writer.

The most common and effective word-study method is an analysis of the ways a word was used in other ancient literature: secular literature, the Septuagint (the Greek translation of the Old Testament made before the time of Christ), and other biblical writings by the same or a different author.

The first step in a word study is to identify which words in a passage require attention. Is there a word that is translated in significantly different ways in various English translations? Is there a word that is repeated or that is clearly central to the passage? Is there a word that simply needs to be clarified? Such words make good choices for further work.

After identifying a word needing further study, one must determine the original Hebrew (if working with an Old Testament text) or Greek (New Testament text) word. It is the word in the original language, rather than its English translation, that is needed to determine the range of meaning known to the biblical author. Consider a typical scenario. A believer reads the English words in his Bible. As an English speaker, he knows their various nuances, and he draws conclusions and says this is what this word means here. Many times he is right. But sometimes the English word, a good translation of the original Greek or Hebrew, has meanings or nuances that were not present in the Greek or Hebrew word. The original meaning—the author's intent—could not have been a nuance or meaning that the word did not possess for him.

Consider the following example. Luke 13 describes the account of Jesus healing a crippled woman who is bent over. Through Jesus' miraculous power the woman was "made straight/straightened." In modern English, the word *straight* has various connotations, one of which involves sexuality. If we were to read this biblical passage as proof that homosexuals can be healed by Jesus and thus made straight, we will be very far away indeed from what Luke intended to communicate! Never mind that the context is clearly not talking about sexuality; the Greek word *anorthoō*, "to be made straight," does not have this as one of its possible meanings. If you look it up in the Greek dictionary, you will see that "straight" as opposed to "gay" is simply not a lexical option. Thus it is clear that our word studies must employ the original language words.

To determine the word in the original language, the student familiar with the biblical languages needs to simply read the passage in a Hebrew or Greek Bible. Those whose language skills need assistance can consult an analytical lexicon in order to move from the form of the word that appears in the text to the form that appears in the dictionary (see further discussion about analytical lexicons in the "Syntax" section below).

The student who does not know the original languages will rely on several kinds of lexical tools that are available to assist the modern student of Scripture with this and other steps of word study. While a knowledge of Hebrew and Greek certainly enhances one's ability to do word studies, the following chart presenting the Hebrew and Greek alphabets in alphabetical order will enable the student who does not know the original languages to make effective use of many original language resources.

The Hebrew Alphabet

Letter	Name	Transliteration	Letter	Name	Transliteration
א	aleph	'	מ/ם	mem	m
ב	bet	b or bh	נ/ן	nun	n
ג	gimel	g or gh	ס	samek	s
ד	dalet	d or dh	ע	ayin	'
ה	he	h	פ/ף	pe	p or ph
ו	waw	w	צ/ץ	tsade	ts
ז	zayin	z	ק	koph	q or k
ח	het	h	ר	resh	r
ט	tet	t	שׂ	sin	s
י	yod	y	שׁ	shin	sh
כ/ך	kaph	k or kh	ת	taw	t or th
ל	lamed	l			

The Greek Alphabet

Letter	Name	Transliteration	Letter	Name	Transliteration
A α	alpha	a	N ν	nu	n
B β	beta	b	Ξ ξ	xi	x
Γ γ	gamma	g	O o	omicron	o
Δ δ	delta	d	Π π	pi	p
E ε	epsilon	e	P ρ	rho	r
Z ζ	zeta	z	Σ σ/ς	sigma	s
H η	eta	ē	T τ	tau	t
Θ θ	theta	th	Y υ	upsilon	u/y
I ι	iota	i	Φ φ	phi	ph
K κ	kappa	k	X χ	chi	ch
Λ λ	lambda	l	Ψ ψ	psi	ps
M μ	mu	m	Ω ω	omega	ō

Additionally, an increasing number of lexical tools are being keyed numerically to *Strong's Exhaustive Concordance of the Bible*, making it possible for the person with no knowledge of Hebrew or Greek (or whose knowledge is "rusty") to do word studies in these languages. The most important kinds of lexical tools are described below.

Concordances. To find the original-language word behind an English word that has been selected for study, the interpreter should consult a concordance. A concordance contains a listing of all the occurrences of a given word in Scripture. To examine the various ways a given Hebrew or Greek word was used, consult a Hebrew or Greek concordance, which lists all the passages in which the word appears.

An English concordance lists all the passages in which various Hebrew and Greek words were translated into a given English word. Each English concordance will follow a given English translation of Scripture. Be sure to look up the English word that occurs in the same English translation as the one to which your concordance is keyed. For example, *Strong's Exhaustive Concordance* shows that the word *peace* occurs more than four hundred times in the King James Version, and it lists each reference. Using a numbering system, it also identifies the various Hebrew and Greek words that are translated into our English word *peace* (there are ten Hebrew words and six Greek words). With the use of *Strong's* numbering system, it is a relatively simple matter to turn to the back of the concordance and find the Hebrew or Greek word used in any particular passage so that a valid analysis can be made. The back of the concordance includes brief definitions of the meaning of each Hebrew and Greek word, which can be supplemented by consulting a lexicon, the next step in the word study. *The New Englishman's Hebrew and Chaldee Concordance of the Old Testament* and *The New Englishman's Greek Concordance of the New Testament*, both edited by G. V. Wigram, function in much the same way as *Strong's* and are keyed to *Strong's* numbering system.

Lexicons. A lexicon is a dictionary of Hebrew or Greek words. Like an English dictionary, it lists the various denotations of each word found in it. Many lexicons survey the usage of words in both secular and biblical literature and give specific examples. Words are often listed in Hebrew and Greek alphabetical order, so it is helpful to know the Hebrew and Greek alphabets in order to use these tools.

Among the most widely used Hebrew lexicons are

- Francis Brown, S. R. Driver, and Charles A. Briggs. *A Hebrew and English Lexicon of the Old Testament*. New York: Oxford, 1952.
- Wilhelm Gesenius. *Hebrew and Chaldee Lexicon to the Old Testament Scriptures*. 1846. Reprint, Grand Rapids: Eerdmans, 1949.

William L. Holladay. *A Concise Hebrew and Aramaic Lexicon of the Old Testament.* 1971. 12th corrected impression, Grand Rapids: Eerdmans; Leiden: Brill, 1988.

Widely used Greek lexicons include

- Walter Bauer, F. W. Danker, W. F. Arndt, and F. W. Gingrich. *A Greek-English Lexicon of the New Testament and Other Early Christian Literature.* 3rd ed. Chicago: University of Chicago Press, 2000.

  Johannes P. Louw and Eugene A. Nida. *A Greek-English Lexicon of the New Testament Based on Semantic Domains.* 2 vols. 2nd ed. New York: United Bible Societies, 1989.

  James H. Moulton and George Milligan. *The Vocabulary of the Greek Testament: Illustrated from the Papyri and Other Non-Literary Sources.* Grand Rapids: Eerdmans, 1949.

- Joseph H. Thayer, ed. *Greek-English Lexicon of the New Testament.* 1896. Reprint, Grand Rapids: Zondervan, 1956.

Recent editions of some of these works are so constructed that the person with little or no Hebrew or Greek can use them. Recent editions of both Gesenius's and Thayer's lexicons are keyed to the numbering system found in *Strong's Exhaustive Concordance.* An index to Bauer's lexicon, in a separate volume by John R. Alsop, makes it readily usable for someone without a knowledge of the Greek alphabet.

Midway between an English dictionary and a Greek lexicon are E. W. Bullinger's *Critical Lexicon and Concordance* and William Mounce's *Complete Expository Dictionary of Old and New Testament Words.* These volumes list English words (in English alphabetical order) and beneath each word list the various Greek or Hebrew words translated into that particular English word. With each original-language word is a short definition of its meaning. Someone with little or no knowledge of the original languages can easily use both of these volumes.

English, Hebrew, and Greek concordances can be used together to do word studies. For example, if you wished to study a particular kind of *fear* found in a given passage, you could use *Strong's* to identify the Hebrew or Greek word from which your English word was translated. Having gained a general sense of the range of meaning of this word by consulting a lexicon, you could then do your own analysis of other occurrences of this word in Scripture. Using the same reference numbers from *Strong's*, you could also consult the *New Englishman's Hebrew and Chaldee Concordance* or the *New Englishman's Greek Concordance* to find a listing of all the passages in which that Hebrew or Greek word was used. By analyzing these passages, you could draw your own conclusions about the exact denotation(s) of that word. Such an analysis should enable you to reach a solid conclusion about the range of meaning of your word in various contexts. However, it is also worth checking what other scholars have said about your word and its use in various contexts. A theological wordbook can assist with this step.

Theological Wordbooks. These books give more extensive definitions of words than are found in lexicons or books of synonyms. The best-known is the ten-volume *Theological Dictionary of the New Testament* (*TDNT*), edited by Gerhard Kittel and Gerhard Friedrich. This monumental work provides an extensive examination of the usages of important Greek New Testament words. A typical article will discuss the role of that word in (1) secular Greek sources; (2) the Old Testament; (3) Philo, Josephus, and pseudepigraphical and rabbinical literature; (4) the various New Testament books; and (5) the Apostolic Fathers.[6]

While *TDNT* is a valuable source in many ways,[7] it has several disadvantages for the average pastor or evangelical Christian who wishes to do word studies. First, the frequent appearance of Hebrew and Greek words in the text makes *TDNT* difficult reading for those who are not familiar with these languages. Second, the entries are extensive (fifteen or more pages on many important words) and often do not include summaries that would help put the discussion into perspective. Third, the theological position of its authors varies considerably, and the influence of liberal presuppositions on some of the articles is significant. Fourth, the price of this ten-volume set places it beyond the reach of many students of Scripture.[8]

The *New International Dictionary of New Testament Theology*, edited by Colin Brown, is a multi-volume reference work providing word studies midway between the concise definitions of a lexicon and the very extensive discussions of the *TDNT*. The articles are scholarly and up-to-date and appear generally to be written by orthodox theologians. It includes frequent references to and summaries from *TDNT*. Most of the text is in English and in regular-sized print (in contrast to the small print in *TDNT*). The average length of a word discussion is three to five pages;

6. A comparable work for the Old Testament is the seventeen-volume *Theological Dictionary of the Old Testament*, ed. G. J. Botterweck and H. Ringgren (Grand Rapids: Eerdmans, 1974–). Fifteen volumes are currently available. Volume 16 will focus on Aramaic words, and volume 17 will be an index.

7. The fact that *TDNT* has been accused of committing the word-study fallacy that suggests that one's language determines one's thought patterns is an important consideration in the use of this source, but it by no means diminishes the overall contribution made by *TDNT*. See Carson, *Exegetical Fallacies*, 44.

8. The one-volume abridged version, also called *Theological Dictionary of the New Testament* (Grand Rapids: Eerdmans, 2002), is a more affordable alternative.

the total price of the set is approximately one-third the price of *TDNT*. For these reasons the *New International Dictionary* set probably represents a more usable tool for the average pastor and student of Scripture than does *TDNT*.[9]

METHODS OF DISCOVERING THE DENOTATION INTENDED IN A SPECIFIC CONTEXT

Having discovered the range of meaning a word possessed in its contemporary culture, we must next ascertain which of those denotations the author intended when he used the word in the passage under study.

An objection occasionally voiced is that the author may have intended more than one denotation simultaneously and was thus communicating a variety of meanings concurrently. However, a consideration of our own use of language reveals that the simultaneous use of more than one denotation of a word runs counter to all normal communication (with the exception of puns, which are humorous precisely because they do use words in two senses simultaneously). Also, if we press words into all their denotations, we soon produce heretical exegesis. For example, the Greek word *sarx* (flesh) may have these meanings:

- the solid part of the body except bones (1 Cor. 15:39)
- the whole substance of the body (Acts 2:26)
- the sensuous nature of man (Col. 2:18)
- human nature as dominated by sinful desires (Rom. 7:18)

Although this is only a partial list of its denotations, we can see that if all these meanings were applied to the word as it is found in John 6:53, where Christ talks about his own flesh, the interpreter would be attributing sin to Christ.

Exercise 20. If you still are not convinced that words should not be understood in all their denotations in each context, try the following exercise:

Write a three-sentence communication similar to statements you normally make. Then, using a regular dictionary, write each of the

---

9. A comparable work for Old Testament words is the five volume *New International Dictionary of Old Testament Theology and Exegesis*, ed. Willem VanGemeren (Grand Rapids: Zondervan, 1997). Typical articles review the use of the Hebrew word in the ancient Near Eastern literature, the Old Testament, and postbiblical texts and discuss its Greek translation in the New Testament. Similarly, the two-volume *Theological Wordbook of the Old Testament*, ed. R. L. Harris (Chicago: Moody, 1980), is a very usable source for Old Testament words.

> denotations for the nouns, verbs, adjectives, and adverbs you used in these three sentences. Combine those various denotations in all their possible arrangements and write the resulting sentences. Is the meaning expressed in your first three sentences the same as the meaning expressed by all the combinations?

There are several methods for discerning the specific denotations intended by an author in a particular context.

First, examine definitions or explanatory phrases that the authors themselves give. For example, 2 Timothy 3:16–17 states that the Word of God was given so that "the man of God may be perfect" (KJV). What does the author mean by *perfect* here? Does he mean sinless? Incapable of error? Incapable of error or sin in some specific area? The best answer is supplied by his own explanatory phrases immediately following—"that the man of God may be perfect, thoroughly furnished unto all good works." In this context Paul meant for this word, translated into our language as *perfect*, to convey the idea of being thoroughly equipped for godly living.

Second, determine if the subject and the predicate of a sentence may explain each other. For example, the Greek word *mōranthē* found in Matthew 5:13 can mean either "to become foolish" or "to become insipid." How do we determine the intended denotation? In this instance the subject of the sentence is "salt," so the second denotation ("if the salt has lost his savour," KJV) is selected as the correct one.

Third, examine parallelism if it occurs within the passage. As mentioned earlier, one-third of the Old Testament (and some of the New Testament) is poetry. Hebrew poetry is characterized by parallelism, a feature that can shed light on the meaning of words that are in question.

Hebrew parallelism can be categorized into three basic types: synonymous, antithetic, and synthetic.[10] In *synonymous parallelism* the second line of a stanza repeats the content of the first but in different words. Psalm 103:10 is an example:

> He does not treat us as our sins deserve
> or repay us according to our iniquities.

In *antithetic parallelism* the idea of the second line sharply contrasts with that of the first line. Psalm 37:21 provides an example:

10. Recent scholarship suggests that Hebrew poetry includes more kinds of parallelism than these three types, although a consensus about a new set of categories to add to these traditional three has not been reached.

111

> The wicked borrow and do not repay,
>   but the righteous give generously.

In *synthetic parallelism* the second line carries further or completes the idea of the first line. Psalm 14:2 is an example:

> The LORD looks down from heaven
>   on the sons of men
> to see if there are any who understand,
>   any who seek God.

Thus, if a passage is poetry, recognition of the type of parallelism employed may give clues to the meaning of the word in question.

Fourth, determine if the word is being used as part of a figure of speech. Sometimes words or phrases are used in ways that deviate from simple, normal speech in order to produce a fanciful or vivid impression. Such phrases, often called figures of speech, are intended to have a meaning different from the literal. If a figure persists and becomes widely accepted within a culture, it is called an idiom. Some English examples of figures of speech or idioms are

> His eyes were bigger than his stomach.
> This fog is as thick as pea soup.
> I'm broke.
> The White House said . . .
> We'll hit Athens about 2:00 pm
> The thermometer is going up.
> The furnace has gone out.
> She made the cake from scratch.
> Take a bus.

Figures of speech, as can be seen from the above list, are ubiquitous—we use them frequently in everyday speech, as did the biblical authors. In addition, figures of speech convey a definite meaning just as surely as do literal usages. To say that something is a figure of speech does not imply that the meaning of the phrase is ambiguous. Figures of speech convey a specific meaning just as other speech does.

Interpreting a figure of speech by using the normal denotations of a word will usually result in a radical misunderstanding of the author's intended meaning. For example, if I were to interpret literally the phrases "his eyes were bigger than his stomach" or "it's raining cats and dogs," I would seriously misinterpret the meaning of these phrases. For this reason, those who proudly boast that they believe everything in the Bible literally (if by this they mean that they fail to recognize figures of speech and special features of poetry and prophecy) may be doing a disservice to the very Scripture they respect so highly.

Figures of speech are common in the biblical text. A good procedure to follow whenever doing an in-depth study of a passage is to consult Bullinger's *Figures of Speech Used in the Bible*. Index 3 of Bullinger's book indicates whether there are any figures of speech in a passage and provides appropriate explanations of them. Bullinger's book must be used with discretion (it reflects his personal judgments and knowledge of Hebrew and Greek), but it does provide much important and useful information.

Fifth, study parallel passages. To understand the meaning of an obscure word or phrase, look for additional data in clearer parallel passages. It is important, though, to distinguish between verbal parallels and real parallels. *Verbal parallels* are those that use similar words but refer to different concepts. The concept of God's Word as a sword, found in Hebrews 4 and Ephesians 6, is an example of a verbal, but not a real, parallel. Hebrews 4 speaks of the Bible's function as a divider that differentiates between those who are truly obedient to its message and those who profess obedience but inwardly remain disobedient. In Ephesians 6, Paul also speaks of the Bible as a sword but in this instance refers to it as a defensive weapon to be used against the temptations of Satan (v. 11). (Christ used the Word in this way when Satan tempted him in the desert.)

Real parallels, in contrast, are those that speak of the same concept or same event. They may use different words and frequently add data not found in the passage under study. The marginal references found in most Bibles are designed to identify real parallels, although occasionally such parallels seem to be more verbal than real. A careful examination of the context is the best method of determining whether the passages are verbal or real parallels.

In summary, there are five ways of ascertaining the specific intended denotation of a word in a given passage: (1) examine definitions or explanatory phrases that the author gives, (2) use the subject and the predicate to explain each other, (3) examine parallelism if it occurs in a passage, (4) determine if the word or phrase was intended as a figure of speech, and (5) study parallel passages.

Syntax

Syntax deals with the way thoughts are expressed through grammatical forms. Each language has its own structure, and one of the problems that makes learning another language so difficult is that the learner must master not only the word definitions and pronunciations of the new language but also new ways of arranging and showing the relationship of one word to another.

English is an analytic language: in English, word order is a key to meaning. For example, nouns normally precede verbs, which normally precede direct objects or predicate adjectives. By changing word order we change meaning. For instance, the sentence "the boy chased the dog" paints a picture different from "the dog chased the boy" even though each contains identical words. Hebrew is also an analytic language but less so than English. Greek, in contrast, is a synthetic language: in Greek, meaning is understood only partially by word order and much more by word endings or case endings.[11]

Several tools are helpful in discovering the information syntax can contribute to your understanding of the meaning of a passage.

Interlinear Bibles. These Bibles contain the Hebrew or Greek text with the English translation printed between the lines (hence the name *interlinear*). By juxtaposing the two sets of words, they enable you to identify easily the Greek or Hebrew word(s) that you wish to study further. (Those more proficient in Hebrew and Greek can, of course, go directly to the Hebrew or Greek texts rather than to interlinears.)

Analytical Lexicons. Often the word you encounter in the text is a variation of the lexical form of the word, that is, the form as it would appear in the dictionary or lexicon. For example, in English you might encounter various forms of the verb *to speak*:

spoke
spake
had spoken
will speak
will have spoken

Nouns likewise may take different forms and play different roles within sentences.

An analytical lexicon does two primary things: (1) it identifies the lexical form of which the word in the text is a variation, and (2) it identifies which part of speech the variation is. For example, if you wished to study the Greek word *thymon*, by looking in an analytical Greek lexicon you would find that this is the accusative singular of the noun *thymos*, which means "anger" or "wrath." Two good analytical lexicons are John Owens' multivolume *Analytical Key to the Old Testament* and William Mounce's *Analytical Lexicon to the Greek New Testament*.

11. Ramm, *Protestant Biblical Interpretation*, 136.

Hebrew and Greek Grammars. If you are unfamiliar with the meaning of the term "accusative singular" to describe the form of a word, a third set of syntactical aids will be valuable. Hebrew and Greek grammars explain the various forms that words can take in their respective languages and the meaning of the words when they appear in one of these forms. Well-respected Hebrew grammars include Friedrich Gesenius's *Hebrew Grammar* and Jacob Weingreen's *Practical Grammar for Classical Hebrew*. Gary Pratico and Miles Van Pelt's recent *Basics of Biblical Hebrew Grammar* is also a very accessible resource. Greek grammars include A. T. Robertson's *Grammar of the Greek New Testament in the Light of Historical Research* and Friedrich Blass and Albert Debrunner's *Greek Grammar of the New Testament and Other Early Christian Literature*. Likewise, William Mounce's *Basics of Biblical Greek Grammar* may be the most accessible for the student with no previous exposure to the language. Most seminary courses in exegesis will describe the above processes in much more detail.

Although it is important to understand the steps in the above process, much of this work has already been done and compiled. For example, exegetical commentaries such as A. T. Robertson's *Word Pictures in the New Testament* include lexical-syntactical analyses of nearly every important word and phrase in the New Testament. Expository commentaries, such as *The Expositor's Bible Commentaries,*[12] attempt to provide both a historical-cultural/contextual analysis and a lexical-syntactical analysis.

Many of the resources described in this chapter are now available in electronic versions. Numerous computer-based resources, including computer programs and Internet sites, can make it much easier to do exegetical work in general and lexical-syntactical work in particular. Notable electronic resources and the benefits they offer to the exegetical process are discussed in appendix D.

Restatement

Put the results of your lexical-syntactical analysis into nontechnical, easily understood words that clearly convey the author's intended meaning to the English reader. There is always the danger in lexical-syntactical analysis of becoming so involved with technical details (e.g., Bullinger's technical names or grammatical case names) that we lose sight of the *purpose of the analysis*, namely, to communicate the author's meaning as clearly as possible. There is also the temptation to impress others with

---

12. Frank E. Gaebelein, ed. *The Expositor's Bible Commentary: With the New International Version of the Holy Bible*. 12 vols. (Grand Rapids: Zondervan, 1976–92).

115

our erudition and profound exegetical abilities. People need clarity, not an attestation of our erudition. Technical work must be done as part of any exegesis, but it should be part of the *preparation* for exposition: most of the analytical details need not appear in the product (except in the case of academic or technical theological papers).[13]

Laborious technical discussions often succeed only in putting an audience to sleep. A good exposition is easily recognized, not by its massive technical discussion, but because it "rings true"—the audience senses that it fits naturally into its context—and because it represents an exposition of the original writer's ideas rather than those of the interpreter. This factor undoubtedly accounts for the popularity of newer translations of the Bible that are more interpretive paraphrases than true translations. A paraphrase that results from solid exegetical work offers significant benefits. Creating a paraphrase based on one's own exegesis requires the interpreter to commit to an interpretive decision and express it in clearly understood terms.

Chapter Summary

The following seven steps are part of a lexical-syntactical analysis:

1. Identify the general literary form.
2. Trace the development of the author's theme and show how the passage under consideration fits into the context.
3. Identify the natural divisions (paragraphs and sentences) of the text.
4. Identify the connecting words within the paragraphs and sentences and show how they aid in understanding the author's progression of thought.
5. Determine what the individual words mean.
   a. Identify the range of meaning a word possessed in its time and culture.
   b. Determine the single meaning intended by the author in a given context.

13. When technical documentation is necessary in written material, it can be inserted as a footnote to avoid distracting the reader from the exposition. However, Hebrew or Greek words can be introduced into a written text in transliterated form. Transliteration involves rendering a Hebrew or Greek word with English letters that have approximately the same sound as the original word. Transliteration can be done easily by anyone who knows the sounds of the Hebrew and Greek letters. Transliterations of all Hebrew and Greek words in Scripture can be found in the back of *Strong's Exhaustive Concordance of the Bible*. When a transliterated word is included in a written text, it is placed in italics.

6. Analyze the syntax to show how it contributes to the understanding of a passage.
7. Put the results of your analysis into nontechnical, easily understood words that clearly convey the author's intended meaning to the English reader.

Exercises

(Note: these exercises and the ones in the following chapters incorporate hermeneutical skills learned in all previous chapters.)

21. A pastor preached a sermon using 1 Corinthians 11:29 as a precommunion text. He interpreted the phrase "not discerning the Lord's body" (KJV) as a reference to Christ's body, the church. His message from the text was that we are not to partake of communion when we have unresolved negative feelings toward a brother or sister, because to do so would be to eat and drink without "discerning the Lord's body." Is this a valid use of this text?

22. A devout young Christian became actively involved in the charismatic movement. Within this movement he was exposed to several powerful speakers who taught that every Spirit-filled Christian should possess all the spiritual gifts (glossolalia, interpretation of tongues, prophecy, healing, etc.). He prayed earnestly that God would give him these gifts so that he might be a more effective Christian. Even after several months, however, he still had not received some of them and became angry and bitter toward God. Use your hermeneutical skills to analyze 1 Corinthians 12, and then outline the scriptural teachings of this passage that you would use in counseling this person.

23. Most people assume that the girl spoken of in Matthew 9:18–26 was dead, but others suggest that she was comatose rather than dead.

a. What lexical-syntactical factors would you consider as you attempt to answer this question?

b. What factors suggest that she was dead? Evaluate the strength of these factors.

c. What factors suggest that she was comatose rather than dead? Evaluate the strength of these factors.

d. Do you think she was comatose or dead?

24. Much discussion by Christians on the topic of anger has been based on Ephesians 4:26 ("Be angry . . ." NASB). Analyze the meaning of this verse and discuss whether it supports the positive view of human anger normally drawn from it.

25. In Matthew 5:22, Jesus says that one who calls a brother a fool is in danger of hellfire, yet he calls the Pharisees fools in Matthew 23:17–19. How do you explain this apparent contradiction?

26. There has been much discussion concerning the nature of "worldly" (neurotic?) versus "godly" guilt (2 Cor. 7:10) by pastors and Christian counselors. Applying your knowledge of hermeneutics to this particular text, differentiate the two as best you can.

online

27. Some Christian groups maintain a very strong stand on the issue that creation took six literal twenty-four-hour periods, believing that to do otherwise suggests a less-than-faithful adherence to the biblical record. Do a word study of the Hebrew word for *day* (*yôm*) as used in the early chapters of Genesis, and state your conclusions. What does your word study indicate regarding the question of whether creation occurred in six days or six periods of unspecified duration?

28. A well-known Christian psychologist in a Christian psychological journal published an article based on the thesis that since humans are created in the image of God, we can learn about God by studying human beings. Two years later he published a second article using the thesis that since humans are created in the image of God, we can learn about human beings by studying God. Do you agree with his theses? Why, or why not?

29. Using Romans 9:13 as a text ("Jacob I loved, but Esau I hated"), a well-known Bible teacher analyzed these two brothers to show why God hated one and loved the other. Is this a valid use of this text? Why, or why not?

30. A Christian student was studying the psychological effects of conversion. In his study of 2 Corinthians 5:17 ("If anyone is in Christ, he is a new creation"), he looked up other biblical usages of the word *creation* (*ktisis*) and found that this word is almost always used of the creation of the world, implying the creation of something out of nothing (ex nihilo). If this is so, he reasoned, the psychological characteristics of the new Christian are something new that did not exist before. However, in studying the psychological literature, he could find no evidence of a new personality dimension in Christians that is not present in non-Christians. (In some cases there does seem to be a reorganization of the preexisting personality patterns, but no newly created personality dimension has been detected.) How would you help him reconcile the psychological data with his understanding of 2 Corinthians 5:17?

31. There is much discussion today among Christians about whether Scripture speaks of human beings as trichotomous (three parts—body, soul, and spirit), dichotomous (two parts—body and soul-spirit), or holistic (a unit—with body, soul, and spirit as different aspects, different ways of viewing that total unit). What hermeneutical principle(s) should be applied when attempting to resolve this question?

32. Judges 19:25 says, "But the men would not listen to *him*. So *the man* took *his* concubine and sent her outside to them." The context of Judges 19 has introduced two different men, a traveling Levite and an old Ephraimite. Read Judges 19 and determine who is meant by "him," "the man," and "his" in Judges 19:25. How did you reach your conclusion?

33. During a Bible study on Genesis 2, a discussion arose about God's intention for the relationship between man and woman. One participant read Genesis 2:18 from the NIV: "The Lord God said, 'It is not good for the man to be alone. I will make a helper suitable for him.'" He argued that the word *helper* is a clear indication that God intended for women to be nothing more than helpers for men. Another participant countered with the rendering from the NEB: "Then the Lord God said, 'It is not good for the man to be alone. I will provide a partner for him.'" He argued that the word *partner* clearly indicates the full equality between male and female. What word-study error did each participant make? How would you instruct them to resolve the matter?

Class

34. Matthew 28:18–20 reads: [Jesus said,] "All authority in heaven and on earth has been given to me. Therefore go and make disciples of all nations, baptizing them in the name of the Father and of the Son and of the Holy Spirit, and teaching them to obey everything I have commanded you." The two English commands *go* and *make disciples* in this verse make this Great Commission passage a popular rallying cry for foreign missions. Investigate the grammar of the verse to discover the mood of these two Greek verbs. Which one is a command and which is a participle? As a result of this grammatical knowledge, what would you encourage a pastor to emphasize when he preaches this verse?

35. The doctrine of "soul sleep" is the belief held by some Christians that believers who die prior to Christ's return exist in a sleeplike state until his second coming. Does 1 Thessalonians 4:14, "We believe that Jesus died and rose again and so we believe that God will bring with Jesus those who have fallen asleep in him," support a doctrine of soul sleep? Why, or why not?

119

36. In Luke's record of the Triumphal Entry (Luke 19:28–44), the disciples brought a colt to Jesus, "threw their cloaks on the colt and put Jesus on it" (19:35). In Matthew's parallel account (Matt. 21:1–11), the disciples retrieved both a donkey and a colt. "They brought the donkey and the colt, placed their cloaks on them, and Jesus sat on them" (21:7). Do these passages contradict one another? Why, or why not?

FIVE

THEOLOGICAL ANALYSIS

After completing this chapter, you should be able to

1. Identify five steps in the process called theological analysis.
2. Define the following terms:
   a. theological analysis
   b. analogy of Scripture
   c. analogy of faith
3. Identify five major positions on the nature of God's relationship to humanity and summarize each in a few sentences.
4. State a personal position on the nature of the divine-human relationship, summarizing the reasons for your decision in one or two pages.

Two Basic Questions

The basic question asked in theological analysis is, How does this passage fit into the total pattern of God's revelation? This question can be asked in two parts: (1) How does this passage fit into the total pattern of God's revelation that was revealed prior to its writing? (2) How does this passage fit into the total pattern of God's revelation that has been revealed at any time? The first part is concerned with the analogy of Scripture and the field of biblical theology, while the second addresses the analogy of faith and the field of systematic theology.

If we believe that each individual writing found in the Bible has a common divine author, then our exegetical exploration expands beyond the relationship between a text and the single biblical writing in which it is found to include questions about its relationship to the entire biblical canon. We are compelled to explore how each part is in continuity with, is consistent with, and must be interpreted by the whole of biblical teaching. As a result we simultaneously maintain the individual contributions of, for example, Malachi while checking our interpretation of his words against passages by other biblical authors to see how they support, nuance, or pose potential problems for our interpretation.

When we ask these questions, however, it immediately becomes evident that another question must also be answered, namely, What *is* the pattern of God's revelation? The hermeneutical challenge is which question to answer first. Once again the "hermeneutical circle"—the recognition that our interpretation of parts of Scripture is dependent on our interpretation of the whole of Scripture, while at the same time our interpretation of the whole cannot be separated from our interpretation of the parts—becomes evident. This book itself illustrates the hermeneutical circle with regard to theology. Although we have argued that exegesis must precede doctrine, we have also maintained that Scripture is truthful, consistent, and inerrant, and we have developed our hermeneutical methodology accordingly. But is not the belief in inerrancy a theological position?

What becomes apparent is that interpretation cannot take place in a theological vacuum. We must take a preliminary theological position and begin the exegetical process from a mindful commitment to that perspective. If as we proceed we encounter biblical data that do not easily fit our framework, we must reassess. Moisés Silva explains the danger of this approach:

> Sometimes we *make* the fact fit our preconceptions and thus distort it. The remedy, however, is neither to deny that we have those preconceptions nor to try to suppress them, for we would only be deceiving ourselves. We are much more likely to be conscious of those preconceptions if we deliberately seek to identify them *and then use them* in the exegetical process. That way, when we come across a fact that resists the direction our interpretation is taking, we are better prepared to recognize that anomaly

for what it is, namely an indication that our interpretive scheme is faulty and must be modified.[1]

Aware that we have begun with a view of biblical inerrancy, and having found it to be confirmed by our exegesis of individual biblical passages, we now take the position more firmly than at first. We thus believe that the theological question can appropriately be the initial question and concur with Silva that "exegesis stands to gain, rather than to lose, if it is *consciously* done within the framework of one's theology."[2]

Therefore, before we ask how a biblical passage fits into the total pattern of God's revelation, we must first become aware of what we believe to be God's pattern of revelation. This question is so important that the greater part of this chapter will be spent discussing it. Once the pattern of divine revelation has been tentatively determined, the question of how a particular passage fits into that total pattern becomes much easier to answer.

There are several theories regarding the best way to conceptualize the nature of God's relationship to human beings. Within salvation history (defined in this book as the history of God's saving work for humanity), some theories see significant discontinuity; others stress the continuity within salvation history. Probably most dispensationalists view the nature of God's relationship to humans as more discontinuous, with a secondary emphasis on continuity; most covenantal theologians view the divine-human relationship as primarily continuous, with a lesser emphasis on discontinuity.

Both continuity and
discontinuity present

Primary continuity
Secondary discontinuity

Primary discontinuity
Secondary continuity

**Theories regarding the Nature
of God's Relationship to Man**

Complete continuity

Complete discontinuity

1. Walter C. Kaiser Jr. and Moisés Silva, *An Introduction to Biblical Hermeneutics: The Search for Meaning* (Grand Rapids: Zondervan, 1994), 263. Emphasis in original.
2. Ibid., 260. Emphasis added.

John Feinberg has said: "The relation of the Testaments has occasioned much debate throughout church history. Whether one sees more continuity or discontinuity will become evident at various points in one's theological system. No theological system can escape addressing this issue either explicitly or implicitly."[3]

Hypotheses about the pattern of God's relationship to humans are necessary because they provide an organizational framework around which the biblical data can be understood. Without some sort of organizing principle, the amount of biblical data (the entire Old and New Testaments) would be too great to comprehend. However, there are at least two major dangers in accepting a certain system or hypothesis about the nature of divine revelation. First is the danger of imposing one's own system *onto* the biblical data rather than deriving the system *from* the data. F. F. Bruce has cautioned that "there is a great danger, when once we have adhered to one particular school of thought or adopted one particular system of theology, of reading the Bible in the light of that school or system and finding its distinctive features in what we read."[4]

A second and perhaps even greater danger is that of accepting a theory about the pattern of divine revelation without recognizing it as a theory or without looking at other theories to see which one fits the data best. Quite frequently, for example, someone who has been taught in a church that adopts one of these positions is not aware that the position is a theory or that there are other ways of conceptualizing biblical data.

The first part of this chapter presents five of the most common conceptual systems that have been proposed to explain the nature of God's relationship to humanity. Following this is a discussion of the areas of agreement between those who emphasize continuity and those who emphasize discontinuity and a discussion of the areas in which there is ongoing disagreement. The final section of the chapter identifies the steps and principles involved in theological analysis.

The Relevance of the Continuity-Discontinuity Issue

God has sent his message to us in two Testaments. But how do these two Testaments relate to each other and to us?

3. John S. Feinberg, "Systems of Discontinuity," in *Continuity and Discontinuity: Perspectives on the Relationship between the Old and New Testaments*, ed. John S. Feinberg (Westchester, IL: Crossway, 1988), 63.

4. F. F. Bruce, foreword to *God's Strategy in Human History*, ed. R. Forester and V. Marston (Wheaton: Tyndale, 1973), vii.

Chapter 3 emphasized the importance of ascertaining the recipient of a given passage or command. Those who understand salvation history as primarily continuous generally view all Scripture as relevant for the believer today, since they believe there is a basic unity between themselves and believers throughout Old and New Testament history. Dispensationalists in the first half of the twentieth century, who saw salvation history as primarily discontinuous, tended to believe that only the book of Acts and the Church Epistles possessed primary relevance for the church, since the remainder of Scripture was directed to believers who were under a different biblical economy.[5] Since the Epistles comprise only 10 percent of the Bible, the issue of whether the remaining 90 percent possesses primary relevance to contemporary believers is of paramount importance.

Many significant theological issues are affected by the way one resolves this question. For example, is Israel in the Old Testament to be considered the equivalent of the church in the New Testament? If so, how do we apply the promises given to the nation of Israel to ourselves? Do we "spiritualize" those physical and temporal promises to make them applicable to us? What about the ceremonial, civil, and moral commands given to Old Testament believers? Do they continue to be binding on us as New Testament believers? Are some binding and others not, and how do we determine which ones we must obey? In the same vein, what is the biblical future for the nation of Israel? Does Israel still have promises of a future physical existence in the land of Palestine, or should those promises of a physical existence be spiritualized and applied to the church?

On a more general level, the position one takes regarding the continuity-discontinuity issue significantly affects both preaching and teaching. In contrast to the discontinuity theorists, those who believe there is a basic continuity between the Old and New Testaments tend (1) to use the Old Testament more frequently in teaching and preaching, and (2) to find more examples of Old Testament principles that possess continuing relevance for Christians today.

Other examples can be found in both general theological issues and specific counseling issues, but the conclusion is inescapable: the way we resolve this question will have major implications for our own lives and for the lives we influence.

5. Lewis Sperry Chafer, in *Dispensationalism* (Dallas: Dallas Seminary Press, 1951), 34, states that the only Scriptures addressed specifically to Christian believers are the Gospel of John (particularly the Upper-Room Discourse), the book of Acts, and the Epistles.

Representative Theoretical Systems

The "Theologies but No Theology" Model

Liberal theologians, as mentioned in earlier chapters, typically view Scripture as a product of the evolutionary development of Israel's religion. As Israel's religious consciousness became more sophisticated, so did its theology. Consequently, liberal theologians see in Scripture a variety of theologies—writings that reflect different levels of theological sophistication, sometimes conflicting with one another. Rather than viewing the Bible as God's truth revealed by God to humanity, they believe Scripture to be humanity's thoughts about God. Since humans' ideas change over time, they believe that Scripture reveals a number of developing theological ideas and movements rather than any single, unified theology. As such, this position tends to view biblical history as discontinuous, with a lesser emphasis on continuity (although no generalization is valid for every person within this group). E. W. Parsons's book *The Religion of the New Testament* is an example of applying this type of theory to the New Testament.

Lutheran Theory

Luther believed that for a proper understanding of Scripture we must carefully distinguish between two parallel and ever-present truths of Scripture: law and gospel. As mentioned in chapter 2, *law* refers to God in his hatred of sin, his judgment, and his wrath. *Gospel* refers to God in his grace, his love, and his salvation.

Both aspects of God's nature exist side by side in Scripture throughout both the Old and New Testaments. The law reflects the holiness of God's character; were he to dispense with it, he would become an amoral rather than a holy God. Grace is God's response to the fact that man can never meet the standard of holiness that the law demands.

One way of distinguishing law from gospel is to ask, Is this text speaking judgment on me? If so, it is likely law. In contrast, if a passage brings comfort, it is likely gospel. Using these criteria, determine whether the following passages would be considered law or gospel under a Lutheran framework:

1. Genesis 7:1: "The LORD then said to Noah, 'Go into the ark, you and your whole family, because I have found you righteous in this generation.'"
2. Matthew 22:37: "Jesus replied: 'Love the Lord your God with all your heart and with all your soul and with all your mind.'"
3. John 3:36: "Whoever believes in the Son has eternal life, but whoever rejects the Son will not see life, for God's wrath remains on him."

[Answers: (1) gospel; (2) law; (3) gospel, law]

126

For Lutheran theologians, law and gospel reveal two integral aspects of God's personality: holiness and grace. Thus they see law and gospel as inseparable parts of salvation history, from the story of Adam and Eve's sin to the close of the millennium.

Law and gospel have continuing purposes in the lives of both unbelievers and believers. For the unbeliever the law condemns, accuses, and shows him his need for the Lord. For the believer the law continues to demonstrate the need for grace and provides guidelines for daily living. The gospel shows the unbeliever a way to escape from condemnation, while it motivates the believer to keep God's moral law.

The careful differentiation between, but maintenance of, both law and gospel has been an important hermeneutical tool and hallmark of orthodox Lutheran preaching. The Lutheran position strongly emphasizes continuity. God continues to respond to humans with both law and grace as he has from the beginning of human history. Law and grace are not two different epochs in God's dealing with humanity but are integral parts of all his relationships. For further reading on the Lutheran position, the following two books are recommended:

Paul Althaus. *The Theology of Martin Luther*. Philadelphia: Fortress, 1966.

C. F. W. Walther. *The Proper Distinction between Law and Gospel*. St. Louis: Concordia, 1929.

Dispensational Theory

Dispensational theology emphasizes discontinuity rather than continuity, though for very different reasons than the "theologies but no theology" movement. Whereas liberal theologians see discontinuity in the biblical record as reflecting human beings' struggles to understand God, dispensationalists are almost always orthodox in their view of inspiration, believing that any discontinuity in the pattern of salvation history occurs because God intended it.

DEVELOPMENTAL STAGES WITHIN DISPENSATIONALISM

There have been several stages in the development of dispensationalism.[6] The movement itself was initiated by John Nelson Darby and the British Plymouth Brethren. The second stage of the movement involved the Niagara Bible conferences in the late 1800s. These Bible conferences

---

6. The following discussion is adapted from Craig Blaising, "The Search for Definition," in *Dispensationalism, Israel and the Church: The Search for Definition*, ed. Craig Blaising and Darrell Bock (Grand Rapids: Zondervan, 1992), 19–20.

consisted of weeklong meetings where clergy and laypersons of various denominations met for Bible study. Although participants were probably not conscious of developing dispensationalism as such, the word was frequently used in their meetings.

The third stage in the development of dispensationalism is marked by the emergence of the *Scofield Reference Bible* in 1909. C. I. Scofield had attended the Niagara Bible conferences in their latter years. His annotated Bible was widely used in fundamentalist circles and Bible colleges and became the focus of vigorous debates between covenantalists and dispensationalists. Lewis Sperry Chafer developed his multivolume *Systematic Theology*, which also promoted this approach. Scofield and Chafer's approach became the dominant form of dispensationalism from 1910 to 1965.

In 1965 Charles Ryrie wrote *Dispensationalism Today*, and two years later the *New Scofield Reference Bible* was published. Both books modified a number of the teachings of earlier dispensationalism. Some theologians have referred to Ryrie's theory as "essentialist dispensationalism" since it identified certain essential features that he believed distinguished dispensationalism from covenantal theology.

From the 1990s to the present the dispensational movement has been referred to as "postessentialist" or "progressive" dispensationalism. It is considered postessentialist because the heterogeneity among both dispensational and covenantal theologians has made it increasingly difficult to identify essential differences that consistently differentiate one group from the other.

Dispensationalism as a Changing Theory

One of the cardinal characteristics of dispensationalism has been the use of Scripture to constantly correct its theory.[7] As a result, a dispensational study group continues to meet regularly at the annual meetings of the Evangelical Theological Society to clarify and modify its theory. Many of the beliefs that were harshly criticized in earlier periods of dispensationalism have been revised or withdrawn as a result of this continued study.

Recognizing these changes is important for several reasons. Dispensational theology is widely found among many evangelical denominations, including Baptist, Assemblies of God, Church of God, Nazarene, Christian and Missionary Alliance, independent Bible churches, and independent charismatic churches. Because the changes accepted by dispensational theologians often take considerable time to filter down to

7. Stan Gundry, foreword to Blaising and Bock, *Dispensationalism, Israel and the Church*, 11.

dispensational laypersons, the latter often continue to believe and teach things that dispensational theologians no longer affirm. Also, covenantal theologians have often strongly criticized earlier dispensationalism. It is important for covenantal theologians and laypersons to be aware of the changes that have occurred in dispensational teaching, especially in the last quarter of the twentieth century. Therefore, this discussion will begin with a brief description of dispensationalism as it was taught during the middle of the twentieth century and then clarify the changes that have occurred since then.

Scofield defined a dispensation as "a period of time during which man is tested in respect of obedience to some *specific* revelation of the will of God."[8] The pattern of salvation history was seen as three regularly recurring steps: (1) God gives human beings a specific set of responsibilities or patterns for obedience; (2) humankind fails to live up to that set of responsibilities; and (3) God responds in mercy by giving a different set of responsibilities, that is, a new dispensation.

Dispensationalists historically have recognized between four and nine dispensations; the usual number is seven (or eight if the tribulation period is considered a separate dispensation). The following description of the seven dispensations, summarized from Charles C. Ryrie,[9] is typical, but there are many variations within this school.

Dispensation of Innocence or Freedom. This dispensation included the time when Adam and Eve were in a state of innocence, before the fall, and terminated at the time they sinned through disobedience. It is described in Genesis 1:28–3:6.

Dispensation of Conscience. During this period "obedience to the dictates of conscience was man's chief stewardship responsibility." It ended as humans became increasingly wicked and God brought judgment through the flood. This dispensation is described in Genesis 4:1–8:14.

Dispensation of Civil Government. During this dispensation God gave humankind the right to capital punishment, implying with it the right to develop human government. Instead of scattering and filling the earth, humanity expressed its rebellion by building the tower of Babel. God's judgment came through the confusion of languages. This period is described in Genesis 8:15–11:9.

Dispensation of Promise. This interval covered the time of the patriarchs; its name derives from God's promise to Abraham of a land and subsequent blessings. The disobedience of Jacob in leaving the land of

---

8. *Scofield Reference Bible*, new and improved ed. (New York: Oxford University Press, 1917), 5. Most contemporary dispensational writers stress the concept of various stewardship arrangements rather than time periods.

9. Charles C. Ryrie, *Dispensationalism Today* (Chicago: Moody, 1965), 57–64.

promise and going to Egypt resulted in slavery. This period is described in Genesis 11:10–Exodus 18:27.

Dispensation of Mosaic Law. This period lasted from Moses until the death of Christ. During this time God gave commandments covering all phases of life and activity. Israel's failure to abide by these commandments led to division of the kingdom and bondage. The dispensation of law is described in Exodus 18:27–Acts 1:26.

Dispensation of Grace. During this period (which includes the present) humankind's responsibility is to accept God's gift of righteousness. This age will end with humanity's rejection of God's gracious gift, leading to the tribulation. The dispensation of grace is described in Acts 2:1–Revelation 19:21.

Dispensation of the Millennium. During the millennial kingdom, humanity's responsibility will be obedience to the personal rule of Christ. At the end of this period a final rebellion will erupt and end in the final judgment. The best-known biblical passage describing this period is Revelation 20.

One point of debate has been whether the dispensational regulations represent various means of salvation or various guidelines for obedient living *after* salvation. A common belief among dispensational *laypersons* is that the dispensations of law and grace represent alternative means of salvation. This belief is based, in part, on a note in the original *Scofield Reference Bible.* The note accompanying John 1:17 stated:

> As a dispensation, grace begins with the death and resurrection of Christ (Rom. 3:24–26; 4:24–25). The point of testing is no longer legal obedience as the *condition* of salvation, but acceptance or rejection of Christ, with good works as a fruit of salvation. (emphasis added)

This statement is admittedly poorly worded and did lead to the misunderstanding that dispensationalism recognized at least two means of salvation. However, there is now a strong consensus that "Scofield himself and other dispensationalist writers affirmed elsewhere that salvation was by grace in the Old Testament, and that no one was ever justified by works."[10] The *New Scofield Reference Bible* clarifies that there has always been but one means of salvation. Thus dispensational theologians presently believe that the commands given during the various dispensations were guidelines for godly living given after salvation rather than means of earning salvation.

10. Allen Ross, "The Biblical Method of Salvation: A Case for Discontinuity," in J. Feinberg, *Continuity and Discontinuity,* 162. From the same volume see also Ryrie and Feinberg, cited in Klooster, "The Biblical Method of Salvation: A Case for Continuity," 132. See also Gundry, foreword in Blaising and Bock, *Dispensationalism, Israel and the Church,* 10.

In the last fifty years dispensational teaching has significantly changed with regard to at least four beliefs: the postponed-kingdom theory; the nature of the two kingdoms; the assertion of two entirely separate peoples of God; and the notion of two covenants, one for Israel and one for the church.

The *postponed-kingdom theory* is the belief that at his first coming Christ intended to set up an earthly kingdom with Israel at its center. When the people of Israel rejected him, Christ withdrew the offer of an earthly kingdom, created instead a spiritual kingdom—the church—and postponed the coming of an earthly kingdom with Israel at its center until his second coming. Dispensational theologians now recognize that if Christ had been accepted by the Jews of his time, the crucifixion and resurrection would never have occurred. Walter Kaiser Jr., who does not identify himself as a dispensationalist, reviews the passages that were previously interpreted as the basis for the postponed-kingdom theory to demonstrate that these verses, interpreted in context, simply affirm that God's offer would first be given to the Jews and then to the Gentiles.[11]

In the mid-twentieth century dispensationalists also generally believed in two kingdoms. These included an eternal kingdom, known as the kingdom of God, and an earthly kingdom, known as the kingdom of heaven. It is now recognized that these two terms are synonyms and that both can refer to both a temporal and an eternal kingdom and to both a present and future kingdom.[12]

A third belief that has changed is the notion that there are two entirely separate peoples of God, his heavenly people and his earthly people. However, most scholars now recognize that the biblical language will not support such a strict dichotomy. The phrase "people of God" refers to both Israel and those outside Israel. Robert Saucy reflects the contemporary dispensationalist view of this issue when he says: "In the final sense it is perhaps best to say that 'the people of God' is one people, since all will be related to him through the same covenant salvation. But the affirmation of this fundamental unity in a relation to God through Christ does not eliminate the distinctiveness of Israel as a special nation called of God for a unique ministry in the world as a nation among nations."[13]

A fourth belief that has changed is the dispensational idea of two covenants, one for Israel and one for the church. Although several scriptural passages promise a new covenant (e.g., Jer. 31:31–34; Ezek. 36:26–27),

11. Walter C. Kaiser Jr., "Kingdom Promises as Spiritual and National," in J. Feinberg, *Continuity and Discontinuity*, 295–98.

12. Ibid., 295.

13. Robert Saucy, "Israel and the Church: A Case for Discontinuity," in J. Feinberg, *Continuity and Discontinuity*, 241.

dispensationalists today do not believe that the old covenant was for Israel and the new covenant is for the church.

Bruce Ware summarizes the characteristics of the new covenant that distinguish it from the old:[14]

1. A new mode of implementation (the law is written in their minds rather than on tablets of stone) by the indwelling work of the Holy Spirit (John 14:17).
2. A new result: "they will know me."
3. A new basis: full and final forgiveness (sacrifices are no longer necessary).
4. A new scope of inclusion (from the least to the greatest).
5. The Holy Spirit comes on all believers, not just on select ones.
6. The Holy Spirit's coming is permanent, not temporary.
7. The Holy Spirit's coming is not just to accomplish certain tasks but to enable the believer to live in covenant faithfulness.

Thus the new covenant includes all post-Pentecost believers, whether Jew or Gentile.

Covenantal Theory

Covenantal theory, like Lutheran theory, emphasizes continuity rather than discontinuity in salvation history. Covenantal theologians view all biblical history as covered by two overarching covenants, a covenant of works until the fall and a covenant of grace from the fall to the present.[15] The covenant of works is described as the agreement between God and Adam that promised Adam life for perfect obedience and death as the penalty for disobedience. The covenant of grace is the agreement between God and a sinner in which God promises salvation through faith, and the sinner promises a life of faith and obedience.[16] All Old Testament, New Testament, and contemporary believers are part of the covenant of grace.

Reformed theology, from which covenantal theology developed, has historically viewed the church as existing from the beginning of human

14. Bruce Ware, "The New Covenant and the People(s) of God," in Blaising and Bock, *Dispensationalism, Israel and the Church*, 68–97.

15. Some Reformed theologians speak of a third covenant—the covenant of redemption—that was formed in eternity past. This was an agreement between the Father and the Son, in which the Father pronounced the Son as Head and Redeemer of the elect, and the Son voluntarily agreed to die for those whom the Father had given him.

16. Louis Berkhof, *Systematic Theology*, 4th rev. and enl. ed. (Grand Rapids: Eerdmans, 1941), 211–18, 265–71.

history to the end of the world (as contrasted with dispensationalism, which believes it did not exist until the death and resurrection of Christ). Some of the reasons covenantal theologians believe the church existed in the Old Testament include[17]

1. The Hebrew word for a "called-out" congregation in reference to the nation of Israel is translated in the Septuagint (the Greek translation of the Old Testament) as *ekklēsia*, the same word used for the church in the New Testament. The concept of Israel as a "called-out" assembly begins in the Pentateuch and is also found regularly in the book of Psalms.
2. God's revelation of himself to humans was primarily to Israel in the Old Testament. When Christ came, however, he broke down the dividing wall between Jews and Gentiles such that the church now became all persons who believed in Christ, regardless of nationality (Eph. 2:14).
3. Despite considerable emphasis on temporal blessing in the Old Testament, the heart of the Old Testament message was the Israelites' response to the covenant God offered. The heart of the matter is a spiritual relationship, not temporal blessings. A term often applied to both Old Testament Israel and the church is "the people of God."
4. In 1 Peter 2:9–10 the apostle Peter applies many of the titles given to Old Testament Israel to New Testament Christians.
5. In Galatians 6:16 Paul refers to the church as "the Israel of God."
6. Based on the above understanding, covenantal theology asserts that when Israel as a nation rejected Christ, the church replaced Israel as God's chosen people. They believe that the temporal, physical promises given to Israel in the Old Testament may now be spiritualized and applied to the church. Unlike dispensational theology, most covenantal theologians do not believe God has promised that he will physically restore Israel as a nation to the land of Palestine. Marten Woudstra, a covenantal theologian, says that when we interpret the relationship between the Old Testament and the New Testament properly, "our concern with an earthly restoration of Israel to the land of the fathers will diminish to the vanishing point."[18] Bruce Waltke also says that "kingdom promises are comprehensively fulfilled in the church, not in restored na-

17. Marten Woudstra, "Israel and the Church: A Case for Continuity," in J. Feinberg, *Continuity and Discontinuity*, 221–38.
18. Ibid., 228.

tional Israel." He notes: "No clear passage teaches the restoration of national Israel, its reverse side is imprinted with the hard fact that national Israel and its law have been permanently replaced by the church and the New Covenant."[19]

A question one might raise about covenantal theory concerns the many covenants mentioned in Scripture. The Old Testament speaks of several covenants: a preflood Noachian covenant (Gen. 6:18), a postflood Noachian covenant (Gen. 9:8–17), an Abrahamic covenant (Gen. 15:4–8, 18; 17:6–8), a Mosaic covenant (Exod. 6:6–8), a Davidic covenant (Ps. 89:3–4, 26–37), and a new covenant (Jer. 31:31–34). In light of this, is it proper to speak of a covenant of grace rather than specific covenants? And if there are several covenants, is not the covenantal theory almost the same as the dispensational theory?

Although covenantal theologians recognize each of these individual covenants, there are some basic differences between covenantal and dispensational conceptions of salvation history. In response to the first question above, the covenantal conception of salvation history emphasizes continuity: a general covenant of grace overshadowed each of the specific covenants. Human beings have been called by grace, justified by grace, and adopted into the family of God by grace ever since the fall. Thus covenantal theologians believe it is accurate to group these individual covenants under the more general heading of the covenant of grace.

Dispensational theologians place more emphasis on discontinuity. While dispensationalists agree that salvation has always been by grace, they also believe that significant changes regarding God's commands for obedient living occur across the dispensations. Although contemporary dispensational theologians now stress the continuity between dispensations more than they have in the past, earlier dispensational theologians emphasized the differences between dispensations. Humanity's responsibilities within each dispensation were seen as a different type of test resulting from the previous one. Thus when human beings failed to obey God after receiving the responsibility of following conscience (second dispensation), God gave them the responsibility of obedience through government.

Covenantal theologians place more emphasis on the additive rather than the disjunctive nature of the covenants. For example, the post-flood Noachian covenant was consistent with the preflood covenant; it simply supplied more details of the grace relationship. Similarly, the Mosaic covenant did not abolish the Abrahamic one but rather added

19. Bruce Waltke, "Kingdom Promises as Spiritual," in J. Feinberg, *Continuity and Discontinuity*, 263, 274.

to it (Gal. 3:17–22). Thus, starting from exactly the same biblical data and very similar views of inspiration and revelation, dispensational and covenantal theologians arrive at somewhat different views of the nature of salvation history, views consequently reflected in their theological analysis of the Bible.

Epigenetic Model

The epigenetic model views divine revelation as analogous to the growth of a tree from a seed to a seedling, to a young tree, and then to a fully grown tree. This concept can be contrasted with one that likens divine revelation to the building of a cathedral piece by piece. A cathedral when half built is an imperfect cathedral, whereas a tree when half grown is still a perfect tree. The epigenetic theory views God's self-disclosures as never being imperfect or errant, even though later disclosures may add further information.

The term *epigenetic theory* has not been widely used. Terms such as the *organic unity* of Scripture[20] have also been used, with the adjective *organic* evoking the concept of living growth.

The idea of progressive revelation, which is almost unanimously held by evangelical scholars, is highly consistent with an epigenetic theory. Progressive revelation is the concept that God's revelation gradually increased in definiteness, clarity, and fullness as it was revealed over time, even as a tree increases its girth and root and branch structures over time. As the trunk and branches of a tree may grow in several directions concurrently, so also have the concepts of God, Christ, salvation, the nation of Israel, and the church grown simultaneously as God's revelation progressed.

Although various theories might be considered epigenetic, the best-known is Walter Kaiser's promise theology. In some ways his model may be viewed as a middle road between dispensational and covenantal theology. Covenantal theologians often criticize dispensationalists for minimizing the essential unity of Scripture. Dispensationalists contend that covenantal theologians fail to maintain important distinctions (e.g., that between Israel and the church). A model that is responsive to both criticisms would emphasize the unity of salvation history but allow for valid differentiation as well. The epigenetic model, with its unified trunk but variegated branch structure, provides this balance.

20. For example, Louis Berkhof, *Principles of Biblical Interpretation* (Grand Rapids: Baker, 1950), 134; J. I. Packer, *"Fundamentalism" and the Word of God* (Grand Rapids: Eerdmans, 1958), 52; John W. Wenham, *Christ and the Bible* (Downers Grove, IL: Inter-Varsity, 1972), 19, 103–4.

135

Kaiser describes the promise as God's pledge to do or be something for Old Testament Israelites, then for future Israelites, and eventually for all nations. The promise thus extends from the past to the present and into the future. It includes temporal, physical promises as well as spiritual promises.

The promise became more defined and differentiated over time. Branches of the promise include (1) material blessings for all humans and animals, (2) a special seed to humankind through Abraham, (3) a land for the nation of Israel, (4) spiritual blessings for all nations, (5) a national deliverance from bondage, (6) an enduring dynasty and kingdom that will one day embrace a universal dominion, (7) forgiveness of sin, and others.[21]

Thus Kaiser's promise theology affirms the continuity of God calling out a people unto himself throughout the Bible but also asserts that there are future promises applying to the nation of Israel and the church as distinct entities.

The promise doctrine is not the only possible organizing principle for the epigenetic model. Lutherans would probably suggest that Christ be the central concept, while J. Barton Payne might have suggested "God's testament."[22] Still other theologians might suggest God's grace in all its manifestations.

Making a Decision about the Continuity-Discontinuity Issue

As mentioned earlier in this chapter, it is crucial to consider this issue carefully and make the best decision one can based on one's understanding of the biblical data. Fortunately, covenantal and dispensational theologians are not as polarized as they were fifty or even twenty-five years ago. Both groups recognize that there is a great deal of continuity within salvation history despite the discontinuity in some areas. Both groups are, in general, closer to the middle point on the spectrum shown at the beginning of this chapter than to the extreme ends, something that was not true in the middle of the twentieth century. There is still significant heterogeneity within each group, so no generalizations can accurately categorize every dispensationalist or covenantal theologian. However, some trends do accurately describe a growing number of persons within each

21. Walter C. Kaiser Jr., *Toward an Old Testament Theology* (Grand Rapids: Zondervan, 1978), 14. For a powerful discussion of and apologetic for this approach, see especially his "Kingdom Promises as Spiritual and National," in J. Feinberg, *Continuity and Discontinuity*, 289–307.

22. J. Barton Payne, *The Theology of the Older Testament* (Grand Rapids: Zondervan, 1962), 71–96.

category. This section will discuss areas of growing consensus, followed by a discussion of areas where there is still significant disagreement.

Areas of Growing Consensus

OLD AND NEW COVENANTS

Ursinus (1534–83) described the similarities and differences between the old and the new covenant in terms on which most covenantalists and dispensationalists can agree:[23]

Old Covenant	New Covenant
forgiveness	forgiveness
eternal life	eternal life
faith	faith
obedience	obedience
temporal blessings	general blessings
ceremonial worship	spiritual worship
mosaic polity	no comment
grace given in anticipation of the coming Messiah	grace given for the sake of the Messiah
many sacraments	two sacraments: baptism and the Lord's Supper
types and shadows	fulfillment
obscure understanding	fuller understanding
limited effusion of the Holy Spirit	full effusion of the Holy Spirit
limited duration	forever
bound to all laws	bound only to the moral law
limited to Israel	open to all nations

UNDERSTANDING OF SALVATION

John S. Feinberg, in discussing salvation by grace throughout the Old and the New Testaments, says that we should consider five factors: (1) the basis or ground of salvation, (2) the requirement for salvation, (3) the ultimate content of salvation, (4) the specific revealed content of salvation to be accepted, and (5) the believers' expression of their salvation.

On the first three of these factors, dispensationalists and covenantalists agree: (1) the basis of salvation is and always has been the life, death,

23. Adapted from Zacharias Ursinus, *The Commentary on the Heidelberg Catechism* (1852; Phillipsburg: Presbyterian & Reformed, 1985), 97. Cited in Willem VanGemeren, "Systems of Continuity," in J. Feinberg, *Continuity and Discontinuity*, 42.

and resurrection of Christ; (2) the requirement for salvation has always been faith in the living God as he has revealed himself; (3) the ultimate object of faith has always been the living God himself. With regard to the fourth factor, involving the specific revealed content of salvation, dispensationalists generally believe that the Old Testament sacrifices pointed forward to the ultimate sacrifice that Jesus would make but that Old Testament believers did not understand this. Covenantal theologians believe that Old Testament believers understood this dimly, based on passages such as Genesis 3:15. Similarly for the fifth factor, covenantal theologians generally believe that Old Testament believers expressed their understanding of salvation in ways similar to New Testament believers, whereas dispensational theologians believe there was more discontinuity between these two groups.[24]

To What Extent Are New Testament Believers under the Law?

This question has been variously answered by dispensationalists over the last century. Although dispensational and covenantal theologians seem to be coming to closer agreement, they use different terms in articulating their positions.

Ezekiel Hopkins, drawing on a long Reformed tradition found in the Westminster Confession (chap. 21), has suggested that the Old Testament law can be divided into three aspects: the *ceremonial* (those ritual observances that pointed forward to the final atonement in Christ), the *judicial or civil* (those laws God prescribed for use in Israel's civil government), and the *moral* (that body of moral precepts that possess universal, abiding applicability for all humanity).[25]

Some theologians have argued against the validity of these distinctions for two reasons: the Old Testament Israelites did not understand their law according to these three categories, and the New Testament does not explicitly make such distinctions.

Old Testament believers probably did not divide their law according to these categories; such division would have been superfluous since all three aspects of the law applied to them in any case. As New Testament believers we must decide whether the New Testament validates these distinctions. Also, while the New Testament may not *explicitly* make such

24. John S. Feinberg, "Salvation in the Old Testament," in *Tradition and Testament: Essays in Honor of Charles Lee Feinberg,* ed. J. S. and P. D. Feinberg (Chicago: Moody, 1981), 49–50. Discussed by Fred Klooster in "The Biblical Method of Salvation: A Case for Continuity," in J. Feinberg, *Continuity and Discontinuity,* 131–60.

25. Ezekiel Hopkins, "Understanding the Ten Commandments," in *Classical Evangelical Essays in Old Testament Interpretation,* ed. Walter C. Kaiser Jr. (Grand Rapids: Baker, 1972), 43.

distinctions, much of our theological study involves making explicit what is implicit in the biblical record.

The *ceremonial aspect* of the law encompasses the various sacrifices and ceremonial rites that served as figures or types pointing to the coming Redeemer (Heb. 7–10). A number of Old Testament texts confirm that the Israelites had some conception of the spiritual significance of these rites and ceremonies (e.g., Lev. 20:25–26; Ps. 26:6; 51:7, 16–17; Isa. 1:16). Several New Testament texts differentiate the ceremonial aspect of the law and point to its fulfillment in Christ (e.g., Mark 7:19; Eph. 2:14–15; Heb. 7:26–28; 9:9–11; 10:1, 9). It is important to stress that the ceremonial law was fulfilled, not annulled or abolished (Matt. 5:17–19).

The *civil, or judicial, aspect* of the law encompasses the precepts given to Israel for the government of its civil state. Although many Gentile governments have adopted principles from this portion of the law as their own, these civil laws seem to have been intended for the government of the Jewish people, and believers from other nations are commanded to be obedient to the civil laws of their own government.[26]

The *moral aspect* of the law reflects the moral nature and perfection of God. Since God's moral nature remains unchanged, the moral law is unchanging and is as relevant for the believer today as for the believers to whom it was originally given. The Christian is dead to the condemning power of the law (Rom. 8:1–3) but still very much under its command of obedience as a guide to right living before God (Rom. 3:31; 6:1; 1 Cor. 5:1–13; 6:9–20).

Thus while some theologians argue against the above distinction within Old Testament law, few who do so have expressed an interest in reviving the ceremonial laws or implementing Jewish civil laws (e.g., stoning rebellious children). Until they can propose a better alternative, this distinction seems a plausible and biblically sound alternative.[27]

New Testament believers are not "under the law" in three senses: (1) they are not under the ceremonial law because it has been fulfilled in Christ, (2) they are not under Jewish civil law because it was not intended for them, and (3) they are not under the condemnation of the law because their identification with the vicarious atoning death of Christ frees them from it. However, the moral law continues to apply because it is rooted in God's moral nature.

The views of dispensational theologians vary regarding the applicability of the Old Testament law to New Testament believers. However, a consensus seems to be emerging, namely, that we are under the "law

26. Ibid., 46.
27. David Wenham, "Jesus and the Law: An Exegesis on Matthew 5:17–20," *Themelios* 4 (April 1979): 95; Knox Chamblin, "The Law of Moses and the Law of Christ," in J. Feinberg, *Continuity and Discontinuity*, 183.

of Christ," which is understood as roughly parallel to what covenantal theologians understand as the moral law but is motivated by love rather than fear. Thus covenantal and dispensational theologians appear to be approaching agreement on this issue, though their terminology may differ.

Areas of Continued Disagreement

Although covenantal and dispensational theologians continue to disagree in several areas, for the purposes of this introductory discussion, we will identify three primary ones.

THE CHURCH IN THE OLD TESTAMENT

As mentioned earlier, covenantal theologians believe that the church has existed throughout human history and was present in the Old Testament. Many of the reasons for this belief were presented in the section on covenantal theology.

In contrast, most dispensational theologians believe that the church did not originate until Pentecost. Some of the reasons they offer include the following:[28] (1) When a person trusts Christ as Savior, he is baptized by the Holy Spirit into the body of Christ (1 Cor. 12:13). However, baptism by (or in) the Holy Spirit did not begin until the day of Pentecost. (2) The Bible speaks of New Testament believers as being "in Christ." This also could not happen until the Messiah had been revealed. (3) Ephesians 4:15–16 and Colossians 1:18 speak of Christ as the head of the church, but Ephesians 1:19–23 says that Christ became the head of the church after his resurrection and ascension. Ephesians 4:15–16 suggests very strongly that the church did not exist before Christ became its head. (4) 1 Corinthians 12 and Ephesians 4:11–12 teach that Christ gave gifts to the church through the Holy Spirit for the work of ministry. But Ephesians 4:8 suggests that Christ did not give those gifts until his ascension. Dispensationalists argue that if the church is a body of spiritually gifted people, ministering in the power of the Holy Spirit, and Christ did not give those spiritual gifts until his ascension, then the church did not exist before that time.

HAS THE CHURCH REPLACED ISRAEL AS THE "PEOPLE OF GOD"? HAS GOD ABANDONED ISRAEL?

As mentioned earlier, most covenantal theologians believe that the people of Israel have been set aside because of their unbelief and that the church has replaced the nation of Israel as the "people of God." Bruce

---

28. John S. Feinberg, "Systems of Discontinuity," 63–86.

Waltke is typical of most covenantal theologians when he asserts that "kingdom promises are fulfilled in the church, not a restored national Israel" and that "national Israel and its law have been permanently replaced by the church."[29] Although a few covenantal theologians have asked that this discussion be reopened (e.g., VanGemeren), only a small minority of covenantalists see a distinctive role for Israel in the future.[30]

In contrast, dispensationalists believe that the church has not replaced the nation of Israel: each has a distinctive role to play in the future. Some of the biblical reasons they give for these beliefs include the following: (1) Old Testament prophecies predict a time of spiritual, social, political, and economic blessing for Israel (e.g., Isa. 60; Jer. 31:27–40; Zeph. 3:11–20; Zech. 12–14). Since those prophecies are still unfulfilled, one can expect them to be fulfilled in the future. (2) In Romans 11:25–29 Paul clearly predicts the future salvation of Israel as a nation and says that "God's gifts and his call are irrevocable" (v. 29).

HERMENEUTICAL ISSUES

While covenantal and dispensational theologians probably agree on hermeneutical principles at a theoretical level, they differ in their application of those principles. Following are two examples.

Symbolic versus literal interpretation of Scripture. Probably the beginnings of this issue can be found with Augustine, who rejected the literal interpretation of Scripture that had led to historic premillennialism and replaced it with a more symbolic interpretation, leading to his adoption of amillennialism. Covenantal theologians have continued, for the most part, to advocate this more symbolic interpretation of Scripture, and the majority of them embrace amillennialism. Dispensational theologians continue to give priority to a more literal interpretation of Scripture, and the majority of them are premillennialists. This is not to say that covenantal theologians do not interpret some things literally or that dispensational theologians do not understand some passages symbolically. The difference is in the amount of literal and symbolic interpretation each group does.

Interpretation of terms such as "Jew," "seed of Abraham," and "chosen people." In Scripture these terms are used in various ways, in a biological sense, a political sense, a spiritual sense (to refer to anyone properly related to God by faith), or a typological sense (where Israel is a type of the church). Covenantal theologians interpret these phrases primarily in their spiritual or typological senses, whereas dispensational theologians are more likely to consider all four senses when interpreting a particular

29. Waltke, "Kingdom Promises as Spiritual," 263, 274.
30. John S. Feinberg, "Systems of Discontinuity," 63–86.

passage.[31] For example, Paul Feinberg makes the following argument: "While historical-grammatical interpretation allows for symbols, types and analogies, I see no evidence that Israel is a symbol for the church, Palestine for the new Jerusalem, *et al.* If that is the case, then I do not see how the requirements of historical-grammatical interpretation have been met by those who would change or reinterpret the Old Testament predictions."[32]

Chapter Summary

Theological analysis asks the question, How does this passage fit into the total pattern of God's revelation? Before answering that question we must have some understanding of the pattern of revelation history.

Various views have been offered—from those that emphasize discontinuity within biblical history to those that emphasize continuity. Five such theories were identified and discussed in relation to the continuity-discontinuity continuum.

The history of the two best-known theories within conservative evangelical circles—covenantal theology and dispensational theology—were discussed, including the primary arguments that each group has used to support their positions, as well as the changes that have occurred in these positions, especially in the last fifty years.

Many exegetical arguments on both sides of the issue are too detailed to include in this chapter. We encourage readers to carefully examine the book *Continuity and Discontinuity: Perspectives on the Relationship between the Old and New Testaments*, edited by John Feinberg. This book discusses many of the important aspects of this issue in a more nuanced way than is impossible in a brief introduction, with companion chapters written by leading dispensational and covenantal theologians.

The steps in theological analysis are

1. *Determine your own view of the nature of God's relationship to human beings*. The collecting of evidence, the framing of questions, and the understanding of certain texts presented in this chapter are undoubtedly biased by the author's conceptions of a biblical view of salvation history. The conclusion of this step is too important to assume from someone else without carefully and prayerfully considering the evidence yourself.

31. Ibid., 72.
32. Paul D. Feinberg, "Hermeneutics of Discontinuity," in J. Feinberg, *Continuity and Discontinuity*, 124.

2. *Identify the implications of this view for the passage you are studying.* For example, a position on the nature of God's relationship to humanity that is primarily discontinuous will view the Old Testament as less relevant for contemporary believers than the New Testament.

3. *Assess the extent of theological knowledge available to the people of that time.* What previous knowledge had been given? (This previ-

Summary of General Hermeneutics

Historical-Cultural and Contextual Analysis	Lexical-Syntactical Analysis	Theological Analysis
1. Determine the general historical and cultural milieu of the writer and his audience.	1. Identify the general literary form.	1. Determine your own view of the nature of God's relationship to human beings.
a. Determine the general historical circumstances.	2. Trace the development of the author's theme and show how the passage under consideration fits into the context.	2. Identify the implications of this view for the passage you are studying.
b. Be aware of cultural circumstances and norms that add meaning to given actions.		3. Assess the extent of theological knowledge available to the people of that time.
c. Discern the level of spiritual commitment of the audience.	3. Identify the natural divisions (paragraphs and sentences) of the text.	4. Determine the meaning the passage possessed for its original recipients in light of their knowledge.
2. Determine the purpose the author had in writing a book by:	4. Identify the connecting words within the paragraphs and sentences and show how they aid in understanding the author's progression of thought.	5. Identify the additional knowledge about this topic that is available to us now because of later revelation.
a. Noting explicit statements or repeated phrases.		
b. Observing paraenetic or hortatory sections.	5. Determine what the individual words mean.	
c. Observing issues that are omitted or emphasized.	a. Identify the multiple meanings a word possessed in its time and culture.	
3. Understand how the passage fits into its immediate context.	b. Determine the single meaning intended by the author in a given context.	
a. Identify the major blocks of material in the book and show how they fit into a coherent whole.	6. Analyze the syntax to show how it contributes to the understanding of the passage.	
b. Show how the passage fits into the flow of the author's argument.	7. Put the results of your analysis into nontechnical, easily understood words that clearly convey the author's intended meaning.	
c. Determine the perspective that the author intends to communicate—noumenological or phenomenological.		
d. Distinguish between descriptive and prescriptive truth.		
e. Distinguish between incidental details and the teaching focus of the passage.		
f. Identify the person or category of persons for whom the particular passage is intended.		

ous knowledge is sometimes referred to in hermeneutics textbooks as the "analogy of Scripture.") The biblical references to earlier texts that appear in the margins of Bibles such as the *Thompson Chain Reference Bible* can provide assistance, as can good biblical theology texts.

4. *Determine the meaning the passage possessed for its original recipients in light of their knowledge.*

5. *Identify the additional knowledge about this topic that is available to us now because of later revelation.* (This knowledge is sometimes referred to in hermeneutics textbooks as the "analogy of faith.") What other, perhaps clearer, passages and teachings do you need to consider in your interpretation of this passage? Topical Bibles and systematic theology texts that provide comprehensive scholarship on major topics such as theology, anthropology, Christology, soteriology, pneumatology, ecclesiology, and eschatology can be helpful in acquiring this type of information.

Exercises

37. Carefully think through the continuity-discontinuity issue, using the text, recommended readings, and your own resources to examine the question further. Write a summary of your position. At this point your position should be tentative, open to modification as new information becomes available.

38. A couple in deep conflict comes to you for counseling about a certain matter. The husband says that they need a new car and wants to finance it through their local bank, since they do not have the money to pay cash for it. His wife, basing her argument on Romans 13:8 ("Owe no man any thing," KJV), believes it is wrong to borrow money to purchase the car. The husband says he does not think the verse refers to their situation and wants to know what you think. What is your response?

39. At least one Protestant denomination refuses to have a paid clergy on the basis of 1 Timothy 3:3. Do you agree with the scriptural basis of this practice? Why, or why not?

class

40. A married couple reveals to you that the husband has been having an affair. The husband professes to be a Christian, so you ask him how he reconciles his behavior with the biblical teaching on marital faithfulness. He replies that he loves both persons and justifies his behavior on the basis of 1 Corinthians 6:12 ("Everything is permissible for me"). What is your response?

144

41. You are part of a Bible study discussion group in which someone offers a point based on an Old Testament passage. Another person responds, "That's from the Old Testament and therefore does not apply to us as Christians." As discussion leader that night, how would you handle the situation?

42. A sincere young Christian attended a teaching series based on Psalm 37:4 ("Delight yourself in the LORD, and he will give you the desires of your heart") and Mark 11:24 ("Whatever you ask for in prayer, believe that you have received it, and it will be yours"). Based on the teaching, he began to write checks "on faith" and was rather dismayed when they "bounced." How would you counsel him regarding the teaching he had received concerning these verses?

43. Your cousin, now attending a neoorthodox seminary, argues against the approach toward hermeneutics that carefully considers historical, cultural, contextual, and grammatical matters because "the letter kills, but the Spirit gives life" (2 Cor. 3:6). He goes on to state that interpretations should be in line with "the spirit of Christianity," and that your grammatical-historical method of interpretation often results in exegesis that is no longer consistent with the gracious spirit of Christ. How would you respond?

44. Some writers have suggested that there is an inconsistency between the doctrine of Paul (as found in Gal. 2:15–16; Rom. 3:20, 28) and the doctrine of James (as found in James 1:22–25; 2:8, 14–17, 21–24). Do you believe these doctrines can be reconciled? If so, how would you reconcile them?

45. Paul's experience in Romans 7:7–25 has long been discussed among Christians, with important implications for pastors and Christian counselors. The main question has been: Is his experience the struggle of a believer, or is it a preconversion struggle only? Using your knowledge of hermeneutics, compare the arguments for each interpretation. You may present an alternative interpretation if it can be justified exegetically. What are the implications of your interpretation for Christian mental health and pastoral counseling?

46. Read and compare the accounts of Jesus' baptism in each of the Synoptic Gospels (Matt. 3:13–17; Mark 1:9–11; Luke 3:21–22). What are their similarities? What are their differences? How would you explain the similarities and differences between the accounts?

47. One of your church members has come to you for counseling about the following matter. His wife has been unfaithful to him, and her unfaithfulness has been substantiated by solid evidence. His parents are very upset and tell him that he has the right to divorce her

online

because of her unfaithfulness and remarry when he chooses to do so, citing Matthew 5:31–32 and 19:3–9. Her parents are also upset but tell him that he should forgive her based on the many passages where believers are commanded to forgive and also the example of Hosea (1:2 and 3:1). How would you counsel him?

SIX

SPECIAL LITERARY FORMS

SIMILES, METAPHORS, PROVERBS, PARABLES, AND ALLEGORIES

After completing this chapter, you should be able to

1. Describe in one to three sentences each of the literary terms mentioned in the chapter title.
2. Identify these literary forms when they occur in the biblical text.
3. Describe the interpretive principles necessary to determine the author's intended meaning when he uses any of these literary devices.

Definitions and Comparisons of Methods of Literary Interpretation

Chapters 3, 4, and 5 have discussed those methods used in the interpretation of all texts, that is, in general hermeneutics. This chapter and the following one focus on special hermeneutics, which studies the interpretation of special literary forms or genres. Good communicators use a variety of literary devices for illustration, clarification, emphasis, and maintenance of audience interest. Biblical writers and speakers also used such devices, including similes, metaphors, proverbs, parables, and allegories.

E. D. Hirsch Jr. likens various types of literary expression to games: to understand them properly it is necessary to know what game you are playing. It is also necessary to know the rules of that game. Disagreements arise in interpretation because (1) there is a question over what game is being played, or (2) there is confusion about the proper rules for playing that game.[1] Fortunately for the modern student of the Bible, careful literary analysis has yielded a substantial body of knowledge concerning the characteristics of these literary forms and the principles necessary to interpret them properly.

Two of the simplest literary devices are similes and metaphors. A *simile* is simply an expressed comparison: it typically uses the words *like* or *as* (e.g., "the kingdom of heaven is like . . ."). The emphasis is on some point of similarity between two ideas, groups, actions, and so on. The subject and the thing with which it is being compared are kept separate (i.e., not "the kingdom of heaven is . . ." but rather "the kingdom of heaven is like . . .").

A *metaphor* is an unexpressed comparison: it does not use the words *like* or *as*. The subject and the thing with which it is being compared are intertwined rather than kept separate. Jesus used metaphors when he said, "I am the bread of life" (John 6:35, 48) and "You are the light of the world" (Matt. 5:14). Although the subject and its comparison are identified as one, the author does not intend his words to be taken literally: Christ is no more a piece of bread than Christians are photon emitters. In both similes and metaphors, because of their compact nature, the author usually intends to stress a single point (e.g., that Christ is the source of sustenance for our spiritual lives or that Christians are to be examples of godly living in an ungodly world).

On the most basic level, the English word *parable* refers to an extended simile. The comparison is expressed, and the subject and the thing compared, explained more fully, are kept separate. Similarly an *allegory* can be understood as an extended metaphor: the comparison is unexpressed, and the subject and the thing compared are intermingled.

Unfortunately the biblical words *parabolē* (Greek) and *mashal* (Hebrew) that are translated into English as *parable* have somewhat broader definitions. Klyne Snodgrass explains, "The Greek word *parabolē* . . . can

1. E. D. Hirsch Jr., *Validity in Interpretation* (New Haven: Yale University Press, 1967), 70.

be used of a proverb (Luke 4:23), a riddle (Mark 3:23), a comparison (Matt. 13:33), a contrast (Luke 18:1–8) and both simple stories (Luke 13:6–9) and complex stories (Matt. 22:1–14)."[2] As a result, not all the biblical texts categorized as parables exhibit identical features, and some scholars even view allegories as one form of a parable.[3] Others call such subcategories unhelpful. What is clear is that the "distinction between *parable* and *allegory* . . . is among the most debated issues in New Testament studies."[4]

The primary question in this discussion is whether those literary devices classified as parables are limited to having a single main point or whether several points of correspondence are also possible. Throughout much of church history, parables were read as though they were allegories with multiple layers of meaning.[5] Beginning in the late nineteenth century, Adolf Jülicher argued that parables had only a single point of comparison between the story and reality.[6] Since that time others have asserted that many parables are semi-allegorical and communicate several truths, perhaps one main point associated with each main character in a parable.[7]

The biblical literature contains a range of extended comparisons, from strict parables that have a single correspondence between the story and reality (Luke 16:1–8) to full allegories in which all features have a comparison with something in reality (Mark 4:1–9, 13–20). Perhaps it is best for biblical interpreters to remember that in many instances a definitive classification may not be possible, and Robert Stein rightly recognizes that "the greater danger for most interpreters is to see too much meaning in specific details rather than too little."[8] Similarly G. B. Caird concludes, "Parable and allegory, then, are partial synonyms, and it is less important to distinguish between them than it is to distinguish

2. K. R. Snodgrass, "Parable," in *Dictionary of Jesus and the Gospels*, ed. Joel B. Green, Scot McKnight, and I. Howard Marshall (Downers Grove, IL: InterVarsity, 1992), 591–601.

3. Ibid., 593. Snodgrass speaks of four forms of parables that are often distinguished: similitudes, which are extended similes; example stories, which highlight a character whose actions are to be emulated or avoided; parables, which are extended metaphors; and allegories, which are a series of related metaphors.

4. Ibid., 594.

5. Augustine's interpretation of the parable of the good Samaritan provides the classic example. See Robert H. Stein, *Playing by the Rules: A Basic Guide to Interpreting the Bible* (Grand Rapids: Baker, 1994), 139–40.

6. A. Jülicher, *Die Gleichnisreden Jesu*, 2 vols. (Tübingen: Mohr Siebeck, 1888–89).

7. Craig L. Blomberg, *Interpreting the Parables* (Downers Grove, IL: InterVarsity, 1990).

8. Stein, *Playing by the Rules*, 142.

between allegory, which the author intended, and allegorical embellishment or interpretation, which he did not."[9]

Exercise 48. Read Luke 15:11–32. One interpreter argues that the single basic point of this passage is that just as the older son will not accept and rejoice in the loving forgiveness that his father has extended to his brother, so the Pharisees and teachers of the law are unwilling to accept God's loving forgiveness of tax collectors and sinners through the ministry of Jesus. Another interpreter believes that three truths are communicated in this text: (1) Sinners may confess their sins and turn to God in repentance, (2) God offers forgiveness for undeserving people, and (3) those who claim to be God's people should not be resentful when God extends his grace to the undeserving. Do you agree with the first or the second interpreter? Can you classify this text as either a parable or an allegory? Explain your answer to each question.

A *proverb* can be understood as a compressed parable or allegory, sometimes exhibiting characteristics of both. Proverbs are typically short, pithy sayings that express general truth in a memorable and catchy manner.

The following sections will discuss the nature and interpretation of proverbs, parables, and allegories at greater length.

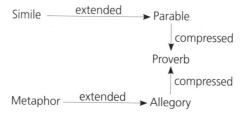

Proverbs

Walter C. Kaiser Jr. has described proverbs as sayings that are "terse, brief, have a little 'kick' to them, and a little bit of salt as well."[10] Many

9. G. B. Caird, *The Language and Imagery of the Bible* (Philadelphia: Westminster, 1980), 167.
10. Walter C. Kaiser Jr., *The Old Testament in Contemporary Preaching* (Grand Rapids: Baker, 1973), 119. This section on proverbs is taken largely from his discussion on pp. 118–20.

people view proverbs as nice slogans—good mottoes to hang on one's wall. Few recognize the tremendous beauty and wisdom often contained in these sayings.

One of the greatest problems religion faces is the lack of practical integration between theological beliefs and daily living. It is possible to divorce our religious life from practical decisions we make each day. Proverbs can provide an important antidote, for they demonstrate true religion in specific, practical, and meaningful terms.

The general focus in the book of Proverbs is the moral aspect of the law—ethical regulations for daily life phrased in universally abiding terms. Specific foci include wisdom, morality, chastity, control of the tongue, associations with others, laziness, and justice. "As Deuteronomy preaches the Law, the Wisdom Books put it into short, understandable phrases that are both quotable and easily digested."[11]

Many of the proverbs are concerned with wisdom, a concept that provides the context for all of them. Wisdom in Scripture is not synonymous with knowledge. It begins with "the fear of the LORD" (Prov. 1:7; 9:10). The fear of the Lord is not normal fear, or even that more profound type known as "numinous awe," but is basically a stance, an attitude of the heart that recognizes our rightful relationship to the Creator God. Wisdom and wise living proceed from this proper stance, this recognition of our rightful place before God. Within this context the proverbs no longer remain pious mottoes to be hung on the wall but become intensely practical, meaningful ways of inspiring a closer walk with the Lord.

From an interpretive standpoint it is helpful to recognize that because of their highly condensed form, proverbs usually have a single point of comparison or principle of truth to convey. Pressing all the incidental points in a proverb usually takes the interpretation beyond the author's intention. For example, when King Lemuel says of the virtuous woman that "she is like the merchant ships" (Prov. 31:14), he probably did not intend this to be a statement about her girth; rather, she is like the ships of the merchants because she goes to various places, gathering food for the needs of her household. Thus, proverbs (like similes and metaphors) usually convey a single intended thought or comparison.

Parables

Even a cursory reading of the New Testament Gospels suffices to show that Jesus regularly taught by means of parables. The Greek word

11. Ibid., 119.

151

for *parable* occurs nearly fifty times in the Synoptic Gospels in connection with his ministry, suggesting that parables were one of his favorite teaching devices. The typical parable uses a common event of natural life to emphasize or clarify an important spiritual truth.

Purpose of Parables

Scripture reveals two basic purposes of parables. The first is to reveal truth to believers (Matt. 13:10–12; Mark 4:11). Parables can often make a lasting impression far more effectively than ordinary discourse. For example, Christ could have said, "You should be persistent in your prayer life," a statement that his hearers would probably have shrugged off and quickly forgotten. Instead he told them of a widow who kept begging an unjust judge to help her, until the judge finally decided to answer her petitions to stop her complaining. Christ then explained the lesson of the parable: if an unjust judge who cares nothing about a widow can be swayed by persistent begging, how much more will a loving heavenly Father answer those who consistently pray to him? Similarly, Christ could have said, "You should be humble when you pray." Instead he told his audience about the Pharisee and the tax collector who went up to the temple to pray (Luke 18:9–14). The ridiculousness of the Pharisee's pride and the authenticity of the tax collector's humility teach Christ's lesson in a simple but unforgettable way.

Because they reveal truth, parables can also be used effectively to confront listeners with wrongdoing in their lives. If a believer possesses basically sound moral standards and yet fails to live up to those standards in some areas of his life, a parable can be a powerful means of pointing out this discrepancy. Consider the case of David and Nathan as told in 2 Samuel 12:1–7. Prior to this incident, David had placed Uriah in the frontlines of battle so that he would be killed and David might then marry his wife, Bathsheba. The text reads:

The Lord sent Nathan to David. When he came to him, he said, "There were two men in a certain town, one rich and the other poor. The rich man had a very large number of sheep and cattle, but the poor man had nothing except one little ewe lamb he had bought. He raised it, and it grew up with him and his children. It shared his food, drank from his cup and even slept in his arms. It was like a daughter to him.

"Now a traveler came to the rich man, but the rich man refrained from taking one of his own sheep or cattle to prepare a meal for the traveler who had come to him. Instead, he took the ewe lamb that belonged to the poor man and prepared it for the one who had come to him."

David burned with anger against the man and said to Nathan. "As surely as the LORD lives, the man who did this deserves to die! He must pay for that lamb four times over, because he did such a thing and had no pity."

Then Nathan said to David, "You are the man!"

David, a man of moral principle, easily identified with the great wrong that had been done to the poor man in the story, and when the parable was applied to his own behavior, he quickly repented of his wrong.

In addition to clarifying and emphasizing spiritual truths for believers, Jesus described a second consequence of his parables—one that seems diametrically opposed to the first. All three Synoptic Gospels record both Jesus' parable of the sower (Matt. 13:1–9; Mark 4:1–9; Luke 8:4–8) and his discussion of this parable with his disciples (Matt. 13:18–23; Mark 4:13–20; Luke 4:11–15). Between the initial presentation of the parable and the ensuing discussion, the evangelists present Jesus' explanation of his use of parables: "The secret of the kingdom of God has been given to [the Twelve and the others around him]. But to those on the outside everything is said in parables so that, 'they may be ever seeing but never perceiving, and ever hearing but never understanding; otherwise they might turn and be forgiven'" (Mark 4:11–12; cf. Matt. 13:10–17; Luke 8:9–10; quoting Isa. 6:9–10).

Jesus' perplexing words about his use of parables to prevent understanding must be interpreted in their literary context. It is quite clear throughout the Gospels that "outsiders" are capable of cognitively understanding the meaning of Jesus' parables (Mark 12:12). Perhaps the answer to this apparent dilemma can be found in the scriptural passages discussed in connection with spiritual factors in the perceptual process (chap. 1). Craig Blomberg similarly expounds: "True, spiritual understanding in the Bible is never merely cognitive but also volitional. That is, unless one acts on Jesus' teaching by becoming an obedient disciple, one has not *truly* understood his message."[12] Blomberg continues, "Parables, once they drive home their lesson, either attract or repel."[13]

The parable of the sower highlights two basic responses to God's Word. "The Word of God is proclaimed and causes a division among those who hear; God's people receive the Word, understand it, and obediently fulfill it; others fail to listen because of a hardened heart, a basic superficiality, or a vested interest in riches and possessions."[14] Jesus' statements about his use of parables additionally highlight the two responses. With this in mind Snodgrass further interacts with Jesus' words:

12. Craig L. Blomberg, *Jesus and the Gospels* (Nashville: Broadman & Holman, 1997), 262.

13. Ibid., 263.

14. Simon Kistemaker, *The Parables of Jesus* (Grand Rapids: Baker, 1980), 29.

In Mark 4:10–12 the Evangelist shows what typically happened in Jesus' ministry. . . . Jesus taught the crowds, but his teaching called for response. Where people responded, additional teaching was given. The pattern of public teaching followed by further private teaching to a circle of disciples is used elsewhere by Mark (7:17; 10:10). The strong words in Isaiah 6:9–10 were not an indication that God did not want to forgive people. They were a blunt statement expressing the inevitable. People would hear, but not really understand.[15]

By its nature a parable requires a response. When the response is one that rejects God's truth, the parable serves as a means of exposing the condition of the heart. Thus the same parables that led to a desire for learning and brought insight to faithful believers prompted other hearers to reject the truth of the parable.

Principles for the Interpretation of Parables

HISTORICAL-CULTURAL AND CONTEXTUAL ANALYSIS

The type of analysis used in interpreting narrative and expository passages should also be used in the interpretation of parables. Since parables were used to clarify or emphasize a truth that was being discussed in a specific historical situation, an examination of the topics under discussion in the immediate context of a passage often sheds valuable light on the parable's meaning.

For example, the parable of the laborers in the vineyard (Matt. 20:1–16) has been given a number of interpretations, many of which have little or no relationship to the context within which this parable was spoken. Immediately preceding Jesus' telling of this parable, the rich young ruler had come to Jesus and asked him what he must do to inherit eternal life. Jesus perceived that the greatest obstacle preventing this young man from total commitment to God was his riches and told him to give away what he possessed and become a disciple. The young man went away sorrowful, unwilling to part with his riches.

Peter asked the Lord, "We have left everything to follow you! What then will there be for us?" (Matt. 19:27). Jesus assured Peter that they would be amply rewarded for their service but then went on to tell the parable of the laborers in the vineyard. In this context it can be seen that Jesus' story was a gentle rebuke to Peter, a rebuke of the self-righteous attitude that says, "See how much I have done. I was willing to give up *all* and follow you, and this young man was not. I should certainly get a large reward for my great sacrifice." Jesus was gently chiding Peter for possessing the attitude of a hireling—"What am I going to get out of

---

15. Snodgrass, "Parable," 597.

this?"—rather than recognizing that the motive for service in the kingdom is love.[16] Interpretations of a parable that fail to consider the historical circumstances surrounding it may pose interesting hypotheses but are unlikely to grasp Jesus' intended meaning.

Sometimes the intended meaning is stated explicitly in the introduction to the parable, either by Jesus or by the biblical author. At other times the intended meaning is conveyed through the application of the parable (see Matt. 15:13; 18:21, 35; 20:16; 22:14; 25:13; Luke 12:15, 21; 15:7, 10; 18:1, 9; 19:11 for examples). At other times, placement of the parables near a certain event in Jesus' ministry or within a grouping of similarly themed teachings adds further meaning.

In addition to historical and contextual clues, knowledge of cultural details often sheds important light on the meaning of a parable. For example, harvest, weddings, and wine were Jewish symbols of the end of the age. The fig tree was a symbol of the people of God. Lamps were put under baskets to extinguish them; thus to light a lamp and put it under a bushel meant to light it and immediately put it out.[17] Joachim Jeremias' book *The Parables of Jesus* abounds with information about cultural details such as these and explains the meaning these stories and symbols had for Jesus and his original hearers.[18]

A significant difference arises in the historical-cultural analysis of parables. The stories expressed within the parables themselves are not historic occurrences. The characters are literary creations rather than actual people. Therefore, Robert Stein observes:

> In a biblical narrative it is perfectly legitimate to ask such questions as, Why did Joseph tell his brothers about his dream (Gen. 37:5–11)? Exactly what was it that defeated the armies of Sennacherib, king of Assyria, as they lay siege to Jerusalem (2 Kings 19:35–37)? . . . On the other hand, we cannot raise such questions with respect to parables. We cannot ask: Why in the parable of the prodigal son was the older brother out in the field when the prodigal returned (Luke 15:25)? There is no historical answer to this question. The two brothers never had historical existence. They are simply literary creations of Jesus. The older brother was out in the field because Jesus wanted him out in the field, and this is Jesus' story.[19]

16. Richard C. Trench, *Notes on the Parables of Our Lord* (1886; repr., Grand Rapids: Baker, 1948), 61–66.

17. Bernard Ramm, *Protestant Biblical Interpretation*, 3rd rev. ed. (Grand Rapids: Baker, 1970), 282.

18. Joachim Jeremias, *The Parables of Jesus*, rev. ed. (New York: Scribner, 1971). Jeremias' literary analysis of the nature of parables is questioned by many evangelical scholars. His work remains valuable, nevertheless, because of his rich knowledge of Hebrew culture and customs.

19. Stein, *Playing by the Rules*, 138.

LEXICAL-SYNTACTICAL ANALYSIS

The same rules of lexical-syntactical analysis that apply to other forms of prose should also be applied to parables. The same tools mentioned in chapter 4—lexicons, concordances, grammars, and exegetical commentaries—can all be used with profit in the exposition of parables.

THEOLOGICAL ANALYSIS

The main theological issue that an expositor must address before he can interpret most of the parables Jesus used is the nature of the kingdom of God/heaven,[20] which is the frequent topic of Jesus' parables. Evangelical scholars almost unanimously agree that in some senses the kingdom has come, in other senses it is continuing, and in some senses it will not ultimately come until the eschatological completion of this age.[21]

In the first sense, Christ taught that the kingdom was already present during his sojourn on earth (Matt. 12:28 and parallels; Luke 17:20–21), that it could be entered by the new birth (John 3:3), and that it was being entered by tax collectors and harlots because they were repenting and believing (Matt. 21:31).

In the second sense, parables speak of the continuing ministry of the kingdom. They tell of sowing and reaping, small seeds growing into magnificent trees, a great net being let down into the sea and not pulled up until the end of the age, and grain and tares growing together. They speak of wise and foolish commitments and of industrious versus slothful use of abilities.

In the third sense, many parables look forward to their ultimate fulfillment when God's kingdom rule will be realized fully, not only in the hearts of believers but in his complete triumph over evil. God will approach man no longer in the form of a servant but as the Ruler, the ultimate Judge, the final Divider.

One other aspect of theological analysis is important in the interpretation of parables. Parables can fix doctrine in our memories in a particularly striking fashion. However, orthodox expositors unanimously agree that no doctrine should be grounded on a parable as its primary

20. The phrase *kingdom of heaven* appears frequently in Jesus' teaching as recorded in Matthew's Gospel, while Mark and Luke regularly record Jesus' words about the *kingdom of God*. This is the case in several parallel texts (Matt. 13:10–15//Mark 4:10–12//Luke 8:9–10; Matt. 13:31–32//Mark 4:30–32//Luke 13:18–19; Matt 5:3//Luke 6:20). Although the note of Matthew 6:33 in the *Scofield Reference Bible* clearly differentiates the kingdom of God from the kingdom of heaven, the corresponding note in the *New Scofield Reference Bible* states that these two terms are in many cases used synonymously but are to be distinguished in some instances. Within New Testament scholarship today the two terms are usually regarded as equivalent.

21. See Ramm, *Protestant Biblical Interpretation*, 280–81.

or only source. The rationale for this principle is that clearer passages of Scripture are always used to clarify more obscure passages, never vice versa. Parables are by nature more obscure than doctrinal passages. Thus doctrine should be developed from the clear prose passages of Scripture and parables used to amplify or emphasize that doctrine.

Church history offers examples of the heresies generated by those who failed to observe this caution. One example is Faustus Socinus, who argued, based on the parable of the unmerciful servant (Matt. 18:23–35), that as the king pardoned his servant merely on the basis of his petition, so in the same way God, without requiring sacrifice or intercessor, pardons sinners on the ground of their prayers.[22] Socinus thus made this parable the basis for doctrine rather than interpreting it in the light of doctrine. Richard Trench offers a second word of warning—one that is important in the interpretation of all of Scripture, including parables—advising that "we are not to expect, in every place, the whole circle of Christian truth to be fully stated, and that no conclusion may be drawn from the absence of a doctrine from one passage which is clearly stated in others."[23]

LITERARY ANALYSIS

As we discussed earlier in this chapter, a central question regarding parables has been, How much is significant? Scholars have argued both sides of this question throughout history. We might do well to recall that on the first two recorded occasions when Jesus spoke in parables, he interpreted their meaning (the sower: Matt. 13:1–23; the wheat and the tares: Matt. 13:24–30, 36–43). His interpretations appear to be midway between the two extremes of requiring all parables to have a single point and of allegorizing all details: in Jesus' own analyses it is possible to discern both a central, focal idea and a significant emphasis on details *as they relate to that focal idea.* Jesus' analysis of the details of the parable contrasts with the practice of those who place significance on the details in such a manner that the details teach an additional lesson unrelated to the central point of the parable.

In the process of literary analysis, the interpreter can look for several clues to the meaning of the parable:

1. Identify the main characters. It is possible that one main point or lesson is demonstrated by each main character.
2. Determine the topic or detail that receives the most attention. This topic is likely to be the focal point.

22. Trench, *Notes on the Parables*, 41.
23. Ibid., 17–18.

3. Observe any elements that occur in direct dialogue. Direct dialogue may serve to emphasize a particular feature within the story.
4. Consider the principle of end stress. Often the main point of the parable occurs at the end.
5. Identify the unexpected twist in the story. Frequently the unexpected shock appears for the purpose of catching the listeners' attention and forcing them to reconsider their perspective.

Another question that has been recently raised regarding parables is whether it is possible to maintain the meaning of a parable if it is explained and translated into nonparabolic language. Consider any good joke. Part of its meaning is the humor with which it surprises the listener. But sometimes we hear jokes and fail to "get" the punch line. Someone might then explain the point of the joke and how the humor is constructed. And yet the explanation of the joke, even as it explains the meaning of the joke, does not have the same effect on the listener. It is just not as funny if it has to be explained.

Some argue that the case of parables is comparable. The details of the parable had immediacy for its original audience. If cultural distance requires an explanation of those details, we do not necessarily lose the ability to understand the parable, but the details lose some of their power to transform thinking.

Consider the parable of the good Samaritan. Because modern readers do not have any particular feelings about Samaritans, the discovery that the Samaritan is the hero of this parable is not particularly shocking. Yet when we research first-century culture and discover the animosity that existed between Jews and Samaritans, we begin to understand how Jesus' parable confronted his audience. Because it does not confront us in quite the same way, some scholars suggest that the best way to understand a parable is to retell it with new points of reference that elicit the same response in today's audience that the original parable did in its own.

Gordon Fee and Douglas Stuart once retold the parable of the good Samaritan to a typical, middle-class, Protestant congregation in the following way:

A family of disheveled, unkempt individuals was stranded by the side of a major road on a Sunday morning. They were in obvious distress. The mother was sitting on a tattered suitcase, hair uncombed, clothes in disarray, with a glazed look to her eyes, holding a smelly, poorly clad, crying baby. The father was unshaved, dressed in coveralls, a look of despair on his face as he tried to corral two other youngsters. Beside them was a rundown old car that had obviously just given up the ghost.

Down the road came a car driven by the local bishop; he was on his way to church. And though the father of the family waved frantically, the bishop could not hold up his parishioners, so he acted as though he didn't see them.

Soon came another car, and again the father waved furiously. But the car was driven by the president of the Kiwanis Club, and he was late for a statewide meeting of Kiwanis presidents in a nearby city. He, too, acted as though he did not see them and kept his eyes straight on the road ahead of him.

The next car that came by was driven by an outspoken local atheist, who had never been to church in his life. When he saw the family's distress, he took them into his own car. After inquiring as to their need, he took them to a local motel, where he paid for a week's lodging while the father found work. He also paid for the father to rent a car so he could look for work and gave the mother cash for food and new clothes.[24]

The points of reference in this telling of the parable connect with today's audience, and Fee and Stuart describe that when one of them delivered this parable, "the startled and angry response made it clear that his hearers had really 'heard' the parable for the first time in their lives."[25]

Resources for Further Reading

Craig Blomberg. *Interpreting the Parables*. Downers Grove, IL: InterVarsity, 1990.

G. B. Caird. *The Language and Imagery of the Bible*. Philadelphia: Westminster, 1980, 160–71.

C. H. Dodd. *The Parables of the Kingdom*. Rev. ed. New York: Scribner, 1961.

Joachim Jeremias. *The Parables of Jesus*. Rev. ed. New York: Scribner, 1971.

Simon Kistemaker. *The Parables of Jesus*. Grand Rapids: Baker, 1980.

Bernard Ramm. *Protestant Biblical Interpretation*. 3rd rev. ed. Grand Rapids: Baker, 1970, esp. pp. 276–88.

Robert H. Stein. *An Introduction to the Parables of Jesus*. Philadelphia: Westminster, 1981.

_____. *The Method and Message of Jesus' Teaching*. Rev. ed. Louisville: Westminster/John Knox, 1994, esp. pp. 60–81.

Milton S. Terry. *Biblical Hermeneutics*. 1883. Reprint, Grand Rapids: Zondervan, 1974, esp. pp. 276–301.

Richard C. Trench. *Notes on the Parables of Our Lord*. 1886. Reprint, Grand Rapids: Baker, 1948.

24. Gordon D. Fee and Douglas Stuart, *How to Read the Bible for All Its Worth: A Guide to Understanding the Bible*, 3rd ed. (Grand Rapids: Zondervan, 2003), 160–61.
25. Ibid., 161.

Allegories

Just as a parable is an extended simile, so an allegory is an extended metaphor. An allegory differs from a strict parable, as noted earlier, in that a parable typically keeps the story distinct from its interpretation or application, while an allegory intertwines the story and its meaning.

Unlike parables, an allegory generally includes several points of comparison, not necessarily centered around one focal point. For example, in the parable of the mustard seed (Matt. 13:31–32) the central purpose is to show the spread of the gospel from a tiny band of Christians (the mustard seed) to a worldwide body of believers (the full-grown tree). The relationship between the seed, the tree, the field, the nest, and the birds is casual, and these details acquire significance only in relationship to the growing tree. However, in the allegory of the Christian's armor (Eph. 6), there are several points of comparison. Each part of the Christian's armor is significant, and each is necessary for the Christian to be "fully armed."

Principles for Interpreting Allegories

1. Use historical-cultural, contextual, lexical-syntactical, and theological analyses as with other types of prose.
2. Determine the *multiple* points of comparison intended by the author by studying the context and the points that he emphasized.

LITERARY ANALYSIS OF ALLEGORY

Scripture contains many allegories. The allegory of Christ as the true vine (John 15:1–17) is analyzed here to show the relationship of the several points of comparison to the meaning of the passage. There are three foci in this allegory. The first is the vine as a symbol of Christ.[26] The entire passage emphasizes the importance of the vine: the pronouns *I*, *me*, and *my* occur thirty-eight times in the seventeen verses and the word *vine* three times, underscoring the centrality of Christ in the spiritual fruit bearing of the Christian. The focus is summarized in verse 4: "No branch can bear fruit by itself; it must remain in the vine. Neither can you bear fruit unless you remain in me."

The second focus is the Father, symbolized as the vinedresser. In this illustration the Father is actively concerned with fruit bearing. He prunes some branches that they may be more fruitful and eliminates those that produce no fruit.

26. Discussion of these points can be found in A. Berkeley Mickelsen, *Interpreting the Bible* (Grand Rapids: Eerdmans, 1963), 232–34.

The third focus is found in the branches, the disciples themselves. "Abiding" speaks metaphorically of relationship, and the present tense speaks of a *continuing* relationship as a necessity for fruit bearing. Obeying God's commands is a necessary part of relationship, and loving fellow believers is an integral part of that obedience. The allegory portrays the need for a continuous, living relationship with the Lord Jesus, coupled with obedience to his Word, as the essence of discipleship and fruit bearing.

The Problem of Paul's Allegorization

One passage that has greatly perplexed evangelicals is Paul's allegorizing in Galatians 4. Liberal theologians have been inclined to view this as an illustration of Paul's adoption of the illegitimate hermeneutical methods of his day. Evangelicals have often retreated in embarrassed silence, for it does seem that in these verses Paul used illegitimate allegorization. If Paul did indeed use illegitimate methods, this would certainly have significant implications for our doctrine of inspiration.

Several evangelical scholars have taken a position similar to that of Richard Longenecker, who in his commentary on Galatians says: "Paul's allegorical treatment of the Hagar-Sarah story is for polemical purposes, countering, it seems, the Judaizers' own contemporization of that story in ad hominem fashion."[27]

Longenecker believes that Paul used allegorization not to give it legitimacy as a method of exegesis but as an *argumentum ad hominem* against opponents who were using these same methods to turn a proper use of the law into a system of legalism.

Alan Cole paraphrases the passage in the following way:

Tell me, do you not listen to what the law says—you who want to be under law as a system? Scripture says that Abraham had two sons, one by the slave-wife and the other by the freeborn wife. The slave-wife's son was born perfectly naturally, but the son of the freeborn wife was born in fulfillment of God's promise. All this can be seen as a symbolic picture [an allegory] for these women could represent two Covenants. The first (i.e., the slave-wife) could stand for the covenant made at Mount Sinai; all her children (i.e., those under that covenant) are in spiritual bondage. That is Hagar for you. So the scriptural character "Hagar" could also stand for Mount Sinai in Arabia. Sinai stands in the same category as the Jerusalem that we know, for she is certainly in slavery, along with her "children." But the heavenly Jerusalem stands for the freeborn wife—and she is our "mother." For Scripture says:

27. Richard N. Longenecker, *Galatians*, Word Biblical Commentary 41 (Dallas: Word, 1990), 200.

"Be glad, you woman who is not in childbirth;
Break into a shout of triumph, you who are not in labour;
For the abandoned wife has more children
Than the wife who has her husband."

Now you, my fellow-Christians, are children born in fulfillment of God's promise, like Isaac was. But just as in those days the son born in the course of nature used to bully the son born supernaturally, so it is today. But what does Scripture say to that? "Expel the slave-wife and her son; for the slave-wife's son is certainly not going to share the inheritance with the freeborn wife's son." And so my summing-up is this: We Christians are not children of the slave-wife, but of the freeborn wife. Christ has given us our freedom; stand firm, and do not allow yourselves to be harnessed again to the yoke that spells slavery.[28]

Paul immediately differentiates his method from that of the typical allegorist by recognizing the grammatical-historical validity of the events. In verses 21–23 he indicates that Abraham had two sons, one by a slave woman and the other by a free woman.

Paul goes on to say that these things could all be allegorized, and then he develops a series of correspondences:

corresponds to

a	1	Hagar, bondmaid = Old Covenant	The present Jerusalem
	2	Sarah, freewoman = New Covenant	Jerusalem above
b	1	Ishmael, child of flesh	Those in bondage to law
	2	Isaac, child of promise	We, Christian brethren (v. 28)
c	1	Ishmael persecuted Isaac	So now legalists persecute Christians
	2	Scripture says: Cast out bondmaid and son	I say (vv. 31; 5:1): Be not entangled in a yoke of bondage (legalism)[29]

Lotto Schmoller, in *Lange's Biblework*, remarks:

Paul to be sure allegorizes here, for he says so himself. But with the very fact of him saying this himself, the gravity of the hermeneutical difficulty disappears. He *means* therefore to give an allegory, not an exposition; he does not proceed as an exegete, and does not mean to say (after the manner of the allegorizing exegetes) that only what he now says is the true sense of the narrative.[30]

28. Alan Cole, *The Epistle of Paul to the Galatians*, Tyndale New Testament Commentaries, ed. R. V. G. Tasker (Grand Rapids: Eerdmans, 1965), 129–30.
29. Terry, *Biblical Hermeneutics*, 322.
30. Cited in Ibid., 323.

To summarize, the following factors suggest that Paul is using allegorization to confound his hypocritical opponents:

1. Paul had made a series of very strong arguments against his Galatian opponents, arguments that by themselves would substantiate his case. This final argument was not needed; it stands more as an example of using the pseudo-apostles' own weapons against them.
2. If Paul regarded allegorizing as a legitimate method, then it seems almost certain that he would have used it in some of his other Epistles, but he did not.
3. Paul differed from the typical allegorist when he admitted the historical validity of the text, rather than saying that the words of the text were only a shadow of the deeper (and truer) meaning. He admitted that these events happened historically and then went on to say that they can be allegorized. He did not say, "This is what the text means" nor claim that he was giving an exposition of the text.

Resources for Further Reading

A. Berkeley Mickelsen. *Interpreting the Bible*. Grand Rapids: Eerdmans, 1963, esp. pp. 230–35.
Milton S. Terry. *Biblical Hermeneutics*. 1883. Reprint, Grand Rapids: Zondervan, 1974, esp. pp. 302–28.

Chapter Summary

The following steps constitute the principles of general and special hermeneutics:

1. Do a historical-cultural and contextual analysis.
2. Do a lexical-syntactical analysis.
3. Do a theological analysis.
4. Identify the literary form and apply an appropriate analysis.
   a. Look for explicit references that indicate the author's intent regarding the method he was using.
   b. If the text does not explicitly identify the literary form of the passage, study the characteristics of the passage deductively to ascertain its form.

    c. Apply the principles of literary devices carefully but not rigidly.

      (1) Metaphors, similes, and proverbs—look for the single point of comparison.

      (2) Parables—determine the central teaching and the significant details surrounding it.

      (3) Allegories—determine the multiple points of comparison intended by the author.

5. State your understanding of the meaning of the passage.

6. Check to see if your stated meaning fits into the immediate context and the total context of the book. If it does not, repeat the process.

7. Compare your work with that of others.

Exercises

49. From the time of Christ until the time of Luther, a major hermeneutical tool was the practice of allegorization. Today most evangelical scholars reject allegorization as an illegitimate hermeneutical device.

    a. Define allegorization and show why this long-used method of interpreting Scripture is now repudiated.

    b. Contrast the genre of allegory with the method of allegorizing and show why one is considered legitimate and the other illegitimate.

50. Use your knowledge of literary methods to identify and interpret the meaning of John 10:1–18. (To gain experience for yourself, do not consult reference Bible study notes or commentaries until after you have completed your interpretation.)

51. Romans 13:1–5 commands Christians to be obedient to their governmental authorities. This command has caused conflicts for Christians who have lived under governments such as in Nazi Germany and in some contemporary totalitarian regimes. What is the meaning of this text and other relevant passages for Christians who encounter a government that commands them to act contrary to their consciences?

52. Some Bible teachers believe that Christians should not experience illness and disease, basing their arguments in part on 3 John 2. Analyze this passage and state whether you think it is intended to teach that Christians should not experience illness.

53. The parable of the wheat and the tares (Matt. 13:24–30) appears to teach that error within the church should not be judged for fear of "uprooting the wheat." How would you reconcile this with the apparent teaching of Matthew 7:15–20, Titus 3:10, and other verses that appear to teach that the church is to judge evil and error within itself?

54. In the parable of the unmerciful servant (Matt. 18:23–35), the first servant was forgiven a large sum of money by his lord and then refused to forgive his fellow servant a small amount. A well-known Christian psychiatrist, counselor, and educator stated that this parable shows that it is possible to be forgiven (by God) without being forgiving (toward others). Do you agree? Why, or why not?

55. Many Christians understand the story of Lazarus and the rich man (Luke 16:19–31) as an actual event and derive a theology of the afterlife from it. Some evangelical scholars are reluctant to do this for hermeneutical reasons. What would be their reasons?

56. In the Old Testament at least two familiar passages seem to contradict what we believe about God's justice. One passage refers to God hardening Pharaoh's heart (Exod. 4:21) and then his punishment of Pharaoh for having a hard heart. The second is when God caused David to take a census (2 Sam. 24:1) and then punished David for doing so (1 Chron. 21:1–7). How do you explain these passages?

57. Nearly every Christian counselor or pastor has some clients or parishioners who come to him believing they have committed the unpardonable sin (Matt. 12:31–32 and parallels). Throughout history this sin has been identified in a number of ways. Irenaeus saw it as a rejection of the gospel; Athanasius equated it with denial of Christ. Origen said it was a mortal sin committed after baptism, and Augustine identified it as persistence in sin until death. Perhaps the most common understanding held by people seeking counseling is that this sin is one of unwittingly insulting Jesus and his works. Use your hermeneutical skills to determine the identity of this sin.

Class

58. Sometimes when godly parents have children who are living in rebellion, other Christians try to comfort them by quoting Proverbs 22:6 to them: "Train a child in the way he should go, and when he is old he will not turn from it." Should this verse be used to promise such parents that their children will definitely return to the Lord sometime in their children's lifetimes?

59. Some have argued that Matthew 13:33 presents a female image of God as a baker woman. From what you know about parables, do you agree or disagree with this use of the passage?

SEVEN

SPECIAL LITERARY FORMS

PROPHECY, APOCALYPTIC LITERATURE, AND TYPES

After completing this chapter, you should be able to

1. Define the former, latter, major, and minor Prophets.
2. Describe the role of the prophet as both foreteller and forthteller.
3. Identify three time frames of prophetic fulfillment.
4. Describe and differentiate between conditional and unconditional prophecy.
5. Recognize six controversial issues in the interpretation of prophecy.
6. Define the terms *prophetic telescoping, progressive prediction*, and *developmental fulfillment*.
7. Identify seven general differences between prophecy and apocalyptic literature.
8. Define the terms *premillennialism, postmillennialism*, and *amillennialism*.
9. Define the terms *type* and *antitype*.

167

10. Distinguish typology from symbolism and allegory.
11. Identify three distinguishing characteristics of a type.
12. Name five classes of types mentioned in Scripture.
13. Correctly interpret the meaning of typological allusions from Scripture.

Prophecy

The interpretation of prophecy is a highly complex subject, not so much because of disagreement regarding proper interpretive principles but because of differences of opinion over how to apply those principles. This chapter introduces the genre of prophecy[1] and the related topics of apocalyptic literature and typology; it also identifies principles about which there is general agreement and issues that are still unresolved. Several books are listed at the end of the chapter for those who wish to study this topic further.

In Scripture "a prophet is a spokesman for God who declares God's will to the people."[2] Within the Old Testament are several categories of prophets. The Former Prophets function within the historical writings of Joshua, Judges, the books of Samuel, and the books of Kings and include such figures as Elijah and Elisha. The remaining prophets for whom respective biblical writings are named are called Latter Prophets and are additionally split into two categories: major and minor. The terms *major* and *minor* do not evaluate the importance of the various prophets but rather indicate the relative length of the prophetic writing. The major prophets include Isaiah, Jeremiah, Ezekiel, and Daniel, while the minor prophets include Hosea, Joel, Amos, Obadiah, Jonah, Micah, Nahum, Habakkuk, Zephaniah, Haggai, Zechariah, and Malachi. When we look at special hermeneutics, it is these Latter Prophets that occupy most of our attention and pose specific interpretive challenges, although additional prophetic passages are also scattered throughout the remainder of Scripture (Matt. 24–25; Mark 13; Luke 13:28–35; 21:5–36).

When people hear the word *prophecy*, they often understand it to refer to words that predict future events. As a result, it is not unusual to find readers of Old Testament prophecy who look for those prophecies to be

1. The reader interested in a more detailed presentation of the variety of prophetic forms is directed to the discussions in Gordon D. Fee and Douglas Stuart, *How to Read the Bible for All Its Worth: A Guide to Understanding the Bible*, 3rd ed. (Grand Rapids: Zondervan, 2003), 194–97; and William W. Klein, Craig L. Blomberg, and Robert L. Hubbard Jr., *Introduction to Biblical Interpretation* (Dallas: Word, 1993), 292–302.

2. A. Berkeley Mickelsen, *Interpreting the Bible* (Grand Rapids: Eerdmans, 1963), 280.

fulfilled in the events around them. However, the office of the biblical prophet includes the functions of both foretelling and forthtelling, and we will examine each role in turn.

Prophets as Foretellers

It is true that the Old Testament prophets predicted various judgments and blessings, and their predictions concerned events in the future. J. Barton Payne calculates that of the Bible's 31,124 verses, 8,352 (27 percent) were predictive material at the time they were first spoken or written.[3] For instance, when Jeremiah spoke God's message of destruction to Jerusalem (Jer. 6), the city was still standing.

Predictive prophecy can serve a number of important functions. It can bring glory to God by testifying to his wisdom and sovereignty over the future. It can grant assurance and comfort to oppressed believers. It can motivate its hearers to stronger faith and deeper holiness (John 14:29; 2 Peter 3:11).[4]

The fulfillment of predictive prophecies involves three different time frames. The majority of the time Old Testament prophecy concerns events in the prophet's near future.[5] Most often the prophetic word was fulfilled within the nation of Israel. But from our perspective, many of these predicted events are now past events. The prophetic fulfillment has already occurred. Jeremiah's prophecy of the fall of Jerusalem was fulfilled at the hands of the Babylonian army in 586 BC. For today's interpreters, then, much of the interaction with prophetic texts involves looking *backward* rather than *forward* to identify the prophetic fulfillment. The second time period of prophetic fulfillment is the messianic period. Finally, other prophecy is eschatological and will be fulfilled in the end times.

Prophetic statements occasionally telescope all three time periods. Prophetic telescoping is best described with a comparison to the perception of a mountain range. When one views a mountain range from a distance, the peaks appear to be quite near to one another. However, on closer examination it becomes evident that wide valleys and many miles separate the individual peaks. When the prophets looked toward

3. J. Barton Payne, *Encyclopedia of Biblical Prophecy* (New York: Harper & Row, 1973), 13.

4. Ibid., 13–16.

5. The exact percentages can be debated. For instance, Payne says there are 535 verses related to Christ's Second Coming, 614 to the Millennium, 279 to the First Judgment, and 128 to the New Jerusalem (*Encyclopedia of Biblical Prophecy*, 680). However, Fee and Stuart claim that "less than 2 percent of Old Testament prophecy is messianic. Less than 5 percent specifically describes the new-covenant age. Less than 1 percent concerns events yet to come in our time," (*How to Read the Bible for All Its Worth*, 182).

the future, they also saw things that appeared to them to be side by side, yet as the time of fulfillment approaches, significant gaps become visible. Thus "biblical prophecy may leap from one prominent peak to another, without notice of the valley between, which may involve no inconsiderable lapse in chronology."[6] The telescoping that sometimes occurred when prophets blended the first and second advents of Christ is an example of this phenomenon.

Prophets as Forthtellers

Although today we typically use the word *prophecy* to speak of foretelling future events, this is only one aspect of biblical prophecy. In Scripture foretelling was usually in the service of forthtelling. The pattern frequently was "in light of what the Lord is going to do [foretelling], we should be living godly lives [forthtelling]."

The Old Testament prophets are best understood as forthtellers, that is, as spokesmen for God who spoke forth God's Word to the people within the context of the covenant. In many instances, the words of the prophets did not bring new revelation; rather, they called the people to remember and abide by the covenant God had made with them. Within the covenant, God's people were to love and serve him and were to express their love and service through obedience to his moral, civil, and ceremonial laws. Such obedience honored God, respected his holiness, and displayed his character to the surrounding nations.

The Old Testament records the great frequency with which the people of God failed to live in obedience to the covenant. In these circumstances, the prophets brought the voice of God to the people, identifying sin, calling for repentance, and reminding the people of the consequences God had promised depending on their response. In so doing they repeated God's promised blessing for repentance and obedience as well as his promised punishment for continued disobedience.

Texts such as Leviticus 26 and Deuteronomy 4 and 28 provide a background for much of the prophetic forthtelling. In Deuteronomy 28, for instance, the people learn that obedience to the covenant will result in God's tremendous blessing on the nation with regard to children, crops, flocks, and protection from enemies (Deut. 28:1–14). Conversely, disobedience will result in a host of punishments including "death, disease, drought, dearth, danger, destruction, defeat, deportation, destitution, and disgrace."[7] Such consequences for disobedience are part of God's grace as he uses these circumstances to draw the people back to cov-

6. Payne, *Encyclopedia of Biblical Prophecy*, 137.
7. Fee and Stuart, *How to Read the Bible for All Its Worth*, 185.

enant fidelity. The prophets, then, also served the purpose of calling the people to return to a life of covenant faithfulness.

Issues in the Interpretation of Prophecy

Before one can begin to interpret prophecy, several theoretical and practical issues must be addressed. Evangelicals agree on some of these issues; on others there are significant differences of opinion.

Hermeneutical principles. A basic question in the interpretation of prophecy is whether this literature can be interpreted using the same hermeneutical principles that apply to other genres or whether some special hermeneutical method is required.

The majority of evangelical scholars (e.g., Bernard Ramm, Louis Berkhof, Merrill Tenney, J. Dwight Pentecost, J. Barton Payne) concur that the interpretation of prophecy starts with the procedures we have labeled as historical-cultural, contextual, lexical-syntactical, and theological analyses. An exposition of Malachi 2:10–16, for example, would begin with an attempt to understand as many of the historical circumstances of that time as possible. Then the context of chapter 1 and the initial section of chapter 2 would be examined for information relevant to the interpretation of what follows. Lexical-syntactical analysis would proceed as with other genres, with the recognition that prophecy tends to use words more frequently in symbolic, figurative, and analogical senses than do other genres. Theological analysis would ascertain how the prophecies fit into other parallel information in Scripture.

Deeper sense. A second major issue is whether a *sensus plenior* exists in prophecy. Is there an additional, deeper meaning in a prophetic text, a meaning intended by God but not necessarily by the human author?

Both views on this issue can be illustrated by the case of Isaiah 7:14. In its historical context, this verse is speaking of a young woman giving birth to a child within whose early lifetime all the destruction that Isaiah prophesies will take place. Advocates of the *sensus plenior* view suggest that Isaiah obviously had no concept of the virgin birth of Christ and therefore was prophesying things he actually did not understand. Opponents of this view would argue that Isaiah did understand what he prophesied but not its full implications. This, they argue, is a natural and frequently occurring phenomenon in communication: people often understand the meaning of what they say without understanding all of its implications. The biblical writers, in the same way, understood what they prophesied but probably did not always understand the implications of their prophecies. Appendix C lists further readings on this issue.

Literal versus symbolic interpretation. A third and very practical issue in the interpretation of prophecy concerns how much of prophecy is to be interpreted literally and how much symbolically or analogically. For example, a literal approach to prophecy often conceives the "beast" of Revelation as a person (note that even this is not *totally* literal); a symbolic approach views it as a personification of the lust for power. A literal approach conceives Babylon as an actual city (often less literally considered to be Rome), whereas a symbolic approach views Babylon as the desire for economic gain. Literalists often view the last battle as an actual physical combat; symbolists see it as a representation of truth overcoming evil.

The question is not between a strictly literal versus a strictly symbolic approach; even the strictest literalist takes some things symbolically. For example, a literal understanding of the passage concerning the woman who sits on seven hills (Rev. 17:9) would suggest either that these were very small hills or that she had a very unusual figure. Conversely, even the most thoroughgoing symbolist interprets some things literally. Thus the differences between literalists and symbolists are relative rather than absolute, involving questions of how much and which parts of prophecy should be interpreted symbolically rather than literally.

In certain parts of prophecy some interpreters prefer an analogical approach, a sort of via media between the strictly literal and the strictly symbolic. In this approach, statements are interpreted literally but then translated into their modern-day equivalents. The battle of Armageddon, for example, is fought not with horses and spears but with modern analogues (perhaps tanks and artillery). The rationale underlying this interpretation is that if God had given John a vision of modern conveyances and equipment, the apostle would not have been able to understand what he saw or to communicate it clearly to his audience.

The question of whether a word or a phrase should be interpreted literally, symbolically, or analogically has no easy answer although G. B. Caird suggests six indicators to help identify when an author does not intend his words to be taken literally: (1) the author makes an explicit statement to that end, (2) a literal interpretation is impossible, (3) a low degree of correspondence exists, (4) the imagery is highly developed, (5) the author piles up multiple images, and (6) the author uses original imagery.[8] The context and the historical uses of the words are the best general guides in making decisions concerning their use within a specific passage.

Universality. A fourth issue, concerning the universality of certain symbols, is whether a symbol means the same thing each time it is used. Some earlier writers tended to ascribe universal symbolic significance to certain numbers, colors, or items; for example, oil was *always* a symbol of the Holy Spirit, leaven *always* a symbol of evil. Probably the major-

---

8. G. B. Caird, *The Language and Imagery of the Bible* (Philadelphia: Westminster, 1980), 186–91.

ity of contemporary evangelical scholars reject the notion of universal symbols but do accept the idea that there is a regularity in the symbolism of some biblical authors. Numbers frequently regarded as symbolic are seven, twelve, and forty. (The issue of whether or not one thousand is symbolic is still unsettled.) Colors that frequently possess symbolic significance are white, red, and purple, often representing the concepts of purity, bloodshed, and royalty, respectively.[9]

Conditionality. A fifth issue is how to distinguish between conditional and unconditional prophecy. Conditional prophecy presents a scenario that may or may not ensue depending on the response of the people, while unconditional prophecy looks only to the faithful character of God as the basis for its realization.

Clearly the fulfillment of certain prophetic utterances depends on human response. For instance, in Jeremiah 18:7–10, God says:

> If at any time I announce that a nation or kingdom is to be uprooted, torn down and destroyed, and if that nation I warned repents of its evil, then I will relent and not inflict on it the disaster I had planned. And if at another time I announce that a nation or kingdom is to be built up and planted, and if it does evil in my sight and does not obey me, then I will reconsider the good I had intended to do for it.

The same willingness to make national prophecies conditional on human response is also found in the actions of God toward individuals who repent (e.g., 1 Kings 21:1–29).

The remaining question is whether prophetic statements are conditional even when a conditional *if* is not stated. Consider the prophet Jonah. In this case God had apparently commanded Jonah to preach the message that Nineveh would be overthrown in forty days. There seemed to be no stated conditions by which that prediction could be averted; however, when the people of Nineveh repented, God also deferred his predicted judgment (Jon. 3:10).

Jonah's ministry probably occurred during the time when Assyria, with its capital city of Nineveh, was a great force and an enemy to the nation of Israel, located just to its south. It is in this context that the command comes from God to Jonah, "Go to Nineveh . . . and preach against it" (3:2 WEB). We would not expect Jonah, an Israelite, to be too disappointed to prophesy the downfall of Nineveh, Israel's enemy. But that is not the reaction that we see from Jonah. Instead of responding to God's call, he flees in the opposite direction to avoid preaching this message to Nineveh.

9. See Mickelsen, *Interpreting the Bible*, 272–78, for a fuller discussion of symbolic numbers, names, colors, metals, and jewels.

The explanation for Jonah's response is that he knew the prophecy was conditional. Inherent in the message he was to deliver was the opportunity for repentance. If Jonah failed to preach the message, he concluded, the Ninevites could not repent and their destruction would be certain. If he did preach it, they might repent, a horrifying prospect to Jonah. When the city does repent, Jonah is angry with God and displeased by God's mercy (4:1–5).

Since an unstated *if* in the prediction of Nineveh's coming judgment is evident both by Jonah's actions and by God's response to the Ninevites, we might wonder whether all prophecies contain an unstated conditional clause. But unconditional prophecy also exists. Walter C. Kaiser Jr. explains, "The actual list of unconditional prophecies is not long, but they occupy the most pivotal spots in the history of redemption."[10] He labels Genesis 15:9–21 as an unconditional prophecy and lists other such prophecies including "God's covenant with the seasons (Gen. 8:21–22); God's promise of a dynasty, kingdom, and a dominion for David and his descendant(s) (2 Sam. 7:8–16); God's promise of the new covenant (Jer. 31:31–34); and God's promise of the new heavens and the new earth (Isa. 65:17–19; 66:22–24)."[11] Nonetheless, it may be necessary to recognize the implied conditionality of a given prophecy even if the condition is not explicitly stated.[12]

Single versus multiple meaning. A final issue, and one about which there is considerable controversy among contemporary evangelicals, is whether prophetic passages have single or multiple meanings. Advocates of the multiple-meaning position use a variety of terms to describe their position, such as "double meaning," "double reference," "manifold fulfillment," or "multiple sense." In earlier chapters we considered the theoretical and practical problems inherent in any system of exegesis that affirms that a passage may have a variety of meanings. Payne presents an excellent critique of the multiple-meaning position and also discusses prophetic interpretive principles that are consistent with the concept of a single intended meaning in each passage. His discussion forms the basis of the following paragraphs.[13]

To affirm that scriptural texts have a single *meaning* in no way negates the fact that that meaning may have a variety of *applications* in different

10. Walter C. Kaiser Jr. and Moisés Silva, *An Introduction to Biblical Hermeneutics: The Search for Meaning* (Grand Rapids: Zondervan, 1994), 148.

11. Ibid., 149.

12. Walter C. Kaiser Jr., *The Old Testament in Contemporary Preaching* (Grand Rapids: Baker, 1973), 111–14. For further discussion of this issue, see Payne, *Encyclopedia of Biblical Prophecy*, 62–68.

13. Payne, *Encyclopedia of Biblical Prophecy*, 121–44.

situations. This same principle applies to prophetic passages and their fulfillments, as Payne illustrates:

> The NT epistles thus repeatedly quote OT prophecies, though not in reference to their actual fulfillments; for example, 2 Corinthians 6:16 cites Leviticus 26:11 (on God's presence with his people in the yet future testament of peace), 6:17 cites Isaiah 52:11 (on Israel's departure from unclean Babylon), and 6:18 freely renders Hosea 1:10 (on the inclusion of Gentiles in the family of God), all to illustrate the Christians' present enjoyment of the presence of God and our need to maintain separation from the uncleanness of the world, though only the last, Hosea 1:10, had this originally in mind. Terry therefore makes it clear that, "We may readily admit that the Scriptures are capable of manifold practical *applications*; otherwise they would not be so useful for doctrine, correction, and instruction in righteousness" (2 Tim. 3:16), though he remains firm in his insistence upon single fulfillment for biblical prophecy.[14]

In place of the concept of multiple meanings, Payne substitutes the concepts of prophetic telescoping, progressive prediction, and developmental fulfillment. *Prophetic telescoping* was introduced above. *Progressive prediction* refers to the fact that although each prophetic passage has a single intended fulfillment, often a series of passages exhibit a pattern of chronological progress in the prophetic enactment. Thus passage A may tell us about certain events, passage B about the events immediately following them, and passage C about the culminating events of the series. The combination of these various passages forms a whole that can be identified as progressive prediction. Sometimes these passages are presented as cycles within the same book, with each cycle presenting additional information. Two well-known examples of progressive predictions that occur in cycles are the books of Zechariah and Revelation.

A third concept of prophetic meaning, *developmental fulfillment*, refers to the realization of a generalized, comprehensive prophecy in several progressive stages. This is also referred to as sequentially fulfilled prophecy. An example is the Genesis 3:15 prophecy, which speaks in general terms of the bruising of Satan's head. The progressive stages in the fulfillment of this prophecy begin with Christ's death, resurrection, and ascension (John 12:31–32; Rev. 12:5, 10), continue in the church (Rom. 16:20), and end with Satan's imprisonment in the abyss (Rev. 20:3) and the lake of fire (Rev. 20:10).[15]

---

14. Ibid., 128–29. The Terry quotation is from Milton S. Terry, *Biblical Hermeneutics*, (1890; repr., Grand Rapids: Zondervan, 1974), 383.

15. Other examples of developmental fulfillment can be found in Payne, *Encyclopedia of Biblical Prophecy*, 135–36.

Apocalyptic Literature

In the twentieth century, students of biblical prophecy spent considerable time investigating a genre called "apocalyptic," a word derived from the Greek *apokalypsis* (found in Rev. 1:1), which means "uncovering" or "revelation." Apocalyptic literature's primary focus is the revelation of what has been hidden, particularly with regard to the end times. Noncanonical apocalyptic writings are found from the time of Daniel until the end of the first century AD and share several characteristics in common. Leon Morris identifies some of these features:

1. The writer tends to choose a great man of the past (e.g., Enoch or Moses) and make him the hero of the book.
2. This hero often takes a journey, accompanied by a celestial guide who shows him interesting sights and comments on them.
3. Information is often communicated through visions.
4. The visions often make use of strange, even enigmatic symbolism.
5. The visions are often pessimistic with regard to the possibility that human intervention will ameliorate the present situation.
6. The vision usually ends with God's bringing the present state of affairs to a cataclysmic end and establishing a better situation.
7. The apocalyptic writer often uses a pseudonym, claiming to write in the name of his chosen hero.
8. The writer often takes past history and rewrites it as if it were prophecy.
9. The focus of apocalyptic is on comforting and sustaining the "righteous remnant."[16]

George Ladd sees the development of apocalyptic as the result of three main factors. The first is "the emergence of a 'Righteous Remnant,'" a minority group, usually without substantial political power, who view themselves as remaining faithful to God while surrounded by those who are not. A second is "the problem of evil." As early as the book of Job, the concept that God rewards the just and punishes evildoers had been recorded. How then could the righteous remnant reconcile the fact that they were oppressed by those much more wicked than themselves? Third, "the cessation of prophecy" (recorded in the noncanonical 2 Baruch 85:3) created a spiritual vacuum: the righteous remnant longed for a word from God, but none was forthcoming. The apocalyptists attempted to bring a word of comfort and reassurance from God to the people of their day.[17]

16. Leon Morris, *Apocalyptic* (Grand Rapids: Eerdmans, 1972), 34–61.
17. George Eldon Ladd, "Apocalyptic, Apocalypse," in *Baker's Dictionary of Theology*, ed. E. F. Harrison (Grand Rapids: Baker, 1960), 50–51.

Apocalyptic literature shares a number of points with biblical prophecy, and some scholars even treat it as a subgenre of prophecy.[18] Both are concerned with the future. Both frequently employ figurative and symbolic language. Both emphasize the unseen world lying behind the action of the visible world. Both emphasize the future redemption of the faithful believer.

There are a number of differences as well, including the following:

1. The initial presentation of prophecy was usually in spoken form and was written at a later time. The initial presentation of apocalyptic literature was usually in writing.
2. Prophetic utterances most often are separate, brief oracles. Apocalyptic literature is often longer, more continuous; cycles of material may be repeated a second or third time in parallel form.
3. Apocalyptic literature tends to contain more symbolism, especially of animals and other living forms.
4. Apocalyptic literature places a greater stress on dualism (angels and the Messiah versus Satan and the antichrist) than does prophecy.
5. Apocalyptic literature primarily comforts and encourages the righteous remnant. Prophecy often castigates the nominally religious.
6. Apocalyptic literature is generally pessimistic about the effectiveness of human intervention in changing the present. Prophecy focuses on the importance of human change.
7. Apocalyptic literature was usually written pseudonymously. Prophecy was usually written or spoken in the name of its author.[19]

These distinctions are matters of degree and emphasis rather than absolute differences. Exceptions can be cited to each of them; however, most conservative Bible scholars would agree with the distinctions.

Apocalyptic sections do occur within the canonical books, most notably in Daniel (chaps. 7–12) and in Revelation. There are also apocalyptic passages in Joel, Amos, and Zechariah. In the New Testament, Jesus' Olivet Discourse (Matt. 24–25 and parallels) contains apocalyptic elements.

Biblical apocalyptic has many elements in common with the apocalyptic literature found in noncanonical books; differences have also been noted.[20] This overlap of characteristics affects the issue of inspiration.

18. Robert H. Stein, *Playing by the Rules: A Basic Guide to Interpreting the Bible* (Grand Rapids: Baker, 1994), 90.

19. Payne, *Encyclopedia of Biblical Prophecy*, 86–87.

20. Morris, *Apocalyptic*, esp. 51–54, 58–67; George Eldon Ladd, *Jesus and the Kingdom* (New York: Harper & Row, 1964), chap. 3.

The question it raises is, How does the use of an enigmatic genre such as apocalyptic affect the authority and trustworthiness of biblical passages in which it is found?

In the study of literary forms in previous chapters, we saw that God revealed his truth using literary forms familiar to the people of that time. The choice of a variety of literary devices to convey information does not affect the validity of that information. Our unfamiliarity with a particular genre such as apocalyptic affects not the trustworthiness of the information contained in apocalyptic passages but only our ability to interpret them with assurance. Perhaps as our understanding of intertestamental apocalyptic increases, our ability to interpret the biblical apocalypse with assurance will increase proportionately.

Varieties of Eschatological Theories

Since there are many unresolved issues regarding the interpretation of prophecy, it is not surprising that a variety of eschatological theories have emerged in the interpretation of Revelation. The New Testament reveals the Christian expectation of Christ's return. Revelation 20:4–6 raises questions about the chronological relationship between Christ's second coming and a millennium, which is understood to be an earthly reign of Christ lasting one thousand years. This section will briefly present the variety of positions theologians hold with regard to the end times.

Premillennialism is the theory that Christ will return before the millennium (*pre*-millennium). He will descend to earth and set up a literal one-thousand-year earthly kingdom with its headquarters in Jerusalem.

Postmillennialism is the view that through evangelism, the world eventually will be reached for Christ. There will be a period in which the world will experience joy and peace because of its obedience to God. Christ will return to earth at the end of the millennium (*post*-millennium).

Amillennialism is conceptually a form of postmillennialism. The millennium in this theory is symbolic and refers to the time between Christ's first and second coming, not to a literal one-thousand-year period. During this time Christ rules symbolically in human hearts. Christ's second coming will mark the end of the period. Some amillennialists believe that Christ will never have an earthly rule, even symbolically. For them the millennium refers to Christ's celestial rule in eternity.

Postmillennialism—the view that the church will eventually win the world for Christ and usher in the millennium—rapidly lost popularity during the first half of the twentieth century. The carnage of the world wars was a grim reminder to most postmillennialists that the world was *not* being won for Christ. Hence the majority of evangelical Christians today identify themselves as either premillennialists or amillennialists.

Hermeneutically, the major issue separating premillennialists from amillennialists is the question of how much of prophecy should be interpreted literally and how much symbolically. The premillennialists interpret most things literally and believe that Christ will actually come to earth, set up a physical earthly kingdom, and reign for one thousand literal years. This position maintains that the promises to Israel and to the church should be kept separate and that it is not valid to take physical promises made to Israel, spiritualize them, and apply them to the church. This hermeneutical method is based on the principle that Scripture should be interpreted literally unless the context definitely suggests that the author intended it otherwise.

The amillennialists interpret things more symbolically, in view of the symbolic language used in prophetic passages. R. Ludwigson gives an example: "Christ bound Satan (symbolically): (1) by resisting him in the wilderness; (2) by paying the penalty of sin to redeem man; (3) by destroying the power of death in his resurrection; and (4) by offering salvation to the Gentiles, making it impossible for Satan to deceive the nations anymore. . . . Satan can still deceive individuals, [but] no longer can he deceive nations."[21] Likewise, the amillennialist interprets Christ's millennial rule symbolically rather than literally: the kingdom is already present in the hearts of believers. Because New Testament believers represent spiritual Israel, Old Testament promises to Israel apply to the new Israel, the church.

There is a hermeneutical basis for both the premillennial and the amillennial model of interpretation. It is correct, as the premillennialists assert, to understand biblical passages literally unless the context suggests otherwise. However, the amillennialists are also correct in asserting that most prophecy and apocalyptic *is* symbolic, justifying a symbolic interpretation.

For those who wish to consider this issue more deeply, a bibliography on the subject is included below. In grappling with the issue, check the internal consistency of each position in relation to all the biblical data. This "goodness of fit" method may be helpful in making a decision about the merits of the two theories. Ultimately, the most important spiritual guidance for all eschatological study can be found in 1 John 3:2–3: "Dear friends, now we are children of God, and what we will be has not yet

21. R. Ludwigson, *A Survey of Bible Prophecy*, 2nd ed. (Grand Rapids: Zondervan, 1975), 109.

been made known. But we know that when he appears, we shall be like him, for we shall see him as he is. Everyone who has this hope in him purifies himself, just as he is pure."

Principles for Interpreting Prophecy and Apocalyptic Literature

Historical-cultural analysis. The wide variety of theories concerning the end times arises not so much from a disagreement concerning principles of prophetic interpretation as from differences in applying those principles. Almost all commentators agree that a careful historical and contextual analysis is a prerequisite for accurate understanding of prophecy. Determination of the identity of all proper names, events, geographical references, and so on remains a crucial first step. Even when such references are used symbolically, as the city of Babylon often is, a knowledge of the historical city of Babylon provides important clues about its symbolic meaning. Careful historical analysis also remains the only way of determining whether a prophecy has already been fulfilled. An analysis of relevant cultural customs is no less important.

Lexical-syntactical analysis. A careful study of the context sometimes reveals whether an author intended his words to be understood literally, symbolically, or analogically. For instance, when John speaks of the seven lampstands in his vision and then declares, "The seven lampstands are the seven churches" (Rev. 1:20), it is clear both that his words are symbolic and that they are symbolic of the seven churches. In many cases, however, the task of interpreting may still be difficult, as Robert Girdlestone observes:

> [What] makes the language of prophecy so vivid and yet so difficult is that it is always more or less figurative. It is poetry rather than prose. It abounds in peculiar words and expressions which are not usually to be found in prose writings of the same date. It is rich with allusions to contemporary life and to past history, some of which are decidedly obscure. The actions recorded in it are sometimes symbolical, sometimes typical. The present, the past, and the future, the declaratory and the predictive, are all combined and fused into one. The course of individuals, the rise and fall of nations, the prospects of the world at large, are all rapidly portrayed in realistic language.[22]

Theological analysis. For the student examining any given prophecy, there are usually several parallel passages that should be consulted.

---

22. Robert B. Girdlestone, *The Grammar of Prophecy* (1901; repr., Grand Rapids: Kregel, 1955), 48. Cited in Bernard Ramm, *Protestant Biblical Interpretation*, 3rd rev. ed. (Grand Rapids: Baker, 1970), 247.

Sometimes such passages occur within the same book, as when prophecy is given in cycles. Frequently other prophets have spoken about the same topic, filling in additional details not contained in the passage under study. The index to Payne's *Encyclopedia of Biblical Prophecy* contains an alphabetical listing of subjects in prophecy together with references to relevant biblical passages and discussions of those passages.

Literary analysis. Once it has been determined that a passage is prophetic or apocalyptic literature, the probability of symbolic and analogical allusions increases. The concepts of progressive prediction, developmental fulfillment, and prophetic telescoping can be incorporated into the understanding of the text as appropriate.

In interpretation of prophecy, as in other types of biblical literature, comparison of one's work with that of others is important. The complexity of the topics, the wide range of parallel passages, and the multitude of unusual allusions make it imperative to draw from the wealth of knowledge of scholars who have studied this area in depth.

Types

The Greek word *typos*, to which the word *type* is related, has a variety of denotations in the New Testament. The basic ideas expressed by *typos* and its synonyms are the concepts of resemblance, likeness, and similarity. David Baker provides a solid general definition identifying a type as "a biblical event, person or institution which serves as an example or pattern for other events, persons or institutions."[23] A typological relationship exists between an initial event that through divine inspiration foreshadows a corresponding event occurring at a later time in salvation history.

This literary device is not without similarities to prophecy. In some ways a type/antitype relationship can be viewed as a prophetic form that nonetheless lacks an overt verbal prediction.[24] The question that remains is whether types are prospective or whether they can only be determined retrospectively.[25] Certainly there is a call for caution in the identification of types that are not overtly recognized as such in the New Testament.

23. David Baker, "Typology and the Christian Use of the Old Testament," cited in Douglas J. Moo, "The Problem of *Sensus Plenior*," in *Hermeneutics, Authority, and Canon*, ed. D. A. Carson and John D. Woodbridge (Grand Rapids: Zondervan, 1986), 179–211.

24. See J. Scott Duvall and J. Daniel Hays, *Grasping God's Word*, 2nd ed. (Grand Rapids: Zondervan, 2005), 195.

25. See Moo, "Problem of *Sensus Plenior*," 195–98.

A well-known example of a biblical type is found in John 3:14–15, where Jesus says, "Just as Moses lifted up the snake in the desert, so the Son of Man must be lifted up, that everyone who believes in him may have eternal life." Jesus points out two corresponding resemblances: (1) the lifting up of the serpent and of himself, and (2) life for those who respond to the object lifted up.[26]

Typology is based on the assumption that there is a pattern in God's work throughout salvation history. God prefigured his redemptive work in the Old Testament and fulfilled it in the New; in the Old Testament are shadows of things to be more fully revealed in the New. The ceremonial laws of the Old Testament, for example, demonstrated to Old Testament believers the necessity of atonement for their sins; these ceremonies pointed forward to the perfect atonement to be made in Christ. The prefigurement is called the *type*; the corresponding figure is called the *antitype*.[27]

Types are similar to symbols and can even be considered a special kind of symbol. However, there are two differentiating characteristics. First, symbols serve as signs of something they represent without necessarily being similar in any respect, whereas types resemble in one or more ways the things they prefigure. For example, bread and wine are symbols of Christ's body and blood; the seven golden lampstands (Rev. 1:20) are symbols of the churches in Asia. There is no necessary similarity between the symbol and the thing it symbolizes as there is between a type and its antitype. Second, types point forward in time, whereas symbols may not. A type always historically precedes its antitype, whereas a symbol may precede, exist concurrently with, or come after the thing it symbolizes.

Typology is also to be distinguished from allegorism. Typology is the search for links between historical events, persons, or things within salvation history; allegorism is the search for secondary and hidden meanings underlying the primary and obvious meaning of a historical narrative. Typology rests on an objective understanding of the historical narrative, whereas allegorizing imports subjective meanings into it.

For example, in the typological allusion in John 3:14–15 we recognize the existence of a real serpent and a real Christ, one as a type, the other as an antitype. The historical circumstances surrounding both present the key to understanding the relationship between them. In contrast, in allegorism the interpreter attributes meaning to a story that would ordinarily not be deduced from a straightforward understanding of it.

26. Mickelsen, *Interpreting the Bible*, 237.

27. *Antitype* as a literary term does not always correspond to the Greek word *antitypos*, which appears occasionally in Scripture (e.g., Heb. 9:24).

For example, one allegorization of the story of Herod's massacre of the infants in Bethlehem states that "the fact that only the children of two years old and under were murdered while those of three presumably escaped is meant to teach us that those who hold the Trinitarian faith will be saved whereas Binitarians and Unitarians will undoubtedly perish."[28]

Characteristics of a Type

Three primary characteristics of types can be identified.[29] First, "there must be some notable point of resemblance or analogy" between the type and its antitype. This does not imply that there are not many points of dissimilarity as well: Adam is a type of Christ, yet Scripture speaks of significant dissimilarity as well as similarity (see Rom. 5:14–19).

Second, "there must be evidence that the type was appointed by God to represent the thing typified." There is some disagreement among scholars regarding how explicit God's declaration must be. Bishop Marsh's famous dictum regarding types states that nothing may be considered a type unless it is explicitly stated to be one in Scripture. At the other end of the spectrum are those who classify as types anything that bears a resemblance to something later. A moderate view, and one held by the majority of scholars (e.g., Milton S. Terry, Louis Berkhof, A. B. Mickelsen, Walther Eichrodt, Bernard Ramm), is that for a resemblance to indicate the presence of a type, there must be some evidence of divine affirmation of the corresponding type and antitype, although such affirmation need not be formally stated.

Third, a type "must prefigure something in the future." Antitypes in the New Testament present truth more fully realized than in the Old Testament. The correspondence in the New Testament reveals what was nascent in the Old. Typology is thus a special form of prophecy.

Jesus illustrated this principle by his frequent typological allusions. R. T. France summarizes Christ's usage of types:

> He uses *persons* in the Old Testament as types of himself (David, Solomon, Elijah, Elisha, Isaiah, Jonah) or of John the Baptist (Elijah); he refers to Old Testament *institutions* as types of himself and his work (the priesthood and the covenant); he sees in the *experiences* of Israel foreshadowing of his own; he finds the *hopes* of Israel fulfilled in himself and his disciples, and sees his disciples as assuming the *status* of Israel; in Israel's *deliverance* by God he sees a type of the gathering of men into

28. Cited in G. W. H. Lampe and K. J. Woollcombe, *Essays on Typology* (Naperville, IL: Allenson, 1957), 31–32.

29. The three characteristics are taken from Terry, *Biblical Hermeneutics*, 337–38.

his church, while the *disasters* of Israel are foreshadowings of the imminent punishment of those who reject him, whose *unbelief* is prefigured in that of the wicked in Israel and even, in two instances, in the arrogance of the Gentile nations.

In all these aspects of the Old Testament people of God Jesus sees foreshadowing of himself and his work, with its results in the opposition and consequent rejection of the majority of the New, while the true Israel is now to be found in the new Christian community. Thus in his coming the history of Israel has reached its decisive points. The whole of the Old Testament is gathered up in him. He himself embodies in his own person the status and destiny of Israel, and in the community of those who belong to him that status and destiny are to be fulfilled, no longer in the nation as such.[30]

In summary, then, for a figure to be a type there must be (1) a notable resemblance or analogy between the type and its antitype, (2) evidence that the type was appointed by God to represent the thing typified, and (3) a future corresponding antitype.

Classifications of Types

Although there are some minor variations among writers regarding the number and names of the various classes of types, the five classes discussed below represent commonly mentioned categories.

Typical persons are those whose lives illustrate some great principle or truth of redemption. Adam is mentioned as a type of Christ (Rom. 5:14): Adam was the representative head of fallen humanity, while Christ is the representative head of redeemed humanity.

Unlike the emphasis on the individual in Western culture, the ancient Jews identified themselves primarily as members of a group. Thus it is not unusual to find a representative person speaking or acting for the entire group. *Corporate identity* refers to that oscillation of thought between a group and an individual who represents that group; it was a common and accepted Hebrew conceptual form.[31] For example, Matthew 2:15 ("Out of Egypt I called my son") refers to Hosea 11:1, in which the son is identified as the nation of Israel. In Matthew it was Christ himself (as a representative of Israel) who was called out of Egypt, so the original

30. R. T. France, *Jesus and the Old Testament* (Downers Grove, IL: InterVarsity, 1971), 75–76.

31. A good discussion of the conceptions of human solidarity in the Old Testament and in early Jewish thought can be found in Russell Shedd, *Man in Community: A Study of St. Paul's Application of Old Testament and Early Jewish Conceptions of Human Solidarity* (London: Epworth, 1958), 3–89.

words are applied to him. Some of the psalms also view Christ as representative of all humanity.[32]

Though largely at odds with contemporary Western thinking, this use of the concepts of fulfillment and corporate identity were accepted devices; that is, they were intended, used, and understood in that culture in certain culturally accepted ways. The fact that those concepts are somewhat different from our own attests only to the differences between cultures, not to the validity or invalidity of the concepts themselves.

Typical events possess an analogical relationship to some later event. Paul uses the judgment on faithless Israel as a typological warning to Christian believers not to engage in immorality (1 Cor. 10:1–11). Matthew 2:17–18 (Rachel weeping for her slaughtered children) is mentioned as a typological analogy to the situation in Jeremiah's day (Jer. 31:15). In Jeremiah's day the event involved a national tragedy; in Matthew's time it involved a local one. The point of correspondence was the grief displayed in the face of personal loss.

Typical institutions are practices that prefigure later salvation events. One example of this is atonement by the shedding of blood by lambs and later by Christ (Lev. 17:11; cf. 1 Pet. 1:19). Another is the Sabbath as a type of the believer's eternal rest.

Typical offices include Moses in his prophetic office (Deut. 18:15) as a type of Christ, Melchizedek (Heb. 5:6) as a type of Christ's continuing priesthood, and David as king.

Typical actions are exemplified by Isaiah's walking naked and barefoot for three years as a sign to Egypt and Ethiopia that Assyria would soon lead them away naked and barefoot (Isa. 20:2–4). Another example of a typical action was Hosea's marriage to a prostitute and his later redemption of her after her infidelity, symbolizing God's covenantal love to faithless Israel.

Principles for Interpretation of Types

Historical-cultural and contextual analysis. An investigation of any two events in salvation history should first consider the historical-cultural situation in which they occurred. Identification of proper names, geographical references, contemporary customs, and historical details and background is a necessary step in understanding how both a type and its antitype fit into the pattern of salvation history. The immediate context sometimes provides clues in this regard; at other times a study of the

32. John W. Wenham, *Christ and the Bible* (Downers Grove, IL: InterVarsity, 1973), 107.

wider context (such as the purpose of the book) provides an understanding of the author's reason for including a certain event.

Lexical-syntactical analysis. Are the words being used literally, figuratively, or symbolically? (See the similar discussion in this chapter under "Prophecy.") The same principles of lexical-syntactical analysis discussed in chapter 4 apply in the interpretation of types.

Theological analysis. The proper interpretation and understanding of types often lead to an increased appreciation of the unity of Scripture and the consistency with which God has dealt with humankind throughout salvation history. One's interpretation of a type will be affected, either consciously or unconsciously, by his view of the nature of salvation history. Interpretation cannot be divorced from the presuppositions one brings to the text.

Literary analysis. Once a type has been identified as such by using the three characteristics mentioned in the preceding section, two steps remain in the analysis: search the text for the point(s) of correspondence, and note the important points of difference between the type and its antitype.

As in any other comparison, the author did not intend every incidental detail of the type and the antitype to be a point of correspondence. Some commentators, for example, have divined from the fact that the serpent in Numbers 21 was made of bronze (a metal inferior to gold or silver) that this was a type of the outward plainness of the Savior's appearance. Other commentators have found in the acacia wood and gold of the tabernacle a type of the humanity and deity of Christ, and other types and symbols have been found in the boards, the sockets of silver, the heights of the doors, the linens, and the coloring or lack of coloring of the draperies, and so on.[33] Such practices seem dangerously akin to the allegorism of the Middle Ages, imputing meaning to the text that the biblical author probably did not intend. The context and the analogy of faith (other related scriptural passages) remain the best sources of discrimination between types and nontypes.[34]

Chapter Summary

The following steps for interpreting types and prophecy have been discussed:

33. C. I. Scofield, *Scofield Reference Bible* (New York: Oxford University Press, 1917), 101–5.

34. A listing of biblical types can be found in J. Barton Payne's excellent volume *Encyclopedia of Biblical Prophecy*, 671–72.

Types	Prophecy and Apocalyptic Writing
1. Historical-cultural and contextual analysis: determine the significance within the time and culture of both the type and the antitype.	1. Historical-cultural and contextual analysis: determine the specific historical situation surrounding the composition of the writing. Study intervening history to see whether or not the prophecy has been fulfilled.
2. Lexical-syntactical analysis: follow the same principles as with other literary forms.	2. Lexical-syntactical analysis: expect more words to be used in symbolic and analogical senses.
3. Theological analysis: search the text for the points of correspondence between the type and its antitype as they relate to salvation history.	3. Theological analysis: study parallel passages or other cycles within the same prophecy for further information.

4. Literary analysis:
  a. Find some notable resemblance or analogy between the type and its antitype.
  b. Find some evidence that the type was appointed by God to represent the thing typified.
  c. Determine the point(s) of correspondence between the type and antitype—typical persons, events, institutions, offices, or actions.
  d. Note the important points of difference between the type and antitype.
	4. Literary analysis:
	  a. Be aware that the style is generally figurative and symbolic.
	  b. Watch for supernatural elements such as information conveyed by the announcement of angels, by visions, or by other supernatural means.
	  c. Notice the emphasis on the unseen world that lies behind the action of the visible world.
	  d. Follow the action to its usual conclusion by a sovereign intervention of God.
	  e. Analyze whether this passage is part of a progressive prediction, is capable of developmental fulfillment, or includes prophetic telescoping.

5. Compare your analysis with that of others; modify, correct, or expand your interpretation as appropriate.	5. Compare your analysis with that of others; modify, correct, or expand your interpretation as appropriate.

Resources for Further Reading

D. E. Aune. *Prophecy in Early Christianity and the Ancient Mediterranean World*. Grand Rapids: Eerdmans, 1983.

Louis Berkhof. *Systematic Theology*. Vol. 2. 4th rev. and enlarged ed. Grand Rapids: Eerdmans, 1949, esp. pp. 708–19.

Robert Clouse, ed. *The Meaning of the Millennium: Four Views*. Downers Grove, IL: InterVarsity, 1977.

Patrick Fairbairn. *The Typology of Scripture*. 2 vols. 1845–47. Grand Rapids: Zondervan, 1967.

C. Forbes. *Prophecy and Inspired Speech in Early Christianity and Its Hellenistic Environment*. Peabody, MA: Hendrickson, 1997.

G. W. H. Lampe and K. J. Woollcombe. *Essays on Typology*. Naperville, IL: Allenson, 1957.

R. Ludwigson. *A Survey of Biblical Prophecy*. 2nd ed. Grand Rapids: Zondervan, 1975.

A. Berkeley Mickelsen. *Interpreting the Bible*. Grand Rapids: Eerdmans, 1963, esp. pp. 280–305.

Leon Morris. *Apocalyptic*. Grand Rapids: Eerdmans, 1972.

J. Barton Payne. *Encyclopedia of Biblical Prophecy*. New York: Harper & Row, 1973.

J. Dwight Pentecost. *Things to Come*. Grand Rapids: Zondervan, 1958.

Bernard Ramm. *Protestant Biblical Interpretation*. 3rd rev. ed. Grand Rapids: Baker, 1970, esp. pp. 241–75.

Merrill C. Tenney. *Interpreting Revelation*. Grand Rapids: Eerdmans, 1957.

Milton S. Terry. *Biblical Hermeneutics*. 1883. Reprint, Grand Rapids: Zondervan, 1974, esp. pp. 405–48.

Walter L. Wilson. *A Dictionary of Bible Types: Examines the Images, Shadows, and Symbolism of Over 1,000 Biblical Terms, Words, and People*. Peabody, MA: Hendrickson, 1999.

Recent Developments in Genre Analysis

In the past thirty years there has been significant elaboration of the genres identified in Scripture. William Klein, Craig Blomberg, and Robert Hubbard's *Introduction to Biblical Interpretation* discusses many of these. For example, narrative sections have been differentiated to include reports, anecdotes, battle reports, construction reports, dream reports, epiphany reports (reports of a conversation with God or an angelic messenger), historical stories, heroic narratives, ancestral epics, prophet stories, comedy, farewell speeches, popular proverbs, riddles, fables, parables, songs, and lists.

The law sections of Scripture have been differentiated into case law, absolute law, legal series, legal instruction, criminal law, family law, civil law, religious law, and charitable law.

Poetry has been subdivided into complaints, imprecatory psalms, funeral laments, thanksgiving songs, songs of praise, coronation hymns, love songs, wedding songs, worship songs, and wisdom psalms.

Wisdom literature has been subdivided into proverbs, instruction, example stories, and disputation speeches (speeches that attempt to persuade the audience of some truth).

In the New Testament, the Gospels are viewed as theological biographies, written in the style of the times and not necessarily in the same ways as modern biographies (e.g., various teachings that relate to the same theme may be gathered together, rather than presented chronologically in the sequence they occurred). The Gospels contain various genres, including parables, miracle stories, pronouncement stories, legal maxims, beatitudes and woes, announcement and nativity stories, calling and recognition scenes, and farewell discourses. Many of these genres are used in Acts.

The Epistles include exhortational letters, diatribes (instructional letters in which objections and answers to those objections are presented), letters of self-recommendation, family letters, creeds or hymns, domestic codes, slogans, and vice and virtue lists.

Many of the above genre or form differentiations are self-evident and require little explanation. The reader interested in an excellent, comprehensive discussion of these various genre distinctions is directed to *Introduction to Biblical Interpretation,* by Klein, Blomberg, and Hubbard, pages 215–374.

Exercises

60. It has been stated that the Bible prophesies the use of Christmas trees in Jeremiah 10:3–4. Is this a valid interpretation of these verses? Why, or why not?

61. According to some interpreters the Bible also foresees the use of jet airplanes in Ezekiel 10:9–17. More specifically, this passage describes the hubcaps and wheels (vv. 9–11), the windows (v. 12), the jet turbines (v. 13), and a takeoff (vv. 15–16). Is this a valid interpretation? Why, or why not?

62. According to some interpreters there is also a biblical prophecy of police cars, rushing to an emergency with their headlights beaming (Nah. 2:4). Discuss the validity of this interpretation.

63. Many Bible students have understood the seven churches of Revelation 2 and 3 as referring to both the historical churches of John's time and the seven successive epochs in church history. Do you agree or disagree? Give hermeneutical principles to justify your answer. *Class*

64. Interpret Revelation 20:1–10 from both premillennial and amillennial viewpoints. What hermeneutical problems arise with each method?

65. Some early church fathers attempted to find a typological picture of the Trinity in the Old Testament by asserting that the three stories of the ark are types of the three persons of the Godhead. Is this valid typology? Why, or why not?

66. A hermeneutics textbook makes the following points regarding the study of typology of the Old Testament tabernacle. Linen means the Righteous One, Jesus. Brass is always a symbol of judgment.

Silver is always the symbol of redemption. In the tabernacle the pure linen (Jesus) was hung on the pillars of brass and was set in sockets of brass (judgment) but was held together with rods of silver hooks (redemption). Jesus could have come down from the cross, but he would not. Our redemption held him there (the silver hooks of redemption that held the linen to the brass).[35] Is this valid typology? Why, or why not?

67. The same hermeneutics text makes the following points regarding the typological meaning of badger skins (Exod. 26:14 KJV). The fact that these skins were not very pleasing to the eye is typical of the fact that Christ "hath no form nor comeliness" (Isa. 53:2 KJV). People outside the tabernacle tent could see only the outer covering of skins. To see the beautiful linen, one had to be inside. Correspondingly, the world sees only Christ's humanity and not his deity. From inside the tabernacle tent, one could see the purple, scarlet, blue, gold, and silver. The corresponding application is that we must get inside Christ to see his beauty.[36] Is this valid typology? Why, or why not?

68. A minister preached a message on Ezekiel 37 (the vision of the dry bones), saying that although the message was initially to the nation of Israel, it could also be legitimately applied to the church. His message focused on the importance of developing relationships with others in the body of Christ (getting connected to the other bones). Is this a valid use of this text? Why, or why not?

69. Another minister preached a message from Isaiah 18:1–7, saying that although the prophecy was originally intended against Ethiopia, according to the "double fulfillment" theory of prophecy, it could also legitimately be applied to the United States. His rationale included the following points: (1) verse 1 suggests the United States, since it is one of the few countries with a bird as its national symbol, (2) verse 2 describes the United States as a strong and mighty nation, (3) verse 3 refers to the raising of the American flag on the moon, and (4) verse 5 warns us that judgment is coming for the United States. Is this a legitimate use of this text? Why, or why not?

70. Isaiah 14:12–15 has often been interpreted as a typological allusion to Satan. Discuss the hermeneutical pros and cons of such an interpretation.

35. J. Edwin Hartill, *Principles of Biblical Hermeneutics* (Grand Rapids: Zondervan, 1947), 61.
36. Ibid., 62.

71. In Matthew 16:19 Jesus prophesies that he will give to Peter the keys of the kingdom of heaven. What is the meaning of this prophecy?

72. Some people believe that Paul's prophecy in 1 Corinthians 15:22 suggests that everyone will be saved ("For as in Adam all die, so in Christ all will be made alive"). How would you respond to this argument?

73. Some liberal commentators have claimed that Christ was mistaken regarding the time of his second coming, because of verses such as Matthew 24:34 that seem to indicate that he would return within one generation. Are there other legitimate ways of understanding this verse?

74. Sometimes when believers are going through difficult experiences, their friends will quote Jeremiah 29:11 to them: "'For I know the plans I have for you,' declares the Lord, 'plans to prosper you.'" This verse is usually intended to encourage them that their situation will improve in the near future. Is this a valid application of this verse?

EIGHT

APPLYING THE BIBLICAL MESSAGE

A PROPOSAL FOR THE
TRANSCULTURAL PROBLEM

In the first seven chapters we studied the practices of traditional hermeneutics to answer the basic question: What was the author's meaning
when he wrote a particular text? This chapter will address another question that arises for those who believe Scripture to be continually relevant:
What are the implications of that meaning for us in a different time and
culture?

There are two main categories of Scripture to which the above question must be addressed. The first is the narrative portions of Scripture.
How can we approach these portions of the Bible for teaching, reproof,
correction, and instruction in righteousness in a hermeneutically valid
way?

Second, how do we apply the normative commands of Scripture?
Do we transfer them wholesale into our time and culture, regardless of
how archaic or peculiar they might seem to us? Or should we transform
them? What guidelines do we follow to answer these questions?

All too often the movement from historical meaning to modern-day application is assumed to be straightforward and self-evident. Richard Muller assesses the situation, claiming:

> Neither exegesis nor homiletics offers a method of moving from original meaning to contemporary significance. What is left to the exegetically responsible [reader] is "the black box": the results of exegesis are thrown into one door of the box and the application of the text to the present is taken out of another door on the opposite side. One has the impression of a somewhat mysterious and arbitrary passage, of a magical act, rather than of an organic relationship between original meaning and application. What went on inside the box remains a secret and the arbitrariness of the procedure is often obscured from view by a few well-placed anecdotes.[1]

This chapter aims to explicitly describe the movement from meaning to application. It is divided into two parts. The first part describes *principlizing*, a hermeneutically legitimate way of showing the relevance of the narrative portions of Scripture for contemporary believers. The second half of the chapter proposes a model for translating biblical commands from one culture to another.

Principlizing: An Alternative to Allegorizing Biblical Narratives

As we saw in chapter 2, allegorism developed from a valid motive: the desire to show how Old Testament passages are relevant to the New Testament believer. Allegorism has been rejected, however, because it imports meaning into the text that the author never intended. Another method is needed to help the contemporary reader extract the relevance of the long historical sections of Scripture.

A simple recounting of the narrative is an insufficient and ineffective expository method. By itself such a method leads to a "BC message," a message that may have been relevant for believers at the time of the writing but fails to seem applicable to believers today. What is needed, then, is an expository method that identifies the relevance of the narrative portions of Scripture for contemporary believers without making the text say something the original author did not intend. A method of accomplishing this is principlizing.

Principlizing is an attempt to discover in a narrative the spiritual, moral, and/or theological principles that have relevance for the contemporary believer. It is based on the assumption that the Holy Spirit chose

---

1. Richard A. Muller, *The Study of Theology: From Biblical Interpretation to Contemporary Formulation* (Grand Rapids: Zondervan, 1991), 161.

those historical incidents recorded in Scripture for a purpose: to give information, to make a point, to illustrate an important truth, and so on. Principlizing attempts to understand a biblical account in such a way that we can recognize the original reason it was included in Scripture, the principles it was meant to teach.

Unlike allegorizing, which gives a story new meaning by assigning its details symbolic significance not intended by the original author, principlizing seeks to derive its teachings from a careful understanding of the story itself. Unlike demythologizing, principlizing recognizes the validity of both the historical details of a narrative and the principle(s) those details attempt to teach.

This approach uses the same methodology as that employed in the exegesis of any biblical passage. The historical circumstances and the cultural customs that illuminate the significance of various actions and commands are carefully observed. The purpose of the book within which the narrative occurs is studied, as well as the narrower context of the passages immediately preceding and following the section under examination. The state of theological knowledge and commitment among the original audience is also assessed.

Having examined these aspects of the passage, the interpreter is then in a position to understand the fixed meaning of the narrative in its original setting. Finally, based on this understanding and using a process of deduction, the interpreter attempts to articulate the principle(s) illustrated by the story, principles that continue to be relevant for the contemporary believer. We will examine two narratives to illustrate the process of principlizing.

Example 1: The "Unholy Fire" of Nadab and Abihu (Lev. 10:1–11)

The story of Nadab and Abihu is interesting both because of its brevity and because of the sternness and uniqueness of the judgment on them. It raises curiosity because it is not immediately apparent what the "strange fire" (v. 1 NASB) was nor why it brought such a quick and forceful response from God.

THE ACTIONS OF THE NARRATIVE

Aaron and his sons had just been consecrated to the priesthood (Lev. 8); after commanding that the fire be kept burning continually (6:13), God confirmed their sacrificial offering by kindling it miraculously (9:24).

Nadab and Abihu, Aaron's two oldest sons, took "strange fire" and made an incense offering to the Lord. Immediately they were struck dead by fire from God. Moses uttered a prophecy and then commanded Aaron's relatives to remove the dead bodies of Nadab and Abihu from the camp. Aaron and his two remaining sons, who were also priests, were commanded not to show the traditional signs of mourning (letting their hair hang loose and tearing their clothes), although their relatives were allowed to do so.

God then gave Aaron three commands (Lev. 10:8–10): (1) neither he nor any of his priestly descendants were to use fermented beverages before entering their sacred duties; (2) they were to distinguish between the holy and the common, the clean and the unclean; and (3) they were to teach the people all of the Lord's statutes.

Significance or Meaning of the Actions

Historical-cultural analysis. Israel had just come out of, and continued to be surrounded by, idolatrous worship. There was an ever-present danger of syncretism, that is, combining the worship of the true God with the practices of pagan worship.

Contextual analysis. This was the inauguration day of Aaron and his sons as initiators of the Levitical priesthood. Their actions would undoubtedly be regarded as precedents for those who followed. Similarly, God's acceptance or rejection of these actions would affect further developments of the priesthood itself and the priestly activities.

Lexical-syntactical and theological analysis. Fire was regarded as a divine symbol in almost all ancient religions, including Judaism. The unholy or "strange" fire that Nadab and Abihu offered is explained as fire that God had not commanded them to offer (Lev. 10:1). A similar expression is found in Exodus 30:9, where incense that had not been prepared according to the directions of the Lord is called "strange incense" (KJV).

Further analysis of the time sequence of chapters 9 and 10 suggests that Nadab and Abihu offered the incense offering between the sacrificial offering (Lev. 9:24) and the sacrificial meal that was to have followed it (10:12–20), that is, at a time other than that designated for an incense offering. C. F. Keil and F. Delitzsch suggest that it is not improbable that

> Nadab and Abihu intended to accompany the shouts of the people with an incense-offering to the praise and glory of God, and presented an incense-offering not only at an improper time, but not prepared from the altar-fire, and committed such a sin by this will-worship, that they were smitten by the fire which came forth from Jehovah. . . . The fire of the holy God (Exod. 19:18), which had just sanctified the service of Aaron as well-pleasing to God, brought destruction upon his two eldest sons, because they had not

sanctified Jehovah in their hearts, but had taken upon themselves a self-willed service.[2]

This interpretation is further borne out by God's prophecy through Moses to Aaron immediately after fire had consumed Nadab and Abihu. "This is what the LORD spoke of when he said: 'Among those who approach me I will show myself holy; in the sight of all the people I will be honored'" (v. 3).

Shortly after this, God spoke directly to Aaron, saying: "You and your sons are not to drink wine or other fermented drink whenever you go into the Tent of Meeting, or you will die. This is a lasting ordinance for the generations to come. You must distinguish between the holy and the common, between the unclean and the clean" (vv. 9–10).

Some commentators have inferred from these verses that Nadab and Abihu were under the influence of intoxicating beverages when they offered the strange fire. The text does not allow us to assert this with absolute certainty, although it is probable that God was giving commands related to the offense that had just brought the judgment of death upon Nadab and Abihu.

The principal lesson of the three commands is clear: God had carefully shown the way by which the Israelites might atone for their sins and maintain a right relationship with himself. The distinctions between holy and unholy, clean and unclean, had been clearly demonstrated by God to Aaron and his sons, who had been instructed to teach these things to the people. Nadab and Abihu, in an act of self-will, had substituted their own form of worship, obscuring the distinction between the holy (God's commands) and the common (man's self-initiated religious actions). These actions, had they not been quickly rebuked, might easily have led to the assimilation of personal pagan practices in the worship of God.

A second lesson is found in the fact that reconciliation with God depends on the grace of God, not on man's self-willed and self-initiated practices. The means of reconciliation and atonement had been given by God. Nadab and Abihu attempted to add something to God's means of reconciliation. As such they stand as an example to all people and all religions that substitute their own actions for God's grace as the means of reconciliation and salvation.

APPLICATION

God is the initiator of his mercy and grace in the divine-human relationship; we are the respondents to that grace. Believers, particularly

2. C. F. Keil and F. Delitzsch, *Commentary on the Old Testament* (Grand Rapids: Eerdmans, 1973), 1:351.

those in positions of leadership within the believing community, have a God-given responsibility to teach carefully that salvation comes by God's grace, not through the works of humans, and to distinguish between the holy and the common (v. 10). To believe and to act as if we are the initiators rather than the respondents in our relationship with God, particularly if we are in positions where others are likely to model their behavior on ours, as in the case of Nadab and Abihu, is to invite God's displeasure on ourselves.

Example 2: An Analysis of the Temptation Process

Sometimes a narrative provides several principles or truths that continue to possess relevance, as does the narrative of the first temptation, found in Genesis 3:1–6. The actions of the narrative are found in a straightforward recounting of the text:

> Now the serpent was more crafty than any of the wild animals the LORD God had made. He said to the woman, "Did God really say, 'You must not eat from any tree in the garden'?"
>
> The woman said to the serpent, "We may eat fruit from the trees in the garden, but God did say, 'You must not eat fruit from the tree that is in the middle of the garden, and you must not touch it, or you will die.'"
>
> "You will not surely die," the serpent said to the woman. "For God knows that when you eat of it your eyes will be opened, and you will be like God, knowing good and evil."
>
> When the woman saw that the fruit of the tree was good for food and pleasing to the eye, and also desirable for gaining wisdom, she took some and ate it. She also gave some to her husband, who was with her, and he ate it.

SIGNIFICANCE OF THE ACTIONS

Satan's temptation of Eve can be conceptualized in six steps, which can be seen in Satan's temptation of believers today. Step 1 is found in the first verse. The Hebrew may be paraphrased in the following way: "Now the serpent was more crafty than any wild creature that the LORD God had made. He said to the woman: 'Is it really a fact that God has prohibited you from eating of *all* the trees of the garden?'"

What is the dynamic here? Why did Satan ask this question? He obviously knew what God had said to Adam and Eve, or he would not have been able to ask what he did. Furthermore, he deliberately distorted what God had said. "Is it really a fact that God has prohibited you from eating of *all* the trees of the garden?" Satan's ploy is obvious: he was getting Eve to take her eyes off all the things God had given her to enjoy and to focus on the one thing that God had forbidden. There were probably a thousand pleasurable things Eve could have done in the garden, but now all her attention was focused on the one thing she could not do. We might call this first step *maximizing the restriction*.

Eve was now prepared for Satan's next step. In response to Eve's statement that God had said that eating of the fruit of the tree would result in death, Satan boldly declared: "You will not surely die." The results of such-and-such an action will not really be as bad as God has said. This might be called *minimizing the consequences* of sin, which Satan did in two ways: first, by telling Eve that the consequences of sin would not be as bad as God had stated, and second, by focusing her attention so completely on the tree that she forgot about those consequences (v. 6).

The third step Satan took might be called *mislabeling the action*. In verse 5 he says: "For God knows that when you eat of it your eyes will be opened, and you will be like God, knowing good and evil." Here Satan planted the suspicion in Eve's mind that God had forbidden her to eat the fruit of the tree not because it would injure her but because he did not wish her to be like him. Satan deftly tried to remove his temptation from the category of sin by mislabeling it. In this particular instance, partaking of the fruit was relabeled as a way of expanding her consciousness. She would become a more complete person if she tried it once. Before this time Eve had thought of the forbidden action as disobedience: now she saw it as a necessity if she were to become a complete and mature person.

Satan then quickly added another step to his temptation, an aspect that might be called *mixing good and evil*. Verse 6 reads: "The woman saw that the fruit of the tree was good for food." C. S. Lewis has commented that evil is often a perversion of something good that God has created. In this instance Satan added potency to his temptation by mixing good with evil: Eve saw that the tree *was* good for food.

The fifth step of Eve's temptation is found in the middle part of verse 6: "She saw that the fruit of the tree was . . . pleasing to the eye." This might be called *mixing sin with beauty*. Temptation often comes wrapped in the form of something beautiful, something that appeals to our senses and desires. It is often necessary to think twice before we recognize that a beautiful object or goal may really be sin in disguise. Eve failed to discriminate between the beautiful package and the sinful contents that the package contained.

Finally Eve took a sixth step: the narrative tells us that "she saw that the fruit of the tree was . . . desirable for gaining wisdom." In essence she swallowed the devil's lie. This step might be called *misunderstanding the implications*. Although this may seem a less significant point in the temptation process, it is perhaps the most crucial. In effect, by accepting Satan's statement, Eve was calling God a liar, even though she might not

199

have recognized those implications of her action. She accepted Satan as the truth teller and God as the prevaricator: by partaking of the fruit she was implicitly stating her belief that Satan was more interested in her welfare than God was. Yielding to the temptation implied that she accepted Satan's analysis of the situation instead of God's.

APPLICATION

Many of the dynamics of Eve's temptation are often present in Satan's temptations of believers today. With only brief introspection we can recognize his tactics of maximizing the restriction, minimizing the consequences, mislabeling the action, mixing good and evil, and mixing sin with beauty operating in our own lives.

Guidelines for Principlizing

1. Principlizing focuses on those principles implicit in a story that are applicable across times and cultures. The details may change, but the principles remain the same: for example, Satan may continue to tempt us by maximizing a restriction but is not likely to do so by using a fruit tree.

2. When deriving the meaning of a story as a basis for principlizing, we must develop the meaning from a careful historical, lexical analysis: the meaning must be the author's intended one.

3. From a theological standpoint, the meaning and principles derived from a story must be consistent with all other teachings of Scripture. A deductive principle drawn from a narrative that contradicts the teaching of some other scriptural passage is invalid.

4. Principles derived by this method may be either normative or non-normative. For example, it is valid to say that Satan sometimes uses the above methods to tempt believers today, but it would be invalid to say that he *always* uses these methods or that he uses *only* these methods.

5. Texts have only one meaning but may have many applications. Principlizing is a method of application. The meaning is the author's intended one, but the applications of that meaning may refer to situations that the author, in a different time and culture, never envisioned. For example, the author of Genesis intended to give us a narrative account of the first temptation—not a psychological analysis of the temptation process. For our application of the text (through principlizing) to be valid, it must be firmly grounded in, and thoroughly consistent with, the author's intention. Thus if the author's intention in a narrative passage was to describe an event of temptation, it is valid to analyze that passage deductively in order to understand the sequence and process of that particular temptation and then see how it might apply to our lives.

It would not be valid to generalize from that same text principles about the way temptation always takes place, since the author did not intend the text to be the basis for normative doctrine.

Translating Biblical Commands from One Culture to Another

In 1967 the United Presbyterian Church in the USA adopted a new confession of faith that contained the following statement:

> The Scriptures, given under the guidance of the Holy Spirit, are nevertheless the words of men, conditioned by the language, thought forms, and literary fashions of the places and times at which they were written. They reflect views of life, history, and the cosmos which were then current. The church, therefore, has an obligation to approach the Scriptures with literary and historical understanding. As God has spoken his word in diverse cultural situations, the church is confident that he will continue to speak through the Scriptures in a changing world and in every form of human culture.

While this statement obviously addresses some very basic cultural issues, it does not give specific guidelines for interpreting the Scriptures in "diverse cultural situations." It does not answer two important questions: To what extent are biblical commands to be understood as culturally conditioned and thus not normative for believer's today? and What kind of methodology should be applied to translate biblical commands from that culture to our own?

At one end of the spectrum are interpreters who believe that often both the scriptural principles and the behavioral command that expresses those principles should be modified in light of historical changes. At the other end of the spectrum are those who believe that scriptural principles and their accompanying behavioral commands should always be applied literally within the church today. Many believers adopt a position somewhere between these two views, or they lack a consistent method and alternate between the two extremes depending on the passage.

The majority of evangelical churches have, by their actions, implicitly agreed that some biblical commands are not to be adopted wholesale into our time and culture. For example, the command to greet one another with the holy kiss is made five times in the New Testament (Rom. 16:16; 1 Cor. 16:20; 2 Cor. 13:12; 1 Thess. 5:26; 1 Pet. 5:14), yet very few churches observe this command today. Likewise, few Protestant churches observe the command for women to wear veils when praying (1 Cor. 11:5). Few churches continue the practice of foot washing mentioned in John 13:14 (except perhaps in an occasional, ritualistic context), because the changing cultures and times have lessened the need and significance of the practice.

More controversially, some evangelical churches now have women who preach, although Paul stated in 1 Timothy 2:12 that he did not permit a woman to teach or have authority over men. Many evangelicals, men and women alike, wonder whether the traditional husband-wife roles delineated in Ephesians 5 and other passages are to be continued in our culture and time. Similar questions are being raised on other issues as well.

In 1973 a conference was convened by the Ligonier Valley Study Center to address the question, Is Scripture culturally bound? Speakers at this conference included leading contemporary evangelical scholars. The difficulty and complexity of the issue are demonstrated by the fact that the major outcome of the conference was refinement of the question rather than any substantive answers. Thus the question is one of immense importance, yet one that has no easy or universally accepted answers at this time.

The approach of principlizing is sufficiently accepted and widespread such that William Klein, Craig Blomberg, and Robert Hubbard Jr. assert, "Recent evangelical analysis has come to a consensus that the key to legitimate application involves what is usually called 'principlizing.'"[3] Nonetheless, recent years have witnessed additional proposals,[4] the most notable of which is called a redemptive-movement hermeneutic. Put forward most explicitly by William Webb,[5] the redemptive-movement hermeneutic is a trajectory approach used most often regarding biblical application in the area of social ethics. On its most basic level, the redemptive-movement hermeneutic "acknowledges that certain features within [the biblical text] reflect a less-than-ultimate ethic, yet that their meaning must be understood in keeping with their redemptive spirit relative to the ancient world and relative to canonical development."[6]

3. William W. Klein, Craig L. Blomberg, and Robert L. Hubbard Jr., *Introduction to Biblical Interpretation* (Dallas: Word, 1993), 407.

4. The following sources are cited in William J. Webb, "A Redemptive-Movement Hermeneutic: Encouraging Dialogue among Four Evangelical Views," *Journal of the Evangelical Theological Society* 48, no. 2 (June 2005): 331–49; I. Howard Marshall, *Beyond the Bible: Moving from Scripture to Theology* (Grand Rapids: Baker, 2004); Gary T. Meadors, "Probing the Redemptive Movement Model" (paper presented at a conference on hermeneutics at Heritage Seminary, Cambridge, Ont., January 17, 2005); the Midwest Evangelical Theological Society meeting held March 24–25, 2006, highlighted at least three "going beyond" models: a narrative model (Lissa Wray Beal, Providence Seminary), a theological model (Daniel J. Treier, Wheaton College), and a redemptive trajectory model (William J. Webb, Heritage Seminary).

5. William J. Webb, *Slaves, Women and Homosexuals: Exploring the Hermeneutics of Cultural Analysis* (Downers Grove, IL: InterVarsity, 2001).

6. William J. Webb, "Bashing Babies against Rocks: A Redemptive-Movement Approach to the Imprecatory Psalms" (paper presented at the annual meeting of the Evangelical Theological Society, November 2003).

For instance, biblical texts on slavery can be found throughout Scripture. In places slaves are viewed as less than human, and the laws concerning them reflect such difference in value (Exod. 21:28–32; Lev. 25:39–46). However, often the biblical directives concerning slaves reflect a substantial departure from the abuse common in the ancient Near Eastern and Greco-Roman cultures (Lev. 25:39–43; Deut. 16:10–12; Col. 4:1). The redemptive-movement hermeneutic recognizes that the biblical commands express a redemptive attitude toward slaves when compared with the original cultural setting, and it also perceives within canonical progression additional development in the direction of redemption. As a result, Webb believes such "movement was sufficient enough to signal a clear direction in terms of the possibility of further improvements for later generations."[7] With regard to slavery, an abolitionist stand is not expressed in Scripture, but the trajectory is established such that the ultimate ethic of abolition is required today. In other words, the underlying spirit of a text, rather than its specific expression in a distant culture, often allows for an ultimate ethic to be embodied in contemporary application even when it could not be expressed in the ancient world.

Wayne Grudem is among the most vocal critics of the proposed redemptive-movement hermeneutic. Grudem objects to this approach because he believes that it nullifies at least in principle the moral authority of the New Testament by establishing an ethic beyond what is clearly expressed in the biblical text[8] and in so doing encourages the interpreter to be overly subjective.[9] Grudem wonders how it is that today's reader knows how much movement is necessary to reach the "ultimate ethic," and he questions how any two interpreters will agree on just where this ultimate ethic lies.[10] Grudem further faults the redemptive-movement hermeneutic for failing to appreciate that Christians are not covenantally bound by the Old Testament[11] and for treating Genesis 2–3 without a full regard for its historicity.[12] He raises additional concerns about Webb's treatment of texts without regard for the difference between description and prescription,[13] faulty exegetical work,[14] and excessive complexity of

---

7. Webb, "Bashing Babies against Rocks," 333–34.

8. Wayne Grudem, "Should We Move beyond the New Testament to a Better Ethic? An Analysis of William J. Webb, *Slaves, Women and Homosexuals: Exploring the Hermeneutics of Cultural Analysis," Journal of the Evangelical Theological Society* 47, no. 2 (June 2004): 299–346.

9. Ibid., 321.

10. Ibid., 306.

11. Ibid., 307.

12. Ibid., 309.

13. Ibid., 312.

14. Ibid., 314.

method.[15] This conversation about whether and how valid applications of Scripture can go beyond the concrete expression of the New Testament ethic will likely continue among evangelicals for the foreseeable future.

Although much is still open for debate, what is evident is that most evangelical Christians adopt the view that some scriptural commands are culturally limited while others are not. As a result it becomes necessary to develop criteria for distinguishing between those commands that apply directly and continually and those that do not. If our procedure is not to be arbitrary, allowing us to dismiss those commands and principles with which we disagree and retain those with which we agree, we must develop criteria, (1) the logic of which can be demonstrated, (2) which can be consistently applied to a variety of issues and questions, and (3) the nature of which is either drawn from Scripture or at least is consistent with Scripture.

Establishing a Theoretical Framework for Analyzing Behavior and Behavioral Commands

First postulate: A single behavior usually has ambiguous significance for the observer. For example, if I look out my study window and see a man walking up the street, I do not know whether he is (a) getting some exercise by taking a walk, (b) on his way to catch a bus, or (c) leaving home after an argument with his wife.

Second postulate: Behavior takes on more meaning for the observer as he ascertains more about its context. As I observe the man in the above example more closely, I hypothesize that he is a student on his way to a class because of his age, dress, bag, and books. However, I also observe a woman, apparently his wife (because of similar clothing styles) following about fifteen feet behind him, walking with her head down. I immediately wonder if they have been fighting and if she is following him in an attempt to pacify him after he left the house in anger. I quickly dismiss this hypothesis when I recognize that the clothing styles indicate this couple is from a culture where it is normal and expected that the wife walk a certain distance behind her husband whenever they are together in public.

Third postulate: Behavior that has a certain meaning in one culture may have totally different significance in another culture. In American society, for a woman to follow her husband at a distance of fifteen feet, with her head down, would usually indicate a problem in their relationship. In another culture, this same behavior may be considered normal and expected.[16]

---

15. Ibid., 318.

16. For other examples of behavior that has different meanings in different cultures, see Edwin Yamauchi, "Christianity and Cultural Differences," *Christianity Today*, June 23, 1972, 5–8.

Let us examine the implications of these three postulates.

First, the meaning of a single behavior cannot be ascertained apart from its context. Analogously, the meaning of (and principle behind) a behavioral command in Scripture cannot be ascertained apart from the context of that command.

Second, the meaning behind a given behavior can be more accurately ascertained the more one knows about the context of that behavior. Similarly, the more we know of the context of a behavioral command, other things being equal, the more we will be able to ascertain accurately the meaning of (and the principle expressed by) that command.

Third, since a given behavior in one culture may have a different meaning in another culture, it may be necessary to change the behavioral expression of a scriptural command in order to translate the principle behind that command from one culture and time to another.

Two aspects of biblical commands need to be differentiated: the behavior specified and the principle expressed through the specified behavior. For example, the holy kiss greeting (behavior) expressed brotherly love (principle).

In making transcultural applications of biblical commands, three alternatives can be considered:

1. Retain both the principle and its behavioral expression.
2. Retain the principle but suggest a change in the way that principle is behaviorally expressed in our culture.
3. Change both the principle and its behavioral expression, assuming that both were culture-bound and are therefore no longer applicable.

As an example, let us look at the oft-debated custom related to women's head coverings discussed in 1 Corinthians 11:2–16. Many believe that the cultural practice expresses an attitude of female submission.[17] Three approaches have been taken by various commentators:

1. Retain both the principle of submission and its expression through the use of head coverings.[18]

---

17. See Letha Scanzoni and Nancy Hardesty, *All We're Meant to Be* (Waco: Word, 1975), 40, 64–67, for a discussion of the cultural significance of veiling among various Mediterranean cultures during biblical times.

18. B. K. Waltke, "1 Corinthians 11:2–16: An Interpretation," *Bibliotheca Sacra* 135 (January 1978): 46–57.

2. Retain the principle of submission but replace the use of head coverings with some other behavior that more meaningfully expresses submission in our culture.[19]
3. Replace both the principle of submission and all expressions of submission with a more egalitarian philosophy, since the concept of hierarchy within the family is a culture-bound one.[20]

Understanding biblical commands in terms of principles and behaviors that express those principles is of little value unless there are some means for differentiating between those principles and behaviors that are culture-bound and those that are transcultural.

Preliminary Guidelines for Differentiating Culture-Bound from Transcultural Principles and Commands

The following guidelines are called preliminary for two reasons. First, they are incomplete in that they do not cover every biblical command and principle; second, at this point they are tentative, intended to initiate discussion and further exploration of the issue.

GUIDELINES FOR DISCERNING WHETHER PRINCIPLES ARE TRANSCULTURAL OR CULTURE-BOUND

First, determine the reason given for the principle. For example, we are to love one another *because* God first loved us (1 John 4:19). We are not to love the world and its values *because* love of the world and love of God are mutually exclusive (1 John 2:15).

Second, if the reason for a principle is culture-bound, then the principle may be also. If the reason has its basis in God's unchanging nature (his grace, his love, his moral nature, or his created order), then the principle itself should probably not be changed.

GUIDELINES FOR DISCERNING WHETHER COMMANDS (APPLICATIONS OF PRINCIPLES) ARE TRANSCULTURAL OR CULTURE-BOUND

First, when a transcultural principle is embodied in a form that was part of the common cultural habits of the time, the form *may* be modified, even though the principle remains unchanged. For example, Jesus demonstrated the principle that we should have an attitude of humility

---

19. Thomas R. Schreiner, "Head Coverings, Prophecies and the Trinity: 1 Corinthians 11:2–16," in *Recovering Biblical Manhood and Womanhood: A Response to Evangelical Feminism*, ed. John Piper and Wayne Grudem (Wheaton: Crossway, 1991), 124–39.

20. An example of one expression of an egalitarian position can be found in Craig S. Keener, *Paul, Women and Wives: Marriage and Women's Ministry in the Letters of Paul* (Peabody, MA: Hendrickson, 1992).

and willingness to serve one another (Mark 10:42–44) by washing the disciples' feet (John 13:12–16), a familiar custom of the day. We retain the principle, although there are other ways to express that principle more meaningfully in our culture.

Again James argued that believers should not show partiality within the church meeting by having the rich sit in chairs and the poor sit on the floor (James 2:1–9). We retain the principle of nonpartiality, but the application of the principle takes on different dimensions in our time and culture.

Second, when a practice that was an accepted part of a pagan culture was forbidden in Scripture, it is probably to be forbidden in contemporary culture as well, particularly if the command is grounded in God's moral (as opposed to ceremonial or civil) law. Examples of practices that were accepted parts of pagan cultures but were forbidden in Scripture include fornication, adultery, spiritism, divorce, and homosexual behavior.

Third, it is important to define the intended recipients of a command and to apply the command discriminately to other groups. If a command was given to only one church or one individual, this *may* indicate that it was meant to be a local rather than a universal practice. For instance, in 2 Timothy 4:9–13 Paul issues a command: "Come to me quickly. . . . Bring the cloak that I left with Carpus at Troas, and my scrolls, especially the parchments." Few readers of this text have felt the need to book the next flight to Troas to gather Paul's belongings and then attempt to deliver them to the apostle! Clearly the command was given to Timothy and no longer applies directly to today's reader.

Suggested Steps in Translating Biblical Commands from One Culture and Time to Another

1. *Discern as accurately as possible the principle behind the given behavioral command.* Sometimes this principle is stated explicitly; other times it must be inferred from the context. For example, Christians are to judge individual sin within their local community of believers because, if unchecked, evil will have an effect on the entire community (1 Cor. 5:1–13, especially v. 6).

2. *Discern whether the principle is timeless or time-bound (transcultural or culture-bound).* Suggestions for doing this were offered in the last section. Since most biblical principles are rooted in God's unchanging nature, it seems to follow that a principle should be considered transcultural unless there is evidence to the contrary.

3. *If a principle is transcultural, study the nature of its behavioral application within our culture.* Will the behavioral application given then be appropriate now, or will it be an anachronistic oddity?

207

The danger of conforming the biblical message to what is considered "politically correct" in our culture is very great. There are times when the expression of a God-given principle will cause Christians to behave in a way different from non-Christians (Rom. 12:2) but not needlessly so, not for the sake of the difference itself. The criterion for whether a behavioral command should be applied in our culture should *not* be whether it conforms to modern cultural practices but whether it adequately and accurately expresses the God-given principle that was intended.

4. *If the behavioral expression of a principle should be changed, suggest a cultural equivalent that would adequately express the God-given principle behind the original command.* For example, J. B. Phillips suggests that "Greet one another with a hearty handshake" may be a good American cultural equivalent to "Greet one another with the holy kiss."[21]

If there is no cultural equivalent, it might be worthwhile to consider *creating* a new cultural behavior that would meaningfully express the principles involved. (In a similar but not strictly analogous manner, some of the newer wedding ceremonies express the same principles as more traditional ones but in very creative and meaningful new ways.)

Missiologists in recent decades have recognized the need to engage in this process of contextualization on the mission field.[22] When we recall that Western culture is not a neutral culture or identical to the biblical cultures, Western audiences are rightly identified as a mission field, and the need for this step should become apparent.

5. *If after careful study the nature of the biblical principle and its attendant command remain in question, apply the biblical precept of humility.* There may be occasions when even after careful study of a given principle and its behavioral expression, we still may remain uncertain about whether it should be considered transcultural or culture-bound. If we must decide to treat the command one way or the other but have no conclusive means to make the decision, the biblical principle of humility can be helpful. After all, would it be better to treat a principle as transcultural and be guilty of being overscrupulous in our desire to obey God? Or would it be better to treat a transcultural principle as culture-bound and be guilty of breaking a continuing requirement of God? The answer should be obvious.

Isolated from the other guidelines mentioned above, this principle of humility could easily be misconstrued as ground for unnecessary conser-

---

21. See Fred Wight, *Manners and Customs of Bible Lands* (Chicago: Moody, 1953), 74–75, for further discussion of this Eastern custom.

22. For a comprehensive overview of the background of contextualization, a variety of proposals for doing contextualization, and tools for analyzing those proposals and their results, see David J. Hesselgrave and Edward Rommen, *Contextualization: Meanings, Methods, and Models* (Grand Rapids: Baker, 1989).

vatism. The principle should be applied only after we have carefully tried to determine whether a principle is transcultural or culture-bound, and despite our best efforts, the issue still is uncertain. This is a guideline of last resort and would be counterproductive if used as a first resort.[23]

Chapter Summary

1. Principlizing: Based on a historical-cultural, contextual, lexical-syntactical, and theological analysis of the narrative portion, ascertain by deductive study (1) the principle(s) that a passage was intended to teach or (2) the principles (descriptive truths) illustrated within the passage that remain relevant for the contemporary believer.
2. Transcultural transmission of biblical commands:
   a. Discern as accurately as possible the principle behind the command.
   b. Discern whether the principle is transcultural or culture-bound by examining the reason given for the principle.
   c. If a principle is transcultural, determine whether the same behavioral application in our culture will express the principle as adequately and accurately as the biblical one.
   d. If the behavioral expression of a principle should be changed, suggest a cultural equivalent that will express the God-given principle behind the original command.
   e. If, after careful study, the nature of the biblical principle and its attendant command remain in question, apply the biblical precept of humility.

Resources for Further Reading

James Oliver Buswell Jr. *Systematic Theology of the Christian Religion*. 2 vols. Grand Rapids: Zondervan, 1962–63, esp. vol. 1, pp. 365–84.

David J. Hesselgrave and Edward Rommen. *Contextualization: Meanings, Methods and Models*. Grand Rapids: Baker, 1989.

William W. Klein, Craig L. Blomberg, and Robert L. Hubbard Jr. *Introduction to Biblical Interpretation*. Dallas: Word, 1993, esp. pp. 292–312, 366–74.

Charles Kraft. "Interpreting in Cultural Context." *Journal of the Evangelical Theological Society* 21 (1978): 357–67.

23. The main ideas and some of the phraseology of these last two paragraphs were taken from R. C. Sproul, "Controversy at Culture Gap," *Eternity*, May 1976, 40. Sproul's discussion refers to a related but slightly different issue.

Charles Kraft with Marguerite Kraft. *Christianity in Culture: A Study in Dynamic Biblical Theologizing in Cross-Cultural Perspective*. Rev. ed. Maryknoll, NY: Orbis Books, 2005.

Donald McGavran. *The Clash between Christianity and Cultures*. Washington, DC: Canon, 1974.

A. Berkeley Mickelsen. *Interpreting the Bible*. Grand Rapids: Eerdmans, 1963, esp. pp. 159–76.

R. C. Sproul. "Controversy at Culture Gap." *Eternity*, May 1976, 13–15, 40.

Merrill Tenney. *New Testament Times*. Grand Rapids: Eerdmans, 1965.

Fred Wight. *Manners and Customs of Bible Lands*. Chicago: Moody, 1953.

George Ernest Wright. *The Old Testament against Its Environment*. London: SCM, 1957.

Edwin M. Yamauchi. "Christianity and Cultural Differences." *Christianity Today*, June 23, 1972, 5–8.

Roy Zuck. "Application in Biblical Hermeneutics and Exposition." In *Rightly Divided: Readings in Biblical Hermeneutics*, edited by Roy Zuck, 278–96. Grand Rapids: Kregel, 1996.

Exercises

(As in other chapters, some of these exercises apply hermeneutical skills discussed in previous chapters.)

75. Basing his view on 1 Corinthians 6:1–8, a pastor stated that it is wrong for a Christian to sue another believer. Is this hermeneutically valid? Why, or why not?

76. Pacifists have sometimes used Matthew 26:52 as part of their argument that Christians should not be involved in military activity. From the standpoint of valid hermeneutics, what principles and/or behavioral commands can we draw from this passage?

77. In Deuteronomy 19:21 God's command is "eye for eye, tooth for tooth." Jesus, claiming that he was fulfilling the law, said: "Do not resist an evil person. If someone strikes you on the right cheek, turn to him the other also" (Matt. 5:39). How do you reconcile these two statements?

78. In 1 Timothy 2:12 Paul says that he does not allow a woman to teach or have authority over men. Using the model presented in this chapter, discuss these questions: (1) What was the meaning of this text for Timothy? (2) What application should it have for us today? (3) What implications does your view have for (a) female Sunday school teachers, (b) female hospital chaplains, (c) female seminary teachers, (d) female pastors, and (e) female missionaries?

79. There are three main types of church government—the episcopal, the presbyterian, and the congregational—and some denominations use a mixed model. Investigate how each of these types functions, then do a word study of the terms *bishop, elder,* and *deacon* as used in the New Testament. What are the implications of your New Testament study for the models of church government?

80. Some believers use Acts 4:32–35 as the basis for Christian communal living today. What hermeneutical considerations are relevant to such an application of this text?

81. Basing his view on Ephesians 6:1–3, a noted Christian teacher argues that children should never go against their parents' wishes but should allow God to direct them through their parents. Is this a valid understanding of the text as Paul originally gave it? If it is, is it as valid to apply it in the same way today in our American culture? If you answered affirmatively to both of the above questions, does this obligation ever end?

82. With the rising divorce rate, many churches are faced with the question of what roles, if any, divorced and remarried persons may play in the leadership/service functions of the church. How do you think the teaching of 1 Timothy 3:2, 12 applies to that question?

83. A number of conservative denominations believe that Christians should totally abstain from the use of alcoholic beverages. Other denominations believe that the Bible teaches moderation. Study the relevant verses on the use of alcoholic beverages. Are there scriptural principles besides the passages specifically dealing with alcohol that might apply to this question?

84. As a preface to his exposition of a text, a minister said, "I have gotten this message from no other man. I have consulted no other commentaries; it comes straight from *the Book*!" Comment on this method of expositional preparation.

85. Some liberal theologians and liberal Christian psychologists and psychiatrists believe that when Jesus and the other New Testament writers spoke about demon possession, they were speaking through the lens of a primitive culture, and that now we know that the illnesses spoken of in biblical times were really mental illnesses. What do you think of this assertion and why? If you believe that demon possession and mental illness both exist, how would you decide if a parishioner was suffering from one instead of the other?

86. Many pastors have taken the story of Jesus stilling the storm in the Sea of Galilee and proceeded to preach that Jesus will calm the storms in your life. Is this valid principlizing?

87. Based on Psalm 127:3–5, some believers teach that Christians should not practice birth control but should have large families. Read these verses in context, and then decide whether you think they should be used to discourage birth control and encourage having large families today.

88. It is becoming common for people in the twenty-first century to have tattoos inscribed on their bodies, and even some Christians engage in this practice. However, other Christians believe that the Bible forbids this based on passages such as Leviticus 19:28 and 21:5. Based on these verses, do you think Christians should abstain from having tattoos?

89. Read the story of Samson in Judges 13–16 and draw illustrative principles from his life that you could use in leading a Bible study or preaching a sermon. Develop those principles in an annotated outline that you could use in leading such a Bible study or preaching a sermon.

90. Many fundamentalist and conservative evangelical parents believe that spanking should be a primary method of discipline based on the teaching of Proverbs. Study the book of Proverbs specifically from the perspective of what it says about discipline and parenting, and summarize what you believe it teaches about the role spanking should play in Christian discipline.

91. Some Christians have argued that churches today should continue to use church discipline such as found in 1 Corinthians 5; however, most churches rarely if ever do so. The arguments they give for not doing so are varied but include the following: (1) Paul was exercising an apostolic prerogative in 1 Corinthians 5, and since we are not apostles, we should not follow his example. (2) The biblical commands were given in a different time and culture and should not be applied to churches today. (3) The threat of lawsuits makes it unfeasible to carry out church discipline today. (4) The frequency of Christians engaging in unbiblical behavior (e.g., the number of Christians initiating divorce for less than biblical reasons, the number of Christians living together before marriage, etc.) is so high that churches would spend all their time punishing members for such behavior, and little time and energy would be left for prayer, fellowship, Bible study, and evangelism, which should be the main activities of the church. (5) It would be complicated and controversial to differentiate between those unbiblical behaviors that are wrong but do not rise to the level of deserving church discipline and those that do. (6) With the easy proximity of other churches, such an approach would be ineffective: offenders would simply

Class

terminate their membership in the church that was attempting to discipline them and move to another church (or stop attending church altogether). (7) An unspoken but probably very real fear: Implementing a church discipline procedure in one church when most other churches do not could significantly reduce church growth and produce a mass exodus of present members.

Study the passages related to church discipline (e.g., Matt. 16:19; 18:15–18; Acts 20:28–31; Rom. 2:21–24; 1 Cor. 5:1–13; 6:1–20; Gal. 6:1; James 2:14–17; Jude 3–23). For those who believe the church is to be a continuation of the nation of Israel, there are passages from the Old Testament that apply as well (e.g., Ezek. 3:20–21). From the passages above and any others you believe are relevant, make a statement about whether you believe the church today should engage in church discipline. If you believe it should, give answers to the seven arguments against church discipline mentioned above.

92. You are a youth leader at a local church. A young man who has dabbled with drugs and believes that he is more spiritually sensitive when he is under their influence comes to you. Attempting to find biblical support for the use of marijuana, he points to Genesis 1:29: "Then God said, 'I give you every seed-bearing plant on the face of the whole earth.'" He argues that God gave us the marijuana plant, and it is meant to be used. What hermeneutical errors are involved in his conclusion? How would you respond to his use of this text?

93. Recently a woman at your church was in a serious car accident. She is recovering but will require strenuous physical therapy if she ever hopes to walk without assistance. You want to encourage her by sending her a card. While card shopping you spot one with Philippians 4:13: "I can do everything through him who gives me strength." Do you buy this card?

94. Read 1 Corinthians 11:23–26. Missionaries have suggested that in countries where bread is not a staple food, it is appropriate to celebrate communion with rice or a tortilla, for instance. In similar fashion, the youth pastor at your church has suggested inviting the young people to a communion service specifically for them that uses red soda and potato chips. Is this a good example of contextualization?

95. The day before her son started his first job, a mother admonished him to be responsible and work hard, even if nobody was watching him. She supported her instruction by reading to him from Ephesians 6:5–6: "Slaves, obey your earthly masters with respect and fear, and with sincerity of heart, just as you would obey Christ. Obey them not only to win their favor when their eye is on you, but like

213

slaves of Christ, doing the will of God from your heart." Is this valid principlizing?

96. Acts 1:21–26 records the process used by the disciples to replace Judas. Based on this passage can we conclude that casting lots is a satisfactory means of determining God's will? On the basis of this passage can we conclude that prayer is a necessary means of determining God's will? Why, or why not?

97. Read Acts 10:44–48. Are the following conclusions warranted from this passage? (1) Speaking in tongues provides the necessary proof of whether someone has received the Holy Spirit. (2) All believers in Christ should be baptized in the name of Jesus Christ. (3) God gave definitive evidence that Gentile believers are among his new covenant people.

98. Read John 13:12–16. This passage describes how Jesus washed the feet of his disciples. Some churches conduct regular foot-washing services as a result of this teaching. Is this the best application of this text? Why, or why not? Include a discussion of the principle contained in the text and several concrete practices that would communicate that principle in your own culture.

99. (Note: This is an expanded exercise.) Bruce Wilkinson has written a best-selling book, *The Prayer of Jabez*, based on a passage from 1 Chronicles 4:9–10.[24] This passage says the following:

> Now Jabez was more honorable than his brothers, and his mother called his name Jabez, saying, "Because I bore him in pain."
>
> And Jabez called on the God of Israel saying, "Oh, that You would bless me indeed, and enlarge my territory, that Your hand would be with me, and that You would keep me from evil, that I may not cause pain." So God granted him what he requested. (NKJV)

In the preface to his book Wilkinson says: "I want to teach you how to pray a daring prayer that God always answers. It is brief—only one sentence with four parts—and tucked away in the Bible, but I believe it contains the key to a life of extraordinary favor with God."

"This little book you're holding is about what happens when ordinary Christians decide to reach for an extraordinary life—which, as it turns out, is exactly the kind God promises" (9).

---

24. Bruce H. Wilkinson, *The Prayer of Jabez* (Sisters, OR: Multnomah, 2000). Page numbers of quotations are given in parentheses in the text.

"When was the last time God worked through you in such a way that you knew beyond doubt that God had done it?" (15–16).

"Let me tell you a guaranteed by-product of sincerely seeking His blessing: Your life will become marked by miracles. How do I know? Because He promises it" (24–25).

On the next few pages Wilkinson notes a couple of passages in which he believes God promises such miracles. He cites, "'Ask,' promised Jesus, 'and it will be given to you' (Matthew 7:7)." "'You do not have because you do not ask,' said James (James 4:2)" (27).

Chapter 3 begins with the quotation: "Oh, that You would enlarge my territory!" Wilkinson comments: "The next part of the Jabez prayer—a plea for more territory—is where you ask God to enlarge your life so you can make a greater impact for Him. . . . When Jabez cried out to God, 'Enlarge my territory!' he was looking at his present circumstances and concluding, 'Surely I was born for more than this!' As a farmer or herdsman, he looked over the spread his family had passed down to him, ran his eye down the fence lines, visited the boundary markers, calculated the potential—and made a decision: *Everything you've put under my care, O Lord—take it, and enlarge it.*

"If Jabez had worked on Wall Street, he might have prayed, 'Lord, increase the value of my investment portfolios.' When I talk to presidents of companies, I often talk to them about this particular mind-set. When Christian business executives ask me, 'Is it right for me to ask God for more business?' my response is, 'Absolutely!'" (30–31).

Wilkinson's goal is to encourage Christians to attempt great things for God, things well beyond their personal abilities (either spiritually or financially), so that when such things come to pass, it will be clear that God was the provider (40–41). In his own words, "When you take little steps, you don't need God. It's when you thrust yourself in the mainstream of God's plans for this world—which are beyond our ability to accomplish—and plead with Him, *Lord, use me—give me more ministry for You!*—that you release miracles" (44).

Wilkinson gives his own explanation of the last phrase of the prayer: *"Lord, keep me safe from the pain and grief that sin brings. For the dangers that I can't see, or the ones that I think I can risk because of my experience (pride and carelessness), put up a supernatural barrier. Protect me, Father, by your power!"* (70).

He concludes: "Let me encourage you, friend, to reach boldly for the miracle. Your Father knows your gifts, your hindrances, and the condition you're in at every moment. And He knows something you can't possibly know—every single person who's in desperate need of receiving His touch *through you*. God will bring you to that person at exactly the right time and in the right circumstances.

"And at that moment, you *will* receive power to be His witness" (82–83).

Question: Do you agree with Wilkinson's hermeneutical analysis and application of this passage? Why, or why not?

USING THE BIBLE
FOR PREACHING
AND DEVOTIONS

The task of the minister, as it relates to the content of this text, is twofold: (1) he is to be a minister of the Word of God, and (2) he must minister the Word of God accurately. We quote with approval the words of Bernard Ramm:

> The preacher is *a minister of the Word of God.* . . . His fundamental task in preaching is not to be clever or sermonic or profound but *to minister the truth of God.* The apostles were called *ministers of the word* (Luke 1:2). The apostles were ordained as *witnesses of Jesus Christ* (Acts 1:8). Their task was to preach what they heard and saw with reference to the life, death, and resurrection of Jesus Christ. The elder (pastor) is to labor *in word and doctrine* (1 Tim. 5:17). What Timothy is to hand on to others is . . . *the truth of Christianity* which he heard from many Christians (2 Tim. 2:2). Paul instructs Timothy . . . to "preach *the message*" (2 Tim. 4:2. Grk: *Kērykson ton logon*). Peter says he is an elder by virtue of having witnessed the sufferings of our Lord (1 Peter 5:1).

The New Testament servant of Christ was not one free to preach as he wished, but one bound to minister the truth of Christianity, to preach the Word of God, and to be a witness of the Gospel.[1]

The servant of Christ must do more than preach the Word. It is possible to be earnest, eloquent, and knowledgeable in Scripture and yet preach it either inaccurately or in less than its full truth (e.g., Apollos in Acts 18:24–28). Paul commands Timothy, "Do your best to present yourself to God as one approved, a workman who has no need to be ashamed, *rightly handling* the word of truth" (2 Tim. 2:15 RSV; emphasis added). A workman would feel ashamed if incompetence or shoddiness were detected in his work. Paul tells Timothy that the way he can stand unashamed and approved before God is by *"rightly handling* the word of truth." Thus the twofold task of the pastor, as defined in the above Scriptures, is (1) to preach the Word of God, and (2) to interpret it accurately.

Types of Contemporary Preaching

Most of the preaching done today can be conceptualized on the following continuum:

Topical
Preaching

Varieties of Contemporary Preaching

Expository
Preaching

Sermonizing

Expository preaching starts with a given passage and investigates it, using the processes we have labeled historical-cultural, contextual, lexical-syntactical, theological, and literary analyses. Its primary focus is an exposition of what God intended to say in that particular passage, leading to an application of that meaning in the lives of contemporary Christians.

1. Bernard Ramm, *Protestant Biblical Interpretation*, 3rd rev. ed. (Grand Rapids: Baker, 1970), 195–96.

Sermonizing begins with an idea in the mind of the preacher—a relevant social or political issue of some kind or a theological or psychological insight—and expands this idea into a sermon outline. As part of the process, relevant Scriptures are added as they come to mind or as they are found with the aid of study helps. The primary focus of this method is the elaboration of a human idea in ways that are consistent with Scripture's general teaching in that area.

Topical preaching begins by selecting a topic related to Scripture (e.g., biblical themes, doctrines, Bible characters). If the sermon is developed by selecting relevant Scripture passages and developing an outline based on exposition of those passages, this might be called "topical-expository preaching." If the sermon outline is developed from ideas that come to the mind of the preacher and are then validated by relating them to a relevant Scripture verse, this might be called "topical sermonizing."

Most sermons preached today appear to be of the sermonizing and topical-sermonizing variety. If the proportion of expository preaching to sermonizing is any indication, the majority of theological schools appear either not to be training their students in the skills needed to do expository preaching or not to be encouraging them to use expository preaching as an alternative to sermonizing. It is also possible that the demands of the pastoral job, which today can include counseling, visitation, making business decisions, and much more, intrude on the time required to adequately study a biblical text and prepare an expository sermon.

From the perspective of two who are primarily "consumers" rather than "producers" of sermons, we would like to offer our observations on some of the similarities and differences we see between sermonizing and expository preaching.

Sermonizing and Expository Preaching: A Comparison

The similarities of these two methods of preaching include, among other things, the fact that both are done by intelligent, God-fearing people who are committed to feeding the flock for whom God has given them responsibility. Both methods are used by articulate, eloquent people who preach with forcefulness and dignity. And both appear to be used by God to feed his flock, if the size of the congregations is in any way a valid measure.

There are some differences as well. First, there is a basic difference in procedure as mentioned above. Expository preaching begins with a passage of God's Word, expounds that text, and then applies it to the lives of contemporary believers. Sermonizing begins with an idea in the mind of the preacher that is elaborated into a sermon outline, with Scripture references sometimes appearing to reinforce a particular point. (These differences are relative rather than absolute and vary from minister to minister and sometimes from sermon to sermon with the same minister.)

Second, there is often a difference in the hermeneutical methods. When listening to sermonizing messages, we have had the common experience of either (1) hearing a verse or a portion of a verse read as the text, followed sometimes by a message that could not be derived from that text if it had been read within its context or (2) hearing a passage read that is not really related to the subsequent sermon. This is not to suggest that eisegesis is confined to sermonizing and exegesis to expository preaching. However, when a minister is constructing a series of messages from a particular book of the Bible, a study of the material before and after a passage presents many built-in safeguards against eisegetical interpretation. When a minister is attempting to find a passage to validate his already-established ideas, there is a greater temptation to use a passage that represents a verbal parallel to that idea even if it is not a real parallel.

Third, there is a difference in the biblical authoritativeness of expository preaching and sermonizing. Biblical authoritativeness should not be confused with human persuasiveness. Human persuasiveness depends on articulateness, colorful use of illustrations, verbal inflection, use of electronic amplifying equipment, and so on, and is not related to the type of sermon—expository preaching or sermonizing. However, sermonizing, no matter how brilliant from the standpoint of human persuasiveness, remains fundamentally a word from one human being to another. Though it may be delivered by a minister highly respected by his congregation, his psychological or social or political theories must compete with the theories of hundreds of other "authorities" who also influence his congregation.

Fourth, one additional benefit of the expository sermon is that it offers models of sound hermeneutical methods to the congregation. As laypeople watch their pastor interact with Scripture in a way that speaks God's message with divine authority, they catch a glimpse of what is needed in their own Bible study and devotional times.

To speak with the authority of "thus saith the Lord," the minister must expound *God's* Word. The thundering authority of Moses, Jeremiah, Amos, Peter, and Paul came from speaking forth as the Holy Spirit empowered them (2 Pet. 1:21). We will not regain that sense of divine authority by dabbling in popular psychology and footnoting our speculations with a verse from God's Word. The only way to regain the authority of "thus saith the Lord" is to return to an exposition of his Word. This is not to say that the teaching in a sermonizing message cannot be in accord with biblical truth. If the pastor is well-grounded in Scripture, his thoughts and opinions will likely flow from this fountainhead. Nonetheless, the method of sermonizing cannot guarantee that the message will be in accord with biblical truth, and thus, as a method, it lacks the authority of God's Word.

Finally, there is no promise to be found in Scripture that God will bless human sermonizing. God does, however, promise to bless the declaration of his Word:

> As the rain and the snow
>   come down from heaven,
> and do not return to it
>   without watering the earth
> and making it bud and flourish,
>   so that it yields seed for the sower
>   and bread for the eater,
> so is my word that goes out from my
>   mouth:
>   It will not return to me empty,
> but will accomplish what I desire
>   and achieve the purpose for which I sent
>   it.
>
>   Isaiah 55:10–11

If Your Pastor Is Not an Expository Preacher

If your pastor is not an expository preacher, there are several supplemental activities that you might consider. For instance, you might use the sermon as the beginning and not the end of your interaction with a given text and complete additional study of the text (or one of the texts, if there were several) in the week that follows. Simply reading the entire chapter in which a text appears and considering historical notes in a study Bible or commentary will augment the pastor's sermon. Some pastors make their selection of biblical text for the week available ahead of time. If this is the case, before the sermon you could spend time reading the text in its context and consulting a basic commentary about the passage. There would also be value in using the text, the surrounding chapters, or real parallels as the topic for daily devotions for yourself or your family.

221

Resources for Further Reading

Andrew Blackwood. *Expository Preaching for Today*. 1953. Reprint, Grand Rapids: Baker, 1975.

John A. Broadus. *A Treatise on the Preparation and Delivery of Sermons*. Rev. ed. New York: Harper & Row, 1944.

Phillips Brooks. *Lectures on Preaching*. London: H. R. Allenson, 1877.

E. P. Clowney. *Preaching and Biblical Theology*. Grand Rapids: Eerdmans, 1961.

Sidney Greidanus. *The Modern Preacher and the Ancient Text: Interpreting and Preaching Biblical Literature*. Grand Rapids: Eerdmans, 1988.

Walter C. Kaiser Jr. *Toward an Exegetical Theology: Biblical Exegesis for Preaching and Teaching*. Grand Rapids: Baker, 1981.

W. L. Liefeld. *New Testament Exposition: From Text to Sermon*. Grand Rapids: Zondervan, 1984.

Mark Miller. *Experiential Storytelling: Discovering Narrative to Communicate God's Message*. Grand Rapids: Zondervan, 2004.

Lloyd Perry. *A Manual for Biblical Preaching*. Grand Rapids: Baker, 1965.

Haddon W. Robinson. *Biblical Preaching: The Development and Delivery of Expository Messages*. Grand Rapids: Baker, 1980.

Haddon W. Robinson and Craig Larson. *The Art and Craft of Biblical Preaching*. Grand Rapids: Zondervan, 2006.

John Stott. *Between Two Worlds: The Art of Preaching in the Twentieth Century*. Grand Rapids: Eerdmans, 1982.

The Devotional Use of Scripture

More than one beginning student has finished a course on hermeneutics only to ask, "How do I use the Bible devotionally? I cannot possibly do all of the exegetical work every day, and yet I do not want to misread Scripture!" Such a statement expresses an appropriate fear of reaching conclusions that lack divine authority if the exegetical method is not used. Several suggestions may help to guard against creating such an unbridgeable gulf between the study of Scripture and its devotional use.

First, God can use a biblical text—or anything else for that matter—to impress his children with a lesson or a word that he has for them. For instance, the observer of a spectacular sunset might be prompted to consider God's majesty and his own minuteness. That realization might provide a legitimate reproach to the observer as he is struggling with pride and yet thinking too highly of himself. This lesson regarding the need for appropriate humility is not the meaning of the sunset. No two observers must necessarily reach this same conclusion. And yet it is perfectly valid for the individual who came to the sunset with an open heart reflecting on God to claim, "God taught me a lesson in humility through the sunset."

This is also the case when the Christian comes to Scripture and reads it with a desire to grow spiritually and be transformed into greater Christlikeness. In any given passage that such a person reads, God may provide conviction or reproach or encouragement in a particular direction. This is not the meaning of the text, but it can be a valid conclusion. The authority of the conclusion rests on the reader's own sensitivity to the Holy Spirit and on the consistency of the lesson with biblical teaching. Much like the sermonizing discussed above, this method cannot guarantee conclusions with divine authority, but it does allow for God to speak through his Word in this manner.

Second, a methodical devotional approach that moves through a book of Scripture chapter by chapter raises contextual awareness and helps guard against misuse of Scripture. D. A. Carson critiques many devotional approaches for their failure in this area:

> Devotional guides tend to offer short, personal readings from the Bible, sometimes only a verse or two, followed by several paragraphs of edifying exposition. Doubtless they provide personal help for believers with private needs, fears, and hopes. But they do not provide the framework of what the Bible says—the "plotline" or "story line"—the big picture that makes sense of all the little bits of the Bible. Wrongly used, such devotional guides may ultimately engender the profoundly wrong-headed view that God exists to sort out my problems; they may foster profoundly mistaken interpretations of some Scriptures, simply because the handful of passages they treat are no longer placed within the framework of the big picture, which is gradually fading from view. Only systematic and repeated reading of the whole Bible can meet these challenges.[2]

Various schemes for reading through the entire Bible in a given time frame exist and can provide guidance and accountability for daily reading. Furthermore, if the daily text is read from a good study Bible that provides historical notes as needed, the best of the historical method can be maintained in the devotional time without being overly distracting.

Finally, exegetically sound devotional guides are a valuable resource. When choosing a devotional guide, review several and choose one that incorporates sound exegetical work into the daily readings. A guide that emphasizes reading more than one verse of Scripture at a time is

2. D. A. Carson, *For the Love of God: A Daily Companion for Discovering the Riches of God's Word,* vol. 1 (Wheaton: Crossway, 1998), x.

generally preferable to aids that treat single verses out of context. Also, always remember that the Scripture is primary and the exposition is secondary. Carson rightly places Scripture above all other texts, and we wholeheartedly agree with his command: "If you must skip something, skip this book; read the Bible instead."[3]

3. Ibid., 13.

SUMMARY

THE PROCESSES INVOLVED
IN INTERPRETATION AND APPLICATION
OF A SCRIPTURAL TEXT

I. Historical-Cultural and Contextual Analysis
  A. Determine the general historical and cultural milieu of the writer and his audience.
   1. Determine the general historical circumstances.
   2. Be aware of cultural circumstances and norms that add meaning to given actions.
   3. Discern the spiritual condition of the audience.
  B. Determine the purpose(s) the author had in writing a book.
   1. Note explicit statements or repeated phrases.
   2. Observe paraenetic or hortatory sections.
   3. Observe issues that are omitted or emphasized.
  C. Understand how the passage fits into its immediate context.
   1. Identify the major blocks of material in the book and show how they fit into a coherent whole.
   2. Show how the passage under consideration fits into the flow of the author's argument.
   3. Determine the perspective that the author intends to communicate: noumenological (the way things really are) or phenomenological (the ways things appear).
   4. Distinguish between descriptive and prescriptive truth.
   5. Distinguish between incidental details and the teaching focus of a passage.

6. Identify the person or category of persons for whom the particular passage is intended.

II. Lexical-Syntactical Analysis
  A. Identify the general literary form.
  B. Trace the development of the author's theme and show how the passage under consideration fits into the context.
  C. Identify the natural divisions (paragraphs and sentences) of the text.
  D. Identify the connecting words within the paragraphs and sentences and how they aid in understanding the author's progression of thought.
  E. Determine what the individual words mean.
    1. Identify the multiple meanings a word possessed in its time and culture.
    2. Determine the single meaning intended by the author in a given context.
  F. Analyze the syntax to show how it contributes to the understanding of a passage.
  G. Put the results of your analysis into nontechnical, easily understood words that clearly convey the author's intended meaning to the English reader.

III. Theological Analysis
  A. Determine your own view of the nature of God's relationship to humankind.
  B. Identify the implications of this view for the passage you are studying.
  C. Assess the extent of theological knowledge available to the people of that time (the "analogy of Scripture").
  D. Determine the meaning the passage possessed for its original recipients in light of their knowledge.
  E. Identify additional knowledge about this topic that is available to us now because of later revelation (the "analogy of faith").

IV. Literary Analysis
  A. Look for explicit references that indicate the author's intent regarding the method he was using.
  B. If the text does not explicitly identify the literary form of the passage, study the characteristics of the passage deductively to ascertain its form.
  C. Apply the principles of literary devices carefully but not rigidly.
    1. Simile
      a. Characteristic: an expressed comparison.

b. Interpretation: usually a single point of similarity or contrast.
2. Metaphor
   a. Characteristic: an unexpressed comparison.
   b. Interpretation: usually a single point of similarity.
3. Proverb
   a. Characteristic: comparison expressed or unexpressed.
   b. Interpretation: usually a single point of similarity or contrast.
4. Parables
   a. Characteristics: an extended simile—comparisons are expressed and kept separate; the story and its meaning are consciously separated.
   b. Interpretation: determine the focal meaning of the story and show how the details fit naturally into that focal teaching.
5. Allegories
   a. Characteristics: an extended metaphor—comparisons are unexpressed and intermingled; story and its meaning are carried along together.
   b. Interpretation: determine the multiple points of comparison intended by the author.
6. Types
   a. Characteristics
      (1) There must be a notable resemblance or analogy between the type and its antitype.
      (2) There must be evidence that the type was appointed by God to represent the thing typified.
      (3) A type must prefigure something in the future.
      (4) Classes of the type and its antitype: persons, events, institutions, offices, and actions.
   b. Interpretation
      (1) Determine the significance within the time and culture of both the type and its antitype.
      (2) Search the text for the point(s) of correspondence between the type and its antitype as they relate to salvation history.
      (3) Note the important points of difference between the type and its antitype.
7. Prophecy
   a. Characteristics
      (1) Be aware that the style is generally figurative and symbolic.

(2) Watch for supernatural elements such as information conveyed by the announcement of angels, by visions, or by other supernatural means.

(3) Note the emphasis on the unseen world that lies behind the action of the visible world.

(4) Follow the action to its usual conclusion by a sovereign intervention of God.

b. Interpretation

(1) Determine the specific historical circumstances surrounding the composition of the writing. Study intervening history to see whether the prophecy has been fulfilled.

(2) Study parallel passages or other cycles within the same prophecy for further information.

(3) Analyze whether this passage is part of a progressive prediction, is capable of developmental fulfillment, or includes prophetic telescoping.

V. Comparison with Others

A. Compare your analysis with that of other interpreters.

B. Modify, correct, or expand your interpretation as appropriate.

VI. Application

A. Principlizing: Based on a historical-cultural, contextual, lexical-syntactical, and theological analysis of the narrative portion, ascertain by deductive study (1) the principle(s) that passage was intended to teach, or (2) the principles (descriptive truths) illustrated within the passage that remain relevant for the contemporary believer.

B. Transcultural transmission of biblical commands.

1. Discern as accurately as possible the principle behind the command.

2. Discern whether the principle is transcultural or culture-bound by examining the reason given for the principle.

3. If a principle is transcultural, determine whether the same behavioral application in our culture will express the principle as adequately and accurately as the biblical one.

4. If the behavioral expression of a principle should be changed, suggest a cultural equivalent that will express the God-given principle behind the original command.

APPENDIX A

A SAMPLE BIBLIOGRAPHY OF WORKS RELATING TO HERMENEUTICS FROM VARIOUS THEOLOGICAL VIEWPOINTS

Barrett, C. K. "The Interpretation of the Old Testament in the New Testament." In *The Cambridge History of the Bible*, vol. 1, edited by P. R. Ackroyd and C. F. Evans, 377–411. Cambridge: Cambridge University Press, 1970. The author believes that the New Testament authors borrowed both legitimate and illegitimate hermeneutical principles from their contemporary culture.

Carson, D. A., and John D. Woodbridge, eds. *Hermeneutics, Authority, and Canon*. Grand Rapids: Zondervan, 1986. A collection of essays that present an evangelical apologetic for issues related to biblical authority and interpretation.

Childs, B. S. *Biblical Theology in Crisis*. Philadelphia: Westminster, 1970. A discussion of the American neoorthodox theology movement by one of its members.

Grant, Robert M. *A Short History of the Interpretation of the Bible*. Rev. ed. New York: Macmillan, 1963. A brief history by a professor of New Testament at the divinity school at the University of Chicago. He believes that a universal and permanent meaning of Scripture was not intended by its authors and that Scripture is the response of human beings to God's revelation rather than God's revelation of himself to humans.

Longman, Tremper III, and Leland Ryken, eds. *A Complete Literary Guide to the Bible*. Grand Rapids: Zondervan, 1993. A text from an evangelical perspective that integrates the best literary approaches with hermeneutics.

Marlé, René. *Introduction to Hermeneutics*. New York: Herder & Herder, 1967. A general text written from a liberal perspective.

McKim, Donald K., ed. *A Guide to Contemporary Hermeneutics: Major Trends in Biblical Interpretation*. Grand Rapids: Eerdmans, 1986. A collection of essays related to the issues of hermeneutics representing most current perspectives.

Osborne, Grant R. *The Hermeneutical Spiral: A Comprehensive Introduction to Biblical Interpretation*. Downers Grove, IL: InterVarsity, 1991. A major work detailing a ten-step hermeneutical process constituting a spiral from text to context. The process is author-centered but recognizes the need for a trialogue between the author, the text, and the reader so that the author's illocutions, mediated by the text, are understood by the reader.

Palmer, R. E. *Hermeneutics*. Evanston, IL: Northwestern University Press, 1969. Excellent text on the "new hermeneutic."

Schüssler Fiorenza, Elisabeth. *But She Said: Feminist Practices of Biblical Interpretation*. Boston: Beacon, 1992. An example of a hermeneutical work from a liberationist feminist perspective.

Thiselton, Anthony C. *New Horizons in Hermeneutics: The Theory and Practice of Transforming Biblical Reading*. Grand Rapids: Zondervan, 1992. A highly philosophical, comprehensive overview of major hermeneutical theories.

Von Rad, G. "Typological Interpretation of the Old Testament." In *Essays on Old Testament Hermeneutics*, edited by J. L. Mays, 17–39. Richmond: John Knox, 1963. An example of typological theory by a scholar who believes that the Old Testament is a product of documentary development, a human recounting of God's actions, and it therefore cannot be trusted as either reliable or accurate.

APPENDIX B

READINGS ON REVELATION, INSPIRATION, AND INERRANCY FROM A VARIETY OF THEOLOGICAL PERSPECTIVES

Achtemeier, Paul J. *The Inspiration of Scripture: Problems and Proposals*. Philadelphia: Westminster, 1980.

Baillie, John. *The Idea of Revelation in Recent Thought*. New York: Columbia University Press, 1956. Neoorthodox perspective.

Beegle, Dewey M. *The Inspiration of Scripture*. Philadelphia: Westminster, 1963. An evangelical who denies inerrancy.

Boice, James Montgomery. *The Foundation of Biblical Authority*. Grand Rapids: Zondervan, 1978. A series of lectures prepared by contributors to the International Council on Biblical Inerrancy.

Bruce, F. F. *The New Testament Documents: Are They Reliable?* Grand Rapids: Eerdmans, 1981. Excellent treatment of the subject by a prominent evangelical scholar.

Brunner, Emil. *Revelation and Reason*. Philadelphia: Westminster, 1946. A neoorthodox approach.

Childs. B. S. *Biblical Theology in Crisis*. Philadelphia: Westminster, 1970. A discussion of the American neoorthodox movement by one of its adherents.

Conn, Harvie M., ed. *Inerrancy and Hermeneutic: A Tradition, a Challenge, a Debate*. Grand Rapids: Baker, 1988.

Dodd, C. H. *The Authority of the Bible*. New York: Harper & Brothers, 1929. A liberal perspective.

Fuller, Daniel P. "Benjamin Warfield's View of Faith and History." *Bulletin of the Evangelical Theological Society* 2 (1968): 75–82.

Fuller, Daniel P., and Clark Pinnock. "On Revelation and Biblical Authority." *Christian Scholar's Review*. Vol. 2 no. 4 (1973). Also reprinted as Daniel P. Fuller and Clark Pinnock. "Biblical Revelation: The Foundation of Christian Theology." *Journal of the Evangelical Theological Society* 16.2 (Spring 1973),

67–72. A short discussion by these two well-known contemporary theologians on the issue of "limited inerrancy."

Geisler, Norman. *Inerrancy*. Grand Rapids: Zondervan. 1980.

Henry, Carl F. H. *God, Revelation and Authority*. 6 vols. Waco: Word, 1976–83; Wheaton: Crossway, 1999.

Hodge, Archibald A., and Benjamin B. Warfield. *Inspiration*. 1881. Reprint, Grand Rapids: Baker, 1979.

Lindsell, Harold. *The Battle for the Bible*. Grand Rapids: Zondervan, 1976. This book traces the history of the debate between advocates of biblical errancy and those of inerrancy and describes the doctrinal changes in groups that have adopted an errant Scripture position.

———. *The Bible in the Balance*. Grand Rapids: Zondervan, 1979.

Marshall, I. Howard. *Biblical Inspiration*. Grand Rapids: Eerdmans, 1982.

McDonald, H. D. *Theories of Revelation: An Historical Study, 1700–1960*. Grand Rapids: Baker, 1979.

Montgomery, John Warwick, ed. *God's Inerrant Word: An International Symposium on the Trustworthiness of Scripture*. Minneapolis: Bethany, 1974. An excellent volume from the conservative evangelical perspective. See especially the chapters by Montgomery, Pinnock, and Sproul.

Nicole, Roger R., and J. Ramsey Michaels, eds. *Inerrancy and Common Sense*. Grand Rapids: Baker, 1980.

Packer, J. I. "An Evangelical View of Progressive Revelation." In *Evangelical Roots*, edited by Kenneth Kantzer, 143–58. Nashville: Nelson, 1978.

———. *"Fundamentalism" and the Word of God*. Grand Rapids: Eerdmans, 1958.

———. *God Has Spoken: Revelation and the Bible*. Rev. ed. London: Hodder & Stoughton, 1979.

Pinnock, Clark. *Biblical Revelation*. Chicago: Moody, 1971. Excellent comparison of various perspectives on the nature of Scripture, revelation, and inspiration, written from a conservative evangelical position.

Radmacher, Earl D., and Robert D. Preus, eds. *Hermeneutics, Inerrancy, and the Bible*. Grand Rapids: Zondervan, 1984.

Rogers, Jack B., ed. *Biblical Authority*. Waco: Word, 1977.

Rogers, Jack B., and Donald K. McKim. *The Authority and Interpretation of the Bible: An Historical Approach*. San Francisco: Harper & Row, 1979.

Schaeffer, Francis. *No Final Conflict*. Downers Grove, IL: InterVarsity, 1975. Five short essays illustrating the author's thesis that Scripture is true whether it is speaking of "upper storey" or "lower storey" knowledge.

Warfield, B. B. *The Inspiration and Authority of the Bible*. Philadelphia: Presbyterian & Reformed, 1948.

Wenham, John W. *Christ and the Bible*. Downers Grove, IL: InterVarsity, 1972. An excellent discussion of Jesus' view of the Bible and of objections to Jesus' views.

APPENDIX C

A BIBLIOGRAPHY ON *SENSUS PLENIOR*[1]

Bergado, G. N. "The 'Sensus Plenior' as a New Testament Hermeneutical Principle." Master's thesis, Trinity Evangelical Divinity School, 1969.

Bierberg, R. "Does Sacred Scripture Have a *Sensus Plenior?*" *Catholic Biblical Quarterly* 15 (1953): 141–62.

———. "Hermeneutics." In *Jerome Biblical Commentary*, edited by R. E. Brown, J. A. Fitzmyer, and R. E. Murphy, 605–23. Englewood Cliffs, NJ: Prentice-Hall, 1968.

———. "Pere Lagrange and the *Sensus Plenior.*" *Catholic Biblical Quarterly* 18 (1956): 47–53.

———. "The *Sensus Plenior* in the Last Ten Years." *Catholic Biblical Quarterly* 25 (1963): 262–85.

———. *The Sensus Plenior of Sacred Scriptures*. Baltimore: St. Mary's University, 1955.

Coppens, J. "Levels of Meaning with the Bible." In *How Does the Christian Confront the Old Testament?* edited by Pierre Benoit, Roland Murphy, and Bastian van Iersel. Concilium Theology in the Age of Renewal 30, 125–39. New York: Paulist Press, 1968.

Franzmann, M. "The Hermeneutical Dilemma: Dualism in the Interpretation of Holy Scripture." *Concordia Theological Monthly* 36 (1965): 504.

Hirsch, E. D. Jr. *Validity in Interpretation*. New Haven: Yale University Press, 1967.

---

1. The original list in the 1st edition was taken from a bibliography prepared by Walter C. Kaiser, Trinity Evangelical Divinity School, and used by permission of the author. The present list also includes newer references to the subject of *sensus plenior*.

Hunt, I. "Rome and the Literal Sense of Sacred Scripture." *American Benedictine Review* 9 (1958): 79–103.

Kaiser, W. C. *Uses of the Old Testament*. Chicago: Moody, 1985.

Klein, William W., Craig L. Blomberg, and Robert L. Hubbard Jr. *Introduction to Biblical Interpretation*. Dallas: Word, 1993, esp. 119–32.

Krimholtz, R. H. "Instrumentality and *Sensus Plenior*." *Catholic Biblical Quarterly* 20 (1958): 200–205.

LaSor, William Sanford. "The *Sensus Plenior* and Biblical Interpretation." In *A Guide to Contemporary Hermeneutics: Major Trends in Biblical Interpretation*, edited by Donald K. McKim, 47–64. Grand Rapids: Eerdmans, 1986.

Longenecker, Richard N. *Biblical Exegesis in the Apostolic Period*. Grand Rapids: Eerdmans, 1975, esp. 214–19.

———. "Can We Reproduce the Exegesis of the New Testament?" *Tyndale Bulletin* 21 (1970): 3–38.

Moo, Douglas J. "The Problem of *Sensus Plenior*." In *Hermeneutics, Authority, and Canon*, edited by D. A. Carson and John D. Woodbridge, 175–211. Grand Rapids: Zondervan, 1986.

Nemetz, A. "Literalness and *Sensus Literalis*." *Speculum* 34 (1959): 76–89.

O'Rourke, J. J. "Marginal Notes on the *Sensus Plenior*." *Catholic Biblical Quarterly* 21 (1959): 64–71.

———. "Theology and the *Sensus Plenior*." *Ecclesiastical Review* 143 (1960): 301–6.

Payne, P. B. "The Fallacy of Equating Meaning with the Human Author's Intention." *Journal of the Evangelical Theological Society* 20 (1977): 243–52.

Ricoeur, P. "The Problem of the Double Sense as a Hermeneutic Problem and as a Semantic Problem." In *Myths and Symbols: Studies in Honor of Mircea Eliade*, edited by J. M. Kitagawa and Charles H. Long, 63–79. Chicago: University of Chicago Press, 1969.

Sutcliffe, E. F. "The Plenary Sense as a Principle of Interpretation." *Biblica* 34 (1953): 334–43.

Vawter, B. "The Fuller Sense: Some Considerations." *Catholic Biblical Quarterly* 26 (1969): 85–96.

APPENDIX D

COMPUTER-BASED RESOURCES FOR EXEGETICAL STUDY

In years past, a thorough examination of a biblical text required hours in a library perusing enormous volumes. For today's student of Scripture, the process can include the use of numerous electronic resources that are often more accessible and allow for more convenient searches for the relevant information. From a simple electronic Bible, to major Bible software, to the Internet, the resources are vast and varied.

Electronic Bibles

The electronic age has seen the advent of the electronic Bible. At its most basic level an eBible is a simple electronic device with only one English translation of Scripture. For instance, Franklin Electronic Publications sells an NIV eBible, a KJV eBible, and an eBible with both translations. Such eBibles allow for chapter-and-verse searches of Scripture. More eBibles can be added to a preexisting handheld or PDA device. Zondervan's NIV Study Bible Suite includes the *NIV Study Bible* with notes as well as cross-references, five additional English translations, and reading and devotional plans. Similarly, Thomas Nelson's eBible for Palm OS presents three English Bible translations, Vine's *Expository Dictionary*, *Strong's Concordance*, Nelson's *New Illustrated Bible Commentary and Dictionary*, plus a Max Lucado devotional. Many other eBibles can be found by searching the Web site of your favorite bookseller. Retailers such as Cokesbury.com and Christianbook.com feature a range of products.

Software

BibleSoft. Designed with specific audiences in mind, five libraries (Discovery Reference, New Reference, Reference Plus, Complete Reference, and Advanced Reference) constitute the current BibleSoft Library. All versions include English Bibles, *Nave's Topical Bible*, basic commentaries, Nelson's and Easton's Bible dictionaries, *Strong's Concordance*, theological works by Martin Luther and John Owen, and resources for devotions and Christian living. The Advanced Reference Library adds valuable texts such as Keil and Delitzsch's *Commentary on the Old Testament*, Vine's *Expository Dictionary of Biblical Words*, and original-language biblical texts and lexicons. Although it is less academic than some software and lacks many of the more recent exegetical resources, it is user-friendly and greatly increases the speed with which basic research can be conducted.

BibleWorks. BibleWorks Version 7 contains numerous English translations of the Bible as well as translations in twenty-two modern languages. The original-language biblical texts are included along with lexical and grammatical references such as Holladay's; Brown, Driver, and Briggs's Hebrew lexicons; and Bauer, Arndt, Gingrich, and Danker's Greek lexicon. Several Bible dictionaries (Easton's, Fausset), *Nave's Topical Bible*, and the abridged *TDNT* add to this collection's value. BibleWorks displays lexical and grammatical information for words and verses as the researcher moves the cursor over the text. The software provides search options and parallel displays for multiple levels of research. Study notes can be inserted and will automatically load each time a verse is accessed.

Libronix (Logos). The Logos library includes seven collections ranging from the Christian Home Library to the Scholar's Library: Gold. The resources in each collection vary significantly; additional electronic books can be purchased and added to the system at any time. The Scholar's Library: Gold is the most complete academic resource available at this time and contains numerous English-language Bibles, original-language texts, lexicons, grammars, language tools, commentaries, maps, and theological resources.

Although Logos is basically a collection of electronic books, it provides a valuable mechanism for searching, organizing, and cataloging the resources to make them accessible to the researcher. The interface allows for studies by topic or by biblical passage. Comparisons of parallel Bible versions are available at the click of a button as are lemma reports for original-language words with links to lexicons, parsing information, and concordances. The researcher can also add and save study notes to the system for future reference.

Pradis (Zondervan). This easy-to-use software includes a library of Bibles, commentaries, devotionals, study guides, and reference books packaged in four versions for the Family, Leader, Professional, or Scholar. The library contains numerous Bible translations as well as the Hebrew text of *Biblia Hebraica Stuttgartensia* and the *United Bible Societies Greek New Testament.* It links four panes, allowing the researcher to simultaneously view the desired version of a biblical passage, lexical and grammatical information, commentary, and encyclopedic sources for that text, even permitting access to multiple sources in a given pane at one time. Functions allow the researcher to insert bookmarks, create and save study notes, and conduct searches for words, phrases, or topics. Individual study sessions can be saved, granting flexibility to the researcher who needs to resume a study at a later time.

One great strength of this program is the speed and ease with which original-language word studies can be completed even by those lacking competence in Greek and Hebrew. Its benefit for historical, cultural, and theological information is somewhat limited, particularly in the Family version.

Internet Sources

The Internet can be a valuable source for information if one knows how to use it wisely. Although there is a plethora of useful and accurate information available on the Internet, it is especially important to use critical analysis skills when accessing information from it. Be aware that anyone can create a Web page on the Internet and give it a professional-sounding name, regardless of the accuracy of the information he or she posts. Thus, when using Internet sources, carefully consider the following questions:

Is the author/creator clearly identified (i.e., an individual or a professional group)?

Does the author have credentials demonstrating education and experience in the topic about which he is writing?

Does the writing style and content demonstrate interaction with other materials in the field?

Is the purpose to inform and educate or to sell something?

Are the content and conclusions compatible with accepted scholarship in the area?

Many of the best academic exegetical resources are not available for free on Internet sites, but they are increasingly available for purchase in electronic versions compatible with the various software programs listed above.

The following are Web sites that you may find valuable for beginning exegetical research:

www.biblegateway.com. Bible Gateway provides searchable Bibles in twenty English translations and numerous other languages. It also allows for topic or keyword searches.

www.bibleresourcecenter.org. This site developed by the American Bible Society contains a basic dictionary of Bible words and people as well as helpful charts, graphs, maps, and a Bible timeline. It also provides a searchable Bible in fifteen English translations.

www.blueletterbible.com. Blue Letter Bible is an excellent source for conducting word studies. It allows for a side-by-side comparison of translations plus original language grammatical information, Greek and Hebrew concordances, and a searchable *Strong's Concordance*, Thayer's lexicon, and Gesenius's lexicon. Also included are twenty basic commentaries and J. Vernon McGee's *Through the Bible* series. The researcher can call up any Bible passage and with one click get a listing of all resources related to it that are available on the site.

www.crosswire.org. Follow the link known as The Sword, a growing collection of downloadable software related to biblical studies including Bible texts, commentaries, lexicons, and dictionaries.

www.earlyjewishwritings.com. This is a fabulous site for primary source texts including the Old Testament, the Old Testament Apocrypha, Pseudepigrapha, Dead Sea Scrolls, the Talmud, Philo, and Josephus.

www.earlychristianwritings.com. A site complementary to the preceding one, it includes primary source texts such as the New Testament, New Testament Apocrypha, gnostic writings, and the church fathers.

www.freebiblecommentaries.org. This site contains solid hermeneutical material as well as commentary on some Old Testament and all New

Testament writings provided by Bible Lessons International. The author is working to have commentaries translated into languages other than English.

> **Exercise 100.** In Matthew 19:24 Jesus says, "It is easier for a camel to go through the eye of a needle than for a rich man to enter the kingdom of God." Although no archaeological evidence supports such a conclusion, this verse has prompted numerous individuals to suggest that during Jesus' time there was a small gate in Jerusalem known as the Eye of a Needle and that camels had to unload and kneel in order to pass through. Use the Internet to research this text, and discover how many sites you can find that integrate this incorrect information.

APPENDIX E

INSTRUCTOR'S RESOURCE CD

A resource CD is available free from Baker Academic for instructors who use this book to teach a course in hermeneutics. This CD includes teaching suggestions, articles that can be used as auxiliary handouts within the course, and suggested answers to the one hundred exercises.

Since some instructors may want to use some of the exercises for graded assignments or tests, distribution of the instructor's CD is limited to those who are actually teaching a hermeneutics course. Some materials on the instructor's CD may be distributed for class use; other materials are not recommended for distribution to students so that they can be used for graded exercises (the difference between these two categories is clearly distinguished on the CD).

If you are a faculty member teaching a course in hermeneutics and would like a copy of the Instructor's Resource CD, please send a request to Baker Academic, P.O. Box 6287, Grand Rapids, MI 49516, on official school letterhead, indicating the course in which you will be using this book, the date of the course, and your willingness to distribute to students only those materials allowed by the authors.

If you will be teaching the course in a local church, please send a similar request and commitment to the address above on official church letterhead, with a confirmation by your pastor that you will be teaching such a course.

GENERAL BIBLIOGRAPHY

Adams, J. McKee. *Biblical Backgrounds*. Nashville: Broadman, 1934.

Alsop, John R., ed. *An Index to the Bauer-Arndt-Gingrich Lexicon*. Grand Rapids: Zondervan, 1968.

Althaus, Paul. *The Theology of Martin Luther*. Philadelphia: Fortress, 1966.

Baly, Denis A. *The Geography of the Bible*. New rev. ed. New York: Harper & Row, 1974.

Barrett, Charles K. *Luke the Historian in Recent Study*. London: Epworth, 1961.

———, ed. *The New Testament Background: Selected Documents*. New York: Harper & Row, 1961.

Bauer, Walter, F. W. Danker, W. F. Arndt, and F. W. Gingrich, *A Greek-English Lexicon of the New Testament and Other Early Christian Literature*. 3rd ed. Chicago: University of Chicago Press, 2000.

Berkhof, Louis. *Principles of Biblical Interpretation*. Grand Rapids: Baker, 1950.

———. *Systematic Theology*. 4th rev. and enl. ed. Grand Rapids: Eerdmans, 1941.

Blackwood, Andrew. *Expository Preaching for Today*. 1953. Reprint, Grand Rapids: Baker, 1975.

Blaising, Craig, and Darrell Bock, eds. *Dispensationalism, Israel and the Church: The Search for Definition*. Grand Rapids: Zondervan, 1992.

Blass, Friedrich W., and Albert Debrunner. *Greek Grammar of the New Testament and Other Early Christian Literature*. Translated and revised by Robert W. Funk. Chicago: University of Chicago Press, 1961.

Braga, James. *How to Prepare Bible Messages*. Portland, OR: Multnomah, 1969.

Broadus, John A. *A Treatise on the Preparation and Delivery of Sermons*. 30th ed. New York: Hoddard & Stoughton, 1899.

Brooks, Phillips. *Lectures on Preaching*. London: H. R. Allenson, 1877.

Brown, Francis, S. R. Driver, and Charles A. Briggs. *A Hebrew and English Lexicon of the Old Testament*. New York: Oxford, 1952.

Bruce, F. F. *The New Testament Documents: Are They Reliable?* 6th rev. ed. Grand Rapids: Eerdmans, 1981.

Bullinger, E. W. *Critical Lexicon and Concordance to the English and Greek New Testament*. Grand Rapids: Zondervan, 1975.

———. *Figures of Speech Used in the Bible*. Grand Rapids: Baker, 1968.

Buswell, James Oliver Jr. *Systematic Theology of the Christian Religion*. 2 vols. Grand Rapids: Zondervan, 1962–63.

Carson, D. A. *Biblical Interpretation and the Church: The Problem of Contextualization*. Nashville: Thomas Nelson, 1984.

Carson, D. A., and John D. Woodbridge, eds. *Hermeneutics, Authority, and Canon*. Grand Rapids: Zondervan, 1986.

Chafer, Lewis Sperry. *Dispensationalism*. Rev. ed. Dallas: Dallas Seminary Press, 1951.

Clouse, Robert, ed. *The Meaning of the Millennium: Four Views*. Downers Grove, IL: InterVarsity, 1977.

Costas, Orlando. *The Church and Its Mission*. Wheaton: Tyndale, 1975.

Cox, William E. *Examination of Dispensationalism*. Phillipsburg, NJ: Presbyterian & Reformed, 1963.

De Vaux, Roland. *Ancient Israel*. 2 vols. New York: McGraw, 1961.

Douglas, J. D., ed. *New Bible Dictionary*. Grand Rapids: Eerdmans, 1962.

Dunnett, Walter M. *The Interpretation of Holy Scripture: An Introduction to Hermeneutics*. Nashville: Thomas Nelson, 1984.

Edersheim, Alfred. *The Life and Times of Jesus the Messiah*. 1883. Reprint, Grand Rapids: Eerdmans, 1972.

Fairbairn, Patrick. *The Typology of Scripture*. 2 vols. 1845–47. Grand Rapids: Zondervan, 1967.

Farrar, Frederic W. *History of Interpretation*. 1885. Reprint, Grand Rapids: Baker, 1961.

Fee, Gordon D., and Douglas Stuart. *How to Read the Bible for All Its Worth: A Guide to Understanding the Bible*. 3rd ed. Grand Rapids: Zondervan, 2003.

Feinberg, John S., ed. *Continuity and Discontinuity: Perspectives on the Relationship between the Old and New Testaments*. Westchester, IL: Crossway, 1988.

France, R. T. *Jesus and the Old Testament*. Downers Grove, IL: InterVarsity, 1971.

Freeman, James M. and Harold Chadwick. *The New Manners and Customs of the Bible*. Gainsville, FL: Bridge-Logos, 1998.

Fullerton, Kemper. *Notes on Hebrew Grammar*. 5th rev. ed. Cincinnati: Lane Theological Seminary, 1898.

Gaebelein, Frank E., ed. *The Expositor's Bible Commentary: With the New International Version of the Holy Bible*. 12 vols. Grand Rapids: Zondervan, 1976–92.

Gesenius, Friedrich H. W. *Hebrew Grammar*. 2nd English ed. Oxford: Clarendon, 1949.

Gesenius, Wilhelm. *Hebrew and Chaldee Lexicon to the Old Testament Scriptures*. 1846. Reprint, Grand Rapids: Eerdmans, 1949.

Girdlestone, Robert B. *Synonyms of the Old Testament*. 1901. Reprint, Grand Rapids: Eerdmans, 1948.

Grant, Robert M. *A Short History of the Interpretation of the Bible*. Rev. ed. New York: Macmillan, 1963.

Gutiérrez, Gustavo. *A Theology of Liberation*. Maryknoll, NY: Orbis, 1973.

Haley, J. W. *An Examination of the Alleged Discrepancies of the Bible*. Grand Rapids: Baker, 1977.

Harrison, Roland K. *A History of Old Testament Times*. Grand Rapids: Zondervan, 1957.

Heaton, E. W. *Everyday Life in Old Testament Times*. New York: Scribner, 1956.

Hirsch, E. D. Jr. *Validity in Interpretation*. New Haven: Yale University Press, 1967.

Jeremias, Joachim. *Parables of Jesus*. Rev. ed. New York: Scribner, 1971.

Johnson, Elliot E. *Expository Hermeneutics: An Introduction*. Grand Rapids: Zondervan, 1990.

Kaiser, Walter C. Jr., ed. *Classical Evangelical Essays in Old Testament Interpretation*. Grand Rapids: Baker, 1972.

———. *The Old Testament in Contemporary Preaching*. Grand Rapids: Baker, 1973.

———. *Toward an Exegetical Theology: Biblical Exegesis for Preaching and Teaching*. Grand Rapids: Baker, 1981.

Kaiser, Walter C. Jr., and Moisés Silva. *An Introduction to Biblical Hermeneutics: The Search for Meaning*. Grand Rapids: Zondervan, 1994.

Kantenwein, Lee L. *Diagrammatical Analysis*. Winona Lake, IN: BMH Books, 1979.

Kitchen, K. A. *Ancient Orient and Old Testament*. Downers Grove, IL: InterVarsity, 1966.

Kittel, Gerhard, and Gerhard Friedrich. *Theological Dictionary of the New Testament*. 10 vols. Grand Rapids: Eerdmans, 1964–76.

Klein, William W., Craig L. Blomberg, and Robert L. Hubbard Jr. *Introduction to Biblical Interpretation*. Dallas: Word, 1993.

Kraft, Charles. "Interpreting in Cultural Context." *Journal of the Evangelical Theological Society* 21 (1978): 357–67.

Ladd, George Eldon. *Crucial Questions about the Kingdom of God*. Grand Rapids: Eerdmans, 1952.

———. *A Theology of the New Testament*. Grand Rapids: Eerdmans, 1974.

Lampe, G. W. H., and K. J. Woollcombe. *Essays on Typology*. Naperville, IL: Allenson, 1957.

Lewis, Gordon R. *Testing Christianity's Truth Claims*. Chicago: Moody, 1976.

Lindsell, Harold. *The Battle for the Bible*. Grand Rapids: Zondervan, 1976.

Longenecker, Richard N. *Biblical Exegesis in the Apostolic Period*. Grand Rapids: Eerdmans, 1975.

Longman, Tremper, III. *Literary Approaches to Biblical Interpretation*. Grand Rapids: Zondervan, 1987.

Ludwigson, R. *A Survey of Biblical Prophecy*. 2nd ed. Grand Rapids: Zondervan, 1975.

Marshall, I. Howard, ed. *New Testament Interpretation: Essays on Principles and Methods*. Grand Rapids: Eerdmans, 1991.

McKim, Donald K., ed. *A Guide to Contemporary Hermeneutics: Major Trends in Biblical Interpretation*. Grand Rapids: Eerdmans, 1986.

Mickelsen, A. Berkeley. *Interpreting the Bible*. Grand Rapids: Eerdmans, 1963.

Miller, Mark. *Experiential Storytelling: Discovering Narrative to Communicate God's Message*. Grand Rapids: Zondervan, 2004.

Miranda, J. *Marx and the Bible*. Maryknoll, NY: Orbis, 1974.

Montgomery, John W., ed. *God's Inerrant Word*. Minneapolis: Bethany, 1974.

Morris, Leon. *Apocalyptic*. Grand Rapids: Eerdmans, 1972.

Moulton, James H., and George Milligan. *The Vocabulary of the Greek Testament: Illustrated from the Papyri and Other Non-Literary Sources*. Grand Rapids: Eerdmans, 1949.

Mounce, William D. *The Analytical Lexicon to the Greek New Testament*. Grand Rapids: Zondervan, 1993.

———. *Basics of Biblical Greek Grammar*. 2nd ed. Grand Rapids: Zondervan, 2003.

———. *Complete Expository Dictionary of Old and New Testament Words*. Grand Rapids: Zondervan, 2006.

Muller, Richard A. *The Study of Theology: From Biblical Interpretation to Contemporary Formulation*. Grand Rapids: Zondervan, 1991.

Noth, Martin. *The Old Testament World*. Translated by Victor I. Gruhn. Philadelphia: Fortress, 1966.

Osborne, Grant R. *The Hermeneutical Spiral: A Comprehensive Introduction to Biblical Interpretation*. Downers Grove, IL: InterVarsity, 1991.

Owens, John Joseph. *Analytical Key to the Old Testament*. 4 vols. Grand Rapids: Baker, 1989–92.

Payne, J. Barton. *Encyclopedia of Biblical Prophecy*. New York: Harper & Row, 1973.

Pentecost, J. Dwight. *Things to Come*. Grand Rapids: Zondervan, 1958.

Perry, Lloyd. *A Manual for Biblical Preaching*. Grand Rapids: Baker, 1965.

Pfeiffer, Charles F., ed. *The Biblical World: A Dictionary of Biblical Archaeology*. Grand Rapids: Baker, 1964.

Pinnock, Clark. *Biblical Revelation*. Chicago: Moody, 1971.

———. "Liberation Theology: The Gains, the Gaps." *Christianity Today*, January 16, 1976, 13–15.

Poythress, Vern S. *Science and Hermeneutics*. Grand Rapids: Zondervan, 1988.

Pratico, Gary D., and Miles V. Van Pelt. *Basics of Biblical Hebrew Grammar*. 2nd ed. Grand Rapids: Zondervan, 2007.

Pritchard, James B. *The Ancient Near Eastern Texts Relating to the Old Testament*. 3rd ed., with suppl. Princeton, NJ: Princeton University Press, 1969.

———, ed. *The Ancient Near East in Pictures Relating to the Old Testament*. Princeton, NJ: Princeton University Press, 1954.

Ramm, Bernard, ed. *Hermeneutics*. Grand Rapids: Baker, 1971.

———. *Protestant Biblical Interpretation*. 3rd rev. ed. Grand Rapids: Baker, 1970.

Robertson, A. T. *A Grammar of the Greek New Testament in the Light of Historical Research*. 1914. Reprint, Nashville: Broadman, 1947.

———. *Word Pictures in the New Testament*. 6 vols. 1930–33. Reprint, Nashville: Broadman, 1943.

Robinson, Haddon W. *Biblical Preaching: The Development and Delivery of Expository Messages*. Grand Rapids: Baker, 1980.

Robinson, Haddon W., and Craig Larson. *The Art and Craft of Biblical Preaching*. Grand Rapids: Zondervan, 2006.

Ryrie, Charles C. *Dispensationalism Today*. Chicago: Moody, 1965.

Schultz, Samuel J., and Morris A. Inch, eds. *Interpreting the Word of God*. Chicago: Moody, 1976.

Schüssler Fiorenza, Elisabeth. "The Will to Choose or Reject: Continuing Our Critical Work." In *Feminist Interpretation of the Bible*, edited by Letty M. Russell, 125–36. Philadelphia: Westminster, 1985.

Scofield, C. I. *Rightly Dividing the Word of Truth*. 1896. Reprint, Grand Rapids: Zondervan, 1974.

Sterrett, T. Norton. *How to Understand Your Bible*. Rev. ed. Downers Grove, IL: InterVarsity, 1974.

Sproul, R. C. "Controversy at Culture Gap." *Eternity*, May 1976, 13–15, 40.

Strong, James. *Strong's Exhaustive Concordance of the Bible*. Nashville: Abingdon, 1890.

Surburg, Raymond. *How Dependable Is the Bible?* Philadelphia: Lippincott, 1972.

Tenney, Merrill C. *Interpreting Revelation*. Grand Rapids: Eerdmans, 1957.

———. *New Testament Times*. Grand Rapids: Eerdmans, 1965.

Terry, Milton S. *Biblical Hermeneutics*. 1883. Reprint, Grand Rapids: Zondervan, 1974.

Thayer, Joseph H., ed. *Greek-English Lexicon of the New Testament*. 1896. Reprint, Grand Rapids: Zondervan, 1956.

Thiele, Edwin. *The Mysterious Numbers of the Hebrew Kings*. Rev. ed. Grand Rapids: Eerdmans, 1965.

Thiselton, Anthony C. *New Horizons in Hermeneutics: The Theory and Practice of Transforming Biblical Reading*. Grand Rapids: Zondervan, 1992.

Thompson, John Arthur. *The Bible and Archaeology*. Grand Rapids: Eerdmans, 1962.

Thomson, William M. *The Land and the Book*. 2 vols. New York: Harper, 1858.

Traina, Robert A. *Methodological Bible Study*. 1952. Reprint, Grand Rapids: Francis Asbury, 1980.

Trench, Richard C. *Notes on the Parables of Our Lord*. 1886. Reprint, Grand Rapids: Baker, 1948.

————. *Synonyms of the New Testament*. Grand Rapids: Eerdmans, 1950.

Tyndale New Testament Commentaries. 20 vols. Grand Rapids: Eerdmans, 1957–74.

Vanhoozer, Kevin J. *Is There a Meaning in This Text? The Bible, the Reader, and the Morality of Literary Knowledge*. Grand Rapids: Zondervan, 1998.

Van Til, Cornelius. *The New Hermeneutic*. Phillipsburg, NJ: Presbyterian & Reformed, 1974.

Vine, William E. *Expository Dictionary of New Testament Words*. Old Tappan, NJ: Revell, 1940.

Walther, C. F. W. *The Proper Distinction between Law and Gospel*. St. Louis: Concordia, 1929.

Weingreen, Jacob. *Practical Grammar for Classical Hebrew*. 2nd ed. New York: Oxford, 1959.

Wenham, John W. *Christ and the Bible*. Downers Grove, IL: InterVarsity, 1973.

Wight, Fred. *Manners and Customs of Bible Lands*. Chicago: Moody, 1953.

Wigram, George V. *The Englishman's Greek Concordance*. Rev. ed. Grand Rapids: Baker, 1979.

————. *The Englishman's Hebrew and Chaldee Concordance*. 1843. Reprint, Grand Rapids: Zondervan, 1978.

Wood, A. Skevington. *The Principles of Biblical Interpretation as Enunciated by Irenaeus, Origen, Augustine, Luther and Calvin*. Grand Rapids: Zondervan, 1967.

Wright, George Ernest. *The Old Testament against Its Environment*. London: SCM, 1950.

Yamauchi, Edwin. "Christianity and Cultural Differences." *Christianity Today*, June 23, 1972, 5–8.

————. *The Stones and the Scriptures*. Philadelphia: Holman, 1977.

Zuck, Roy. B. *Basic Biblical Interpretation: A Practical Guide to Discovering Biblical Truth*. Colorado Springs: Victor Books, 1991.

————, ed. *Rightly Divided: Readings in Biblical Hermeneutics*. Grand Rapids: Kregel, 1996.

SCRIPTURE INDEX

SUBJECT INDEX